D0651811

CHINESE GORDON

BY H. E. WORTHAM

THREE WOMEN

MUSTAPHA KEMAL OF TURKEY

EDWARD VII, MAN AND KING

Gordon in Mandarin's Dress

(A photograph taken specially for the Dowager Empress Tzu Hsi)

CHINESE GORDON

By

H. E. WORTHAM

With Illustrations

BOSTON
LITTLE, BROWN, AND COMPANY
1933

Published April, 1933

THE ATLANTIC MONTHLY PRESS BOOKS
ARE PUBLISHED BY
LITTLE, BROWN, AND COMPANY
IN ASSOCIATION WITH
THE ATLANTIC MONTHLY COMPANY

PRINTED IN THE UNITED STATES OF AMERICA

PREFACE

THE principal source on which I have drawn in this study of Gordon is his own letters. Of these by far the most important collection consists of his letters to his sister Augusta, which have never before in their entirety been at the disposal of any of his numerous biographers. This collection is now in the possession of Lieutenant-Colonel F. W. Moffit, the son of Gordon's sister Helen, and thanks to him I have had full and unimpeded access to the whole of the 1600 odd pieces which comprise it. I think it will be agreed that the result has been to present a more human, if less partial, view of the extraordinary personality of their writer.

I am also indebted to Colonel Louis Gordon, the present head of that branch of the family, for the loan of those of his uncle's letters which are in his possession. Colonel Gordon has given me much assistance in other ways. Besides acknowledging his kindness, I should like also to put on record that of Mrs. Freese, Gordon's neighbor and friend at Gravesend. Mrs. Freese is now in her hundredth year, but her memory is unimpaired, and she has been able to supplement in some important particulars her own vivid little book about Gordon. This rare monograph — it was withdrawn from circulation almost immediately after it was published — is our principal source of Gordon's life during the important years of his spiritual development, from 1867 to 1871.

For the events recorded in Book II (China) I have relied, apart from his own letters, on A. E. Hake's *The Story of Chinese Gordon.* This is obviously based on Gordon's own diary, which is lost. The British official White Papers on China (1864) are another first-hand authority.

For Gordon's career subsequent to his going to Egypt in 1874, I am much indebted to Dr. Bernard M. Allen's *Gordon and the Sudan*. Dr. Allen has brought to bear upon this period of Gordon's life a scholarship and erudition which place him in a class apart from the crowd of authors, eminent and obscure, who have been attracted by the enigmatical figure of Charles George Gordon. Demetrius Charles Boulger's *Life* has helped to create the Gordon legend, and it would be churlish not to include that ill-written book in even the briefest bibliography.

To make a full list of the authorities I have consulted would mean nothing to the general reader for whom this book is intended. So far as possible I have avoided footnote documentation. That tiresome method is the historian's privilege, which it would be impertinent for a mere biographer to usurp.

H. E. W.

CONTENTS

ILLUSTRATIONS

MAPS AND PLANS

CHARLES GEORGE GORDON

January 28, 1833. Birth
1843–1848. Taunton Grammar School
1848–1852. Royal Military Academy, Woolwich
1852–1854. Chatham and Pembroke
1855–1856. The Crimea
1856–1858. Bessarabia and Armenia
1860–1862. War with China
1863–1864. Taeping Rebellion
1865–1871. Gravesend
1871–1873. Galatz
1874–1876. Governor of the Equatorial Provinces
1877–1879. Governor-General of the Sudan
1880. India, China, and Ireland
1881–1882. Mauritius
1882. Cape Colony
1883. Palestine
1884–1885. Khartoum
January 26, 1885. Death

PROLOGUE

Look attentively upon, and take inspiration of what I shall show unto thee. Behold there Asia. Here are Tigris and Euphrates. Lo, there Africa. Here is the Mountain of the Moon — yonder thou mayst perceive the fenny march of Nilus. On this side lieth Europe. Dost thou not see the Abbey of Thélème?

RABELAIS

1. An Incident at St. James's Palace

On February 17, 1880, the Prince of Wales held a levee at St. James's Palace. It was a function in the routine of the Victorian Court, in no way different from any others of its kind. Beside the Prince, already a stout, middle-aged figure looking more than his thirty-eight years, stood his brothers, the Dukes of Edinburgh and Connaught and Prince Leopold. Among the royalties stood "Uncle" George of Cambridge, Commander-in-Chief for many years of his long life. The Prime Minister, Lord Beaconsfield, was there, now old and infirm. Members of the Cabinet, the *corps diplomatique*, Court officials, dignitaries of the Church — all these doubtless looked upon a familiar ceremonial with blasé eyes. Some of the young subalterns may have felt nervous on making their first bow to the Prince as commissioned officers in Her Majesty's Army; all were doubtless impressed by the brilliance of the spectacle, by its air of formal informality, of dignity and ease. But, whatever their sentiments, they are lost, and we do not know what passed in their minds; only their names remain on record in dusty files.

We do know, however, something about the feelings of one person present on that occasion. A Brevet Colonel of the Royal Engineers was attending the levee after absence on special service. There was nothing remarkable in his personal appearance, except for the depth of the eyes, which, as he talked, "shone like blue diamonds." A slight stoop made him seem rather under middle height. Some might observe in the spare, well-knit figure an air of resolution and authority which indicated a man well accustomed to command. His head, broad at the bridge of the nose and rather short, though on the whole well shaped, showed strength of character. Closer study of his features revealed a sensitiveness in the lines round the mouth and eyes unusual in those who have been trained in the calling of arms. His quickness of tongue, sometimes pouring out jostling, almost inarticulate words, and his nervous gestures pointed to impulsiveness and some lack of self-control. But the impression he made on the casual observer was simply that of a soldier whose smartness was entirely innocent of dandyism, who carried his forty-odd years lightly — a man still in the prime of life, as his clear complexion, his curly brown hair and fashionable whiskers, unflecked by grey, sufficiently showed.

This Colonel looked upon the scene with mixed feelings. In some ways it appealed to him, in other ways it made him depressed and irritable. His thoughts, indeed, were always unruly companions, and reacted in odd and conflicting ways to the stimulus of the external world. He was interested in receptions, for he had often held them himself, standing on a dais before a throne and receiving the notables of a country many times larger than England. And, even if he did not allow himself to admit it, he rather liked uniforms and gold lace, and he had an instinctive taste for ritual in spite of the fact that he was continually impelled by his conscience to act in defiance of it. In the present instance this monitor told him that a Christian should not be impressed by the superficial brilliance he saw around him. Were not these things manifestations of the flesh which was ineradicably evil and doomed to pass away? The only real values were those of the spirit, values which had no share in determining the course of a levee. So he prevented his heart from warming to the sight by reminding himself that "all this mass of glitter would be worms in thirty years' time." But the thought did not prevent his feeling annoyance when he, a Colonel and a celebrity, was announced as Captain Gordon.

Perhaps the Prince of Wales saw the shadow of it on his face, for Gordon was quick to take offense. Anyhow, as the Prince shook hands with him, he whispered in a voice comfortably used to making *sotto voce* remarks on ceremonial occasions, "Come and see me at lunch time on Sunday." Gordon bowed and passed on. The levee proceeded, and the so-called Captain of Engineers could pursue his thoughts on the carelessness of Court officials and on the transience of human things, or he could more simply talk to his friends, whom he had not seen during his term of service in the Sudan.

Admittedly he was a person of distinction, a soldier with brilliant exploits to his name, a successful administrator of an enormous slice of tropical Africa. More than that, he was a man who by his life and works had won the respect of humanitarians, Liberals, and Evangelicals. Everyone, indeed, knew Chinese Gordon, who combined pugnacity and piety in such heroic proportions, flattering, while he mystified, his age, which was pleased to think that it had produced in him the very type of Christian knight without fear or stain. His achievements in Asia and Africa touched the Imperialistic imagination, and showed, too, the innate superiority of the Englishman over the American or the dago, and of the white man over the yellow and the brown — a cardinal point, this, in the Victorian philosophy. If his faith, which was lit by compassion for the poor and suffering, seemed to men of the world an awkward, though pardonable, eccentricity, it deeply touched the finer spirits of the time. "Captain" Gordon, in short, was a very remarkable man.

But the Prince of Wales, when he gave him this appointment, had a more definite intention than that of merely listening to an account of his adventures in the Sudan. He knew all about Gordon, about his impulsive character and his wish to leave the Army, and he was anxious that such talents should not be lost to the country. When Gordon, therefore, went to Marlborough House on Sunday morning, he found that the Prince had called in the Duke of Cambridge, who remembered Gordon as a winning, bright-eyed little boy of nine when his father had been stationed at Corfu, to help him persuade this Colonel of Engineers not to give up his career. Only a man of Gordon's quixotic temperament would have considered resignation when in two or three years' time he was certain to reach General's rank, with all that meant in the matter of pay and pension. Both now pressed him not to send in his papers. They asked why he wished to retire at a time when it was so obviously advantageous to himself to remain on the active list. Worldly prudence was all on the side of the argument put forward by the Prince and the Duke.

Gordon, for his part, had too many reasons to make his wish easily intelligible. He could not say that his services had not been properly recognized by the Tories, or that he was disillusioned about the work he had been doing for six years in the Sudan, where, in spite of all his efforts, slavery flourished as vigorously as ever, or that he was unhappy in his own mind and would like to start a new life untrammeled by his past, or that he was merely restless and "queer," as he knew many Englishmen in high places believed him to be. He could not advance such reasons as these, although they would all have contained a measure of truth. Nor does he tell us that he explained to the Prince of Wales and the Duke of Cambridge his idea of entering the service of King Leopold of the Belgians, who had his eye upon the ex-Governor-General of the Sudan for his recently acquired territory of the Congo, where Gordon believed he could scotch the awful evil of the slave trade at its source, and incidentally found an international empire in the heart of Africa.

Into these matters Gordon could not enter. So he declared

that he wanted to resign chiefly because he wished for rest. "Take a year's leave, then, or more," said the bluff Commander-in-Chief, adding, with all the authority of his position, that he would not accept Gordon's resignation. Whether Gordon was flattered at being pressed in this kindly way he does not mention. Assuredly the experience was one which could have befallen few officers of his rank. In any case, Gordon did not resign. He went to Switzerland instead with a young nephew.

On the way he visited Brussels. While he was there, beginning those parleys with a king full of craft and greed which never quite reached fruition, Gordon reflected on the wretchedness of mankind. Such meditations often occupied his mind. But they were not inspired in this case by wicked King Leopold — a small book he picked up at his hotel was responsible. *Souvenirs of the Congress of Vienna* showed him how great people fought for invitations to parties, and related the end of some of the men who played a part in that settlement of Europe — Castlereagh, who cut his throat, Alexander I, who died mad. All, Gordon reflected, were now "in their 6 ft. by 2 ft. 6 in.," and he found consolation — and this was another thought habitual to him — in remembering that life required but "a little patience to bear with the present." The longing for death was bound to be satisfied in the end. Meanwhile one only needed "a profound faith in God's ruling *all* things." He underlined the "all" as he wrote in his quick, flowing hand to his sister Augusta, his confidante on all matters, spiritual and temporal. "It is not the Duke [of Cambridge] or Lord Beaconsfield, it is *He* alone who rules." And Gordon thereupon quoted a remark of Napoleon's that "the smallest trifles produce the greatest results."

Gordon's own life seemed to answer for the truth of this. Trifles were always diverting his destiny, and it is possible, had the Prince of Wales not whispered into his ear at the levee, that the last few disjointed years of his career might well have taken another course. He would have gone to the Congo, and either succumbed to the climate or quarreled with his new master. In this case he would have settled in the East End, as he intended, giving himself up to good works for the young and the sick; and when Major-General Charles George Gordon, C.B., died somewhere about the end of the century, after having completed the natural term of his pilgrimage in a world which he so heartily despised, the newspapers, briefly recording the saintly self-sacrifice of his later years, would have recalled his achievements in China and the Sudan as matters of almost forgotten history.

So it might have been. On the other hand, as one remarks the slender chances which determined Gordon's career and which led up to its heroic and sombre end in Khartoum, it seems plain that fate, fortune, Providence — or, in Gordon's own view, God — would not allow so remarkable a character to elude the fame which he at once deprecated and desired. At any rate, Gordon's statue stands with that of Nelson in Trafalgar Square, and the quixotic officer whom it commemorates is one of the best-known figures of his time.

2. Principles and Paradox

There is no man of the mid-Victorian era who is better known to us than Gordon. How far we can understand him is another matter. Certainly none of his contemporaries ever quite understood this eccentric soldier, half saint and half filibuster. He could not understand himself. As he looked into his heart, which he found more unruly than any Sudan, he noted all kinds of contradictory impulses driving him this way and that. "Talk of two natures in one," he wrote to his sister. "I have a hundred, and they none think alike and all want to rule." They all wanted to rule — an embarrassing possession for a man of action which proved too much for Gordon and, from the worldly point of view, made his career into an effective series of brilliant episodes.

Though the most single-minded of men, Gordon had no singleness of purpose. Or, if that sounds too paradoxical a statement, one may say that he never could decide what he really wanted. He was tortured by ambition, and tortured by his conscience for being ambitious. He burned with a missionary zeal, yet he believed that only in seclusion could the spiritual life be cultivated. A professional soldier who loved war, he yearned for the rôle of mystic. He professed to believe that the spiritual life was the only true one, yet he realized nothing of the intellectual subordination on which this must rest; was, in fact, bored when the solitude of religion presented itself as more than a recreation from the labors and disillusion of the life of action. Gordon knew his own weakness. He never tired of writing about himself. He probed into his mind and laid his feelings bare. He carried self-analysis to a point which might be dangerous even in the cloister. He was contemptuous of the world, and yet he simply could not give the world up. He wrestled with "Agag" — the giant in him who hankered after praise and fame. Holding the views he did, he knew it was wrong to wish, in his own words, "to hail the tram of the world." But he boarded it nevertheless.

His career reflected the complexities of his character. In his early thirties this young officer of Engineers was already famous. He returned in 1865 from China with a well-founded reputation for brilliant leadership in war. The story of his crushing of the Taeping Rebellion in two swift campaigns thrilled and gratified England, always ready to react to the glamour of the East and now also reassured regarding its trade on the Yangtze. "Chinese" Gordon everyone called him. The British public prepared to treat him as a lion. But

Gordon already had a decided antipathy to being lionized, and, like Arabian Lawrence more than fifty years later, he refused to play. Why, he asked, should he be treated like a hero when he had simply put his hand to the day's work? The idea of publicity — still a virginal word in the eighteen-sixties — horrified him. "I had rather be dead than praised" expressed his own feeling about fame, which another Protestant as stern as Gordon has called the "last infirmity of noble minds." Shyness, the philosophy of the Covenanter, pride — all doubtless impelled Gordon to disclaim the plaudits of the crowd, and to shun the social obligations on which the Victorians laid such stress. He disliked showing himself in drawing-rooms. Dinner parties filled him with disgust — or, worse still, with boredom. When he found that his manuscript journal was passing from hand to hand, and that even Secretaries of State were being enchanted by the chronicle of his exploits in China, he destroyed it. Though the use of what was called private influence was an accepted means for securing professional advancement in the British Army, Gordon refused to pull any strings at the Horse Guards or the War Office. He would not attempt to rise at the expense of his brother officers of the Royal Engineers. It was clear that this Brevet Lieutenant-Colonel, who held the rank of captain in his own corps, was an odd and difficult man. But he proved more compliant than Colonel Lawrence in one thing. He accepted a C.B. It was the only honor he ever received from his own sovereign.

Partly as the result of these peculiarities of temperament, partly from regimental officers' jealousy of specialists, as sappers were considered to be, Gordon's talents never secured proper recognition from the military authorities at home. He was looked upon as an engineer, and was kept to the specialist's limited field. Instead of being used at headquarters to help in reorganizing a hopelessly out-of-date military machine, or being employed somewhere on the frontiers of an uneasily expanding empire, he was sent on his return from China to build forts at the mouth of the Thames. His strategical eye, his tactical experience, soon told him that in war they would be useless. His fluent pen passed on the information to his superiors. No attention was paid to his remarks, and he spent six hours a day for six years upon this wasted labor, each year making it more improbable that he would ever find scope for his energy and ability within the British Army. Yet his Gravesend period, if professionally a wasted time, was of vital importance in his spiritual development. The scenes of human misery which he had observed in China had predisposed his naturally serious temperament to seek the consolation of religion. His father's death, soon after his return from the East, assisted in what was not so much a conversion as the natural growth of his character. At Gravesend, Gordon turned to the Bible for a key to the enigma of suffering which he saw around him and experienced in his own mind. In the study of its pages he discovered the truth which the prophet Ruskin afterwards declared Gordon's death had taught, that "for all human love and pain there is no comfort, no interpretation worth a thought, except only in the doctrine of the resurrection." More simply, Gordon declared that he saw the "temporal irradiated with the eternal." The vision never left him. On the contrary, it grew clearer year by year — but it did not blot out worldly ambition.

This was starved at Gravesend. He found little more to satisfy it when he was appointed British representative on the Danube Commission, which was a highly paid sinecure, and Gordon cared nothing for money. But when he happened to be in Constantinople in 1872 he met at the British Embassy Nubar Pasha, Prime Minister to Ismail, the Khedive of Egypt. Nubar asked him to recommend some Engineer officer to succeed Sir Samuel Baker in the Sudan. Ultimately Gordon offered his own services, and early in 1874 he started the work with which posterity has connected his name. It provided problems very different from those he had encountered in China. There he had been only a soldier of fortune, a mercenary engaged in reducing rebels against a government with which his own had recently been at war. On the equatorial Nile, where his command under the Khedive lay, he took part in that opening up of Africa which was the most striking political achievement of Europe in the latter decades of the nineteenth century. He showed an extraordinary activity and resource as he fought against man and nature, as he battled with the slavers and the sudd, the pashas in Cairo and the authorities in Whitehall. When he left Egypt in 1880, as he thought for good, he had made for himself another and a greater reputation. His fame, compounded of daring and saintliness, grew to be something of a legend, his name a talisman with the public — if a *bête noire* of officialdom.

It was at this moment that the Prince of Wales intervened to prevent his leaving the British Army. But the Duke of Cambridge was mistaken if he thought that Gordon would long be content to recuperate in Switzerland. True, he refused to accept command of the colonial forces which the Cape Government, troubled by the Basutos, offered him. And the Congo scheme hung fire. But when Lord Ripon, appointed by the new Gladstone Administration to the Indian Viceroyalty, asked Gordon to accompany him as private secretary, Gordon after some hesitation decided to accept this responsible post. He went to India — and resigned almost as soon as he got there. In the meantime the Chinese Government, now in difficulties with Russia, remembered the honest British Major of Engineers whom the Emperor had made a Marshal and a mandarin. Would Gordon return to China? He asked for leave to go. It was refused him. He cabled resigning his commission, and rushed to Peking. There he gave peaceful counsel in his most self-assertive and authoritarian manner. The punctilious Chinese were shocked, but they took his advice and thus avoided a hopeless war with Russia.

At Hongkong, on his way home, Gordon, who believed he was a free man, learned that his resignation had been refused, and dispatched a sardonic cable to the War Office. "Could you not have trusted me?" he asked. Having nothing to do, he spent part of the winter of 1881 visiting Southern Ireland, investigating the distress there prevalent. On this and other subjects he wrote to the papers. His mind had never been more active. He burned to put the world to rights, and the world would give him nothing to do! Hating his enforced idleness, he telegraphed to the Cape Government offering the assistance to bring the Basuto War to an end which he had previously refused. When he received no answer he decided to visit the Holy Land. By accident he met a brother officer at the War Office who ruefully complained that he had been ordered to Mauritius, and declared that he would rather retire than take up his appointment in that remote and unpopular station. Gordon at once offered to go in his place. He had been there only a few months when the Cape Government decided to ask for his services. Believing that "a man must be like a well-broken horse, ready for anything," Gordon started for the Cape. He reached Cape Town in May 1882, and spent six months in South Africa, leaving in October after having hopelessly quarreled with the Colonial Government.

Back in England, he revived his old project of visiting Palestine, and there he spent nearly the whole of 1883, studying the sites of Biblical history, pondering upon the difficulties, topographical and sacramental, of Christianity, and always reading and rereading his Bible. The results of his researches and meditations were embodied in his *Reflections in Palestine*, published when its author was already shut up in Khartoum.

This Indian summer in a restless life soon came to an end. Gordon wearied of an inactivity which he thought selfish, and listened again to King Leopold's overtures on the subject of employment in the Congo. On January 1, 1884, he reached Brussels from the Holy Land, and it seemed decided that Gordon would serve still another foreign potentate when his strange career took its last and most dramatic turn. The British Cabinet, mortally bothered about the Sudan, where Hicks Pasha and his army of 10,000 had lately been cut to pieces by the Mahdi, decided to use Gordon, the only man, it was thought, who could deal with the situation. Gordon responded with alacrity. By the end of January he was at Korosko, far up the Nile, for the first time in his life undertaking an important mission on behalf of his own government. Before another twelve months had passed he was dead — killed at his post, a victim, as everyone believed, to Ministerial incompetence. And the Sudan, where he had labored and died, was destined to lie for the next thirteen years under the most abominable type of African tyranny.

Such, in brief, was the apparently fruitless career of a man about whom more has been written than of any other British soldier since Wellington.

His death gave him immortality. Yet perhaps he does not owe it altogether to the glory shed upon his memory by his defense of Khartoum. Other British soldiers have fallen at the hands of savages rather than desert their posts, and their names have not been remembered. Nor is it because Gordon, both in China and in Africa, did work that particularly interested an Imperialist age and flattered the white man's racial pride. His military prowess, never tested against white troops, and his political vision, likewise never tried by supreme responsibility, would not have of themselves secured him the worldly fame which he at once shunned and courted. The fact is that Gordon was greater than anything he did or dreamed. Granted that he was "an ideal leader of half-civilized man," granted that his views on the responsibilities of Europe *vis-à-vis* Asia and Africa were extraordinarily enlightened, yet we remember Gordon for what he was, and posterity follows the example of his contemporaries in submitting to the charm of a romantic and fascinating figure who never acted from the dull motive of personal gain. As he strode through the mid-Victorian era his equals bowed willingly to a moral superiority absolutely without either priggishness or pretense. "My hero Gordon, whom I served when he lived and whose memory I shall always cherish" — so wrote hard-headed Lord Wolseley, the most distinguished soldier in Queen Victoria's Army. "Our precious martyr" was the expression used of him by Mohammed Nushi Pasha, one of the Egyptian officers at the siege of Khartoum, who regretted that he had not been able to share his chief's fate. Even the celestials mourned the death of one who possessed the born leader's power of inspiring devotion and confidence. "The men like my justice, candor, my outbursts of temper," he once wrote to his sister from the Sudan. He remains likable to us for the same reasons.

We may sometimes smile, as his contemporaries smiled, at his eccentricities, or what Lord Wolseley called his vanities, but Gordon returns the smile far more enigmatically. He has inspired many biographers to eulogize, vindicate, explain that rich personality. He has been shown as a consummate soldier, a statesman, a hero, an adventurer, a saint, and, to an age in love with exaggeration, as a man half mad and something of a drunkard. With all this, as he passed, contemptuous of the world around him, through life to the death he unceasingly desired, one cannot help seeing that he was happy in his generation, and more in sympathy with his time than he realized. Had he lived in the eighteenth century he might have been another Clive, but his humanitarianism could never have flowered, his piety would have withered, in that skeptical atmosphere; he could never have felt towards the people of India as he felt towards the Chinese and the downtrodden natives of the Sudan. If he had been born fifty years later he would have been beaten by the centralization which now saps the initiative in subordinate ranks of the public service, and is largely responsible for the lack of leadership we deplore in this present day.

Gordon's idiosyncrasies, too, funny as they seem to us at first sight, like the pot hat of the mid-Victorian male and the bustle of the mid-Victorian female, are toned down when we place him in proper perspective against the background of the sixties and seventies. Certainly Augusta Gordon, the dominating influence of his life, was an austere personage, even for that time, when so many daughters of the professional classes grew grim in their spinsterhood. But the Bible, by which Gordon measured every thought and action, was still the universal textbook of the Anglo-Saxon race on both sides of the Atlantic. Mrs. Eddy in New Hampshire, like Miss Gordon in old Hampshire, pored over its pages. It colored Abraham Lincoln's speech and thought. When Gladstone agreed to write some articles about the Old Testament — like his contemporaries, he read the Old Testament more than the New — he retired to Oxford to "make himself safe" in his subject. Even the agnostics could not leave it alone. Soldiers shared the general taste, and piety and war were on better terms than they had been at any time since the Roundheads. Other generals besides Gordon studied the Bible and believed that prayer helped to win battles. Stonewall Jackson bears a striking resemblance to our hero, with his penciled annotations of Scripture, his habit of silent prayer, his passion for exact truth, ordered charity, and early rising. General Lee was another in that gallery of Christian militants, with Havelock and Lawrence and Wolseley. But none followed out their principles with the devotion of Gordon.

And at the end he eludes both praise and blame. "If a man speaks well of me, divide it by millions and then it will be millions of times too favorable. If a man speaks evil of me, multiply it by millions and it will be millions of times too favorable." This was the self-judgment of a man who took Job and Thomas à Kempis for his models, who in the end came to believe that he was chosen to be the scapegoat for the sacrifice, yet who with this conviction grew ever more morbidly sensitive to criticism.

I

YOUTH AND THE CRIMEA
(1833–1860)

Son, it behoveth thee to give all for all and for nothing of thine to be to thyself.

THOMAS À KEMPIS, *The Imitation of Christ*

1. The Influences of Heredity

Gordon was born on January 28, 1833, one of the younger members of a large family. Five sons and six daughters blessed this Gordon hearth, which was ruled by a punctilious and laughter-loving master, a pious yet cheerful mistress. Our hero's breeding would have satisfied any Victorian counterpart of the eugenically minded Dr. Inge. He was a soldier born. In the male line he was the descendant of three generations of men who had followed a military career with more or less distinction. Beyond these his lineage went back to the Gordon clansmen who for centuries lived and perished by the sword. Their staunchness, or a simplicity that blinded them to the fact that they were backing the wrong horse, made them good Jacobites, and Charles was not an uncommon Christian name in the clan. But the great-grandfather of the most famous of all the Gordons, showing an independence of judgment which one remarks in his descendant, went over to the Hanoverians. This David Gordon took part in the battle of Fontenoy, and a few years later actually fought against his own clansmen at Prestonpans, where he was made prisoner by his kinsmen. David Gordon was actuated by the true Gordon zeal for the master he served, a fact sufficiently well indicated when the Duke of Cumberland — the butcher of Culloden, who put so many Gordons to the sword — stood sponsor to his son, William Augustus. This scion of the race in due time entered the British Army, and was present at the capture of Quebec. All his three sons became soldiers in their turn, William Henry, the father of Charles, serving in the Royal Artillery, and proving by his ability in this specialized branch of the army in which he rose to the rank of Lieutenant-General that he had more brains than the average officer in Her Majesty's service. Charles, therefore, inherited Gordon blood whose native willfulness had been sobered by the hard discipline of barrack and camp, while its heat had been maintained by frequent experience in the school of war.

His mother, Elizabeth Enderby, introduced different strains. She was a daughter of Samuel Enderby, a London and New England shipowner, who had large views on the development of world trade. Enderby's whalers, which were registered in both London and Boston, were the first ships to prove that the route round the Horn was a commercial possibility, opening up trading relations with Australia and helping to give the first colonists to New Zealand. They attempted to trade with Japan, then closed to the outer world. It was, too, in Samuel Enderby's bottoms that the famous consignment of tea reached Boston in 1773 — thus our Gordon had slender links through both his grandfathers with the New World. Enderby's ventures were of sufficient importance to attract the favorable notice of the younger Pitt, who backed him in his trade with the western seaboard of South America, an old source of contention with Spain. When the Spanish Government proclaimed that any foreign vessel caught within fifty miles of their coasts would be confiscated, Enderby laid the case before the Prime Minister. "What distance would satisfy you?" he was asked. "Twenty miles," Enderby answered. "Make it five," said Pitt, "and if you are caught within that limit, say you are short of water and need a supply."

But if Samuel Enderby's grandson inherited his English grandfather's vision and power of seeing affairs in broad perspective — faculties denied to his Scots ancestors — he had also from him a legacy of another kind. The Enderbys came of that middle-class Puritan stock which had been untouched by the genial skepticism of the eighteenth century. These solid traders took their religion far more seriously than the gay Gordons. They labored to amass wealth, but the knowledge that they were ever in their great Taskmaster's eye prevented them from enjoying it. Mistrusting institutional religion and the voice of the Church, which was controlled by the class above them, they based their faith on the Bible. It was God's Word, and it contained the sum of all wisdom. Upon its quarto pages lay the truth that made all things plain, or as plain as was good for men. There might be heterogeneous teaching, contradictory doctrine, in Holy Scripture; but these did not worry the normal, workaday Christian, who, so long as he went about his business and scanned no spiritual horizons, found in the Bible a magnificent handbook — a Book to inspire the same self-confidence in dealing with worldly matters as it inculcated in the things of the spirit. British industry and trade would never have written that extraordinary chapter in the economic history of mankind if so many of its leaders had not been formed in the sturdy Evangelical school which taught that every man must work out, unaided, his own salvation in this world and in the next.

2. Gordon's Childhood

This was the religious atmosphere in which Charles Gordon's childish mind was formed. He learned at his mother's knee that every word in the Bible was literally true, that the accounts of Eve eating the apple and Joshua making the sun stand still were just as much chronicles of fact as the grieving of Ruth beside the alien corn or the punishment which fell on Sodom and Gomorrah. In spite of occasional backslidings, he never seriously questioned that early teaching. We find him in after years writing, "There is only one sin, and that is unbelief." Paul had settled the matter in his letter to the Ephesians — salvation came through faith. Believe and be saved! When it came to defining what a Christian should believe, difficulties began for him who looked to the Bible for providing dogmas, and Gordon, who had a dogmatic and logical mind, was later on often to be overwhelmed by the burden which he shouldered so willingly.

In those early years, however, like the Gentile Apostle to whom his admirers afterwards compared him, he thought as a child and spoke as a child. He was a bright and high-spirited, if delicate, boy. His father shed the warmth of a jolly early Victorian parent upon the family circle, a military Mr. Wardle with a twinkle in his eye and a pun upon his lips, yet a man for all that with decided views about right and wrong and the honor of a soldier. Though a more shadowy figure, his mother has also left a memory of cheerfulness to color the natural piety of her temperament. Plenty of fun sweetened life in that large family, which was constantly being transplanted to new quarters. As his father was moved from station to station, from Pigeon House Fort, in Dublin Bay, to Leith, from Leith Fort to Corfu (then a British protectorate), the small boy perhaps acquired that physical restlessness which so strongly marked his character throughout life. Still, it was a good training for the future soldier who, despite his martial breeding, was as a child alarmed by the noise of gunfire. Charlie may have been his mother's favorite — "Oh, how my mother loved me!" he wrote many years later to his sister Augusta. There was little fear, however, with so many children, that any one of them would be coddled or spoiled. Mrs. Gordon, who found plenty to occupy her time and energy in providing for the family wants and in managing her numerous household upon the narrow income of an Army officer, eked out by her own modest jointure, must have delegated a good many of her duties to Augusta, twelve years Charles's senior and a girl of strong character. She came to occupy the chief place in her younger brother's affections, and helped both consciously and unconsciously to mould his nature. Had it not been for her influence, Gordon might never have even developed the mystical tendencies which played so large a part in determining his later life. The psychological reactions of excessive intimacy between mother and son, or, as in this case, between brother and sister, have only recently been understood, and we may trace Gordon's coldness towards other women to his devotion to Augusta. In consequence Gordon, all unconsciously, became in this matter a Platonist, and found an outlet for the emotions generated by intercourse with the opposite sex in the company of boys and young men.

Gordon's childhood held little glamour for him when he looked back on it as a man. He was a determined and courageous little boy, who before he could swim would throw himself into deep Mediterranean water and then expect others to rescue him. The stubbornness of the man showed itself in the child's quickness to resent and slowness to forgive what he considered injustice, as when the threat of not being allowed to go to a circus caused him to stay at home after the ban was lifted.

Churchgoing, then a very formidable matter, bored him, and he never lost his fear of Christmas and New Year's Day, both "feast days" in the Gordon family's religious calendar. Easter, too, was a bad time. "What husks the Evangelical religion is," stands as a comment of thirty years later, when he still shuddered at "the thought of those fearful sermons." They lasted an hour and even made the pious Augusta cross. But he found some compensation in the curtained pews, which afforded good cover for bored and fidgety children. "I remember one somewhere which was like a small hut, where you could have made your toilet and no one would have been any the wiser."

But plain living and Sunday's church services did not depress the Gordon animal spirits. Charlie and his brothers found plenty of scope in Woolwich Arsenal, where their father was now quartered, for satisfying their love of mischief. They played all kinds of pranks. They persuaded the workmen to make them squirts — and what more thrilling weapons can boys have than these? "Splendid articles," Gordon described them, "which would wet you through in a minute." Still more formidable were the crossbows, also surreptitiously turned out in the government workshops at the public expense. These fired screws with a lethal force; twenty-seven broken windows and the narrow escape of a captain, by whose head a screw whizzed, embedding itself in the opposing wall, were the work of a single afternoon — and that a Sunday. Sabbatarianism could not subdue the vivacity of these young Gordons, who found that life was fun in spite of everything they were taught to the contrary. They caught mice and set them scampering in the front hall of the Commandant's house; they made Freddy, who was younger than Charles, pay calls on the officers' wives, insisting that he should stay at least ten minutes, otherwise he had to visit another of the officers' ladies, who thought Freddy a strangely polite little boy. Charlie noticed that as the workmen left the Arsenal after their day's work a certain number were touched on the shoulder by the police at the gates — a sign that they must stop and be searched. One day he and his brother decided to assist the police, and gave so many workmen the signal to go into the police office at the gate that complete confusion reigned. Still more daring, they bombarded one evening with handfuls of shot the lecture room in the Arsenal where a class of cadets were receiving instruction. These rushed out amid the crash of breaking glass to punish the disturbers of the peace, but Charlie and his brothers escaped in the dark through the fieldworks, which they knew better than the cadets who had dug them.

Such were some of the escapades, or, if you like, the unconscious self-preparation of the future soldier, into which Charlie led the junior members of the Gordon family during the holidays. He lived before the days when a boy who had not been at a public school lost caste among his fellows. At the age of ten he went to Taunton Grammar School, for no better reason than that the headmaster was brother of the family governess. There he spent five years, showing no special aptitude except with his pencil, a talent which was to serve him well in his fighting career.

The débris of anecdotage which has been saved from oblivion shows Charlie Gordon the boy as father of the man. At the Woolwich Academy, which he entered in 1848, — ominous year for the peace of Europe, — the youth now growing to manhood proved himself at once wilder and more serious than his fellows. He submitted to authority with bad grace. We see him on one occasion charging, head downwards, a cadet underofficer who by order was barring the usual exit from the mess, and knocking him backwards down a flight of stairs. For this serious breach of discipline Gordon's career nearly comes to an end before it has well begun. When rebuked and told that he will never make an officer, he tears off his epaulettes and throws them at his superior's feet. The father shakes his head over this young Ishmael; "while he is in the Academy," he declares, "I feel I am like a man sitting on a powder barrel." Then Charlie was implicated in a ragging case, and though no one who knew this impulsive but frank youngster believed that he had anything of the bully about him, he was deprived of a term's seniority. The punishment was severe, for it put all the members of his term over his head. But it had a decisive influence in shaping his destiny.

He had none of the facility for mathematics which so

many distinguished soldiers have possessed. He saw, however, that the six months' additional study might enable him to obtain a high enough place in the passing-out examination for a commission in the Royal Engineers. Charlie Gordon worked hard, and the memory of that time remained with him all his life. "I had a fearful dream last night — I was back at the Academy, and had to pass an examination!" he wrote eighteen months before his death. Still, he succeeded in his desire to gain admission to the highest-paid branch of the service, an ambition prompted by the wish to save his parents' pockets, and in 1852 he was duly gazetted a second-lieutenant in the Royal Engineers. The fact that he belonged to this corps led him ultimately to the Sudan. Thus the blow with a broomstick on a fellow cadet's head in the year 1851 was responsible for bringing him and the Mahdi, at that time a naked little Arab boy, together at Khartoum thirty-three years later.

When Gordon looked back on his youth he usually saw it in the sombre tints that covered all the world of his maturity. Certainly there was a more serious side to the seemingly irresponsible young cadet whose ebullient spirits got him into so many scrapes. He had already begun to think about the ways of God to man, and had already established that intellectual compromise to which he consistently adhered between predestination and free will. Helped by the influence of the Reverend Capel Molyneux, minister of Trinity Church, Woolwich, he realized that God ruled all, had ordained all from eternity, that nothing happened except by God's deliberate intention. All this he knew, and yet it was clear to him that man must work out his own salvation.

We find from a later letter that, when the question of his being confirmed arose, Gordon "thought it was a useless sin." It aroused, we may believe, the instinctive aversion of his Protestant Enderby blood to religious authority. Besides, he was wild and he did not intend to alter, though he also understood that the power of being converted did not reside in himself. Conversion could only come from God. In any case, Gordon, though he turned over his first new leaf when he was twenty-one and for a time became a regular communicant, never obeyed the rule of the Church which declares the one sacrament to be a necessary preliminary to the other. He was not one of those who learned to command in the school of obedience.

So this strange young man, with all the jumble of inherited qualities which had come to him from Gordons and Enderbys and the whole spreading line of his ancestry, entered upon the difficult business of life. On the one hand were his brother officers, with whom he could enjoy himself in the bluff, hilarious fashion of the time; on the other was Augusta, already a spinster of over thirty and much given to reading pious books in her own room. Charles used to chaff her particularly when she received the parts of Scott's Commentary as they were published. But the influence of his elder sister was to win in the end — she was the heroine of the tragedy of Gordon's life and his future ally in the battle he came to wage, not with man, but with what he called the flesh.

3. The First Conversion

The idiosyncrasies of the young man's character developed when he exchanged the gregarious life of the Royal Engineers barracks at Chatham for comparative solitude at Pembroke, where he was sent to work on the fortifications of that recently established naval base. At first he found it dull. Time hung heavy on his hands. His military duties were finished by two o'clock; the rest of the day was his own. There is no record of Gordon ever having shown the slightest interest in games, which, in any case, exercised only a mild sway over the Englishman of the eighteen-fifties. Cricket had its votaries, but golf had not yet spread its gospel of leisure for the middle classes, and lawn tennis was still unborn. Sport remained the only recreation for the English gentleman, and while Gordon liked shooting, no record exists of his having been able to gratify his taste at Pembroke. Under similar circumstances of enforced semi-idleness the young Napoleon devoured the history of the past; Gordon, not less open-eyed and also longing to play his part in the world, read "every paper that was published," and so began to develop those political interests which grew to be a devouring passion. Later on he came to think that this taste was a sinful one, but at this stage he was a tyro in spiritual matters, a novice basking in the genial and priggish warmth of his first conversion.

Already the vast fissure running through Gordon's character had appeared.

> It is a great blessing for me that in my profession I can be intimate with whom I like, and have not the same trials among my brother officers as those in a Line regiment have. I ought not to say this, for "where sin aboundeth, grace aboundeth more fully"; but I am such a miserable wretch, that I should be sure to be led away. Dearest Augusta, pray for me, I beg of you.

So he wrote when the ennui of the first few months at Pembroke had had their effect. The sole responsibility for this turning over a new leaf, as Gordon called it, did not lie with his elder sister. He had made friends with "a very religious captain of the 11th" named Drew, whom he drove about the country in his gig, and who became his confidant in things spiritual. Or, rather, they exchanged religious confidences, Gordon reading *The Priceless Diamond*, which Drew kept on his mantelpiece, and in return telling his friend of the merits of the Reverend Capel Molyneux, a minister of a very different stamp from their local pastor, who was "a worldly man" and did "not live up to his preaching."

Others besides Captain Drew helped to make Gordon believe that he had overcome his native restlessness, and this at a time when the Crimean War must have been constantly in his thoughts. He was attracted by Mrs. Drew, "a very stylish person and an ardent admirer of Mr. Molyneux." And he became friendly with many of the humbler folk of the place, one of them being the ferryman who recalled, when Gordon revisited Pembroke a quarter of a century later, how he was "the gent who used to walk across the stream right through the water," an incident in the Spartan training which Gordon then and always imposed on the body which he feared.

So passed the first months of Gordon's service as a full-fledged lieutenant. He flattered himself that he felt happier now that he had some curb for the ambition of which a by-product was envy and backbiting. There was plenty of this in Pembroke, "the most gossiping place in Europe." His anxiety that others should share the light caused him to hope that his "dear father and mother think of eternal things," and to wonder whether he could do or say anything to either to bring this about. These aspirations were communicated in confidence to Augusta. To his parents he wrote of more worldly matters — of the early battles in the Crimea, of his amusement when Sir George Browne was nearly taken by Cossacks, of the nuisance of the changes in uniform imposed by the War Office, which was not too much taken up with the war to issue new regulations about the cut of tunics and the gold braid on full-dress trousers.

As the autumn of 1854 wore on, and it became evident that Russian resistance to the allied armies would be more prolonged than men had supposed, Gordon's chances of going to the front grew brighter. When, therefore, at the end of November he received orders to proceed to Corfu, he reproached his mother for having, as he believed, used her interest to prevent his being sent to the Crimea, where his two elder brothers were already serving. "It is a great shame of you," he wrote, though he consoled himself with the thought that he might have been ordered to the West Indies or New Zealand, where he would have been out of the war for good. However, on this occasion, if on no other, Gordon condescended to pull strings. Through Sir John Burgoyne, an old friend of the family, his destination was changed, and he was told to proceed to the Crimea in charge of huts for the winter quarters of the troops, and to supervise their erection when he got there. It was a modest entry into the life of action for which the young soldier longed. Yet, at the moment of his receiving orders for active service, Gordon's other self, who exchanged texts with Augusta and saw the world as irredeemably evil, refused to yield place, and prompted in him "the sincere hope" that he would be killed. Naturally he said nothing about it; he only mentioned it years afterwards to his sister in a moment of reminiscence. But the confession shows how little Gordon changed in the course of his life, for it was in the same spirit that he undertook all his enterprises and at the end started for Khartoum. If this complete indifference to death, which his desire for the other world prompted even in those early days, was one of the secrets of his power as a leader of fighting men, it also fostered the self-abnegation which grew to be indistinguishable from vanity or pride, and set the seal on Gordon's ultimate failure.

The extremely competent sapper subaltern, however, kept these thoughts in the back of his mind as he rushed to London, reported at the War Office, and, with the assistance of Cox, — that god of the banking machine to countless gentlemen holding their sovereign's commission, — prepared a very complete outfit which included plenty of warm clothing and a good supply of tea. In forty-eight hours he was at Portsmouth, which struck his professional eye as a very strong place, supervising the loading of the hut sections in colliers.

The time was the middle of December, and Gordon, for all his intrepidity, quailed as he looked forward to the passage across the Bay of Biscay in a small tramp steamer. Yielding to his fears, he secured a reversal of his orders to accompany the huts, and he was allowed to travel overland. It caused him some embarrassment when he learned that he would have to pay for his ticket himself and apply for a refund. Had he known this he would almost have been persuaded to face the dreaded seasickness. With such various regrets and hopes did Gordon at the age of twenty-two prepare for his first experience of war.

4. War

Gordon en route for the Crimea was not yet the blasé traveler he afterwards became, when the sight of a new city only stirred in him more strongly the desire to see the City not built with hands, and he appears to have enjoyed his journey. "Very flat and dull" is his rather unobservant description of the country between Calais and Paris, which he reached twenty hours after leaving London. Of the French capital he says nothing, but the bridges of Lyons appealed to his engineering mind, and he enjoyed the journey by boat down the Rhone to Valence. At Marseilles — "we leave this (D.V.) on Monday," he wrote from that Mediterranean port with a characteristic reference to Providence — he embarked on a French boat, and, in spite of the rough weather, was able to observe the gaiety and high spirits of the French troops under conditions of discomfort that, he considered, would have driven British soldiers to mutiny. They landed at Messina, recently swept by the cholera, and put in at the Piræus, "a miserable place." Athens seemed "very ugly and dirty," though he describes the Acropolis as a beautiful ruin, and he submitted to the charm of the view from the Parthenon. Thus, pursuing a leisurely journey, they reached the Dardanelles at one o'clock on Christmas Day. The Straits that were to gain so sinister a reputation in a subsequent war did not appear to Gordon very strongly fortified, for he noticed that the forts, though numerous, were open at the rear and overlooked by the heights behind.

The vessel called at Gallipoli, which had been an English base, and finally reached Constantinople on the afternoon of Boxing Day, Gordon's first impression of New Rome being one of disappointment at the lowness of the hills and the squalor of the city. Santa Sophia passed unnoticed, and the other mosques of the Caliph's city. Later on he visited Justinian's great church, of which the interior reminded him of St. Paul's — not a very apt comparison. The only buildings to attract his attention were the Seraglio, the Russian Embassy, and the hospital at Scutari. He crossed to Asia next day, and was able to inform his parents that the wounded had now all the comforts they wanted. He makes no reference to Florence Nightingale. An action which might appear less in keeping with the mature Gordon, as we know him, was his asking one of the entourage of the Duke of Cambridge, then in Constantinople, to tell the Duke who he was and to say that he had inquired after him. But friendliness, and no desire for advancement, had prompted it. Gordon had already made up his mind that this must come only in the ordinary course of promotion, imposed upon him in any case by the rule in the Royal Engineers, where everything went by seniority. The whole duty of a soldier was "to kill and be killed."

From the first Gordon observed this maxim with an absence of fanaticism refreshing after the bitterness with which civilian mentality has invested the horrors of war. He bore no iota of ill-will to the enemy, admired the skill of their engineers, never doubted the courage of the Russian soldiers, though he rather regretted that they were not as devout as the small copper crosses they wore and the prayer books they carried seemed to indicate, and when an armistice enabled him to converse with Russian officers he found nothing against them except that they did not look particularly clean. Such animosity as Gordon allowed himself was directed against the French, and he specially disliked Canrobert's showy qualities. "From high to low we hate the French much more than the Russians," was his verdict eighteen months later.

He arrived on January 1, 1855, when a lull had succeeded the costly early battles of the war, and for some weeks he was engaged in putting up the huts. Gordon gives us a picture of an army interested in only one thing, — its stomach, — even the "swell English cavalry and Horse Artillery carrying rations," and officers in every conceivable costume foraging for eatables. Bread was very dear, a small loaf costing two shillings, but Gordon, who had absolutely no interest in food, found the commissariat efficient enough, and wanted for nothing in the way of things to eat. There are really no hardships for the officers, he declares, and, while the men suffer, it is partly their fault, because "they are like children, thinking everything is to be done for them." Again he contrasts them with the French soldier, who looks out for himself and in consequence fares much better. Often, too, in his letters he refers to the "atrocious fibs about the conditions at the front which are published in the English papers."

Gordon never submitted easily to the facile prejudices of patriotism, nor subscribed to the complacent Victorian view that an Englishman had an abnormal stock of resourcefulness or courage. Even the public did not believe that the higher ranks of the services were distinguished by brains or possessed any particular foresight. The Crimean campaign proved particularly fertile in negative examples of this quality. Britannia muddled more than her wont, and did not always even rule the waves. Gordon wrote on January 18, 1855: —

I saw Sebastopol yesterday for the first time, and do not think I ever saw a prettier city; it looks quite open, and a Russian steamer was cruising about inside the harbor. Two of their steamers came out the other day and bombarded the French lines for two hours, but our vessels were unable to move out to attack them, as their steam was not up. For the future it will always be up.

The mature Gordon would not have written so mildly.

When he was posted to the trenches he soon found things to criticize, including the conduct of the Line officers, who were too much disposed, he considered, to stay in the shelters when their men were on working parties, leaving them "to do more as they like than as they should." This slackness offended the zeal of the cheerful and observant young subaltern who believed so strongly in the force of example. His first turn of duty in the front line indicated his own powers of leadership. A night operation had been planned to strengthen the advance posts where the French and English trenches met. He collected eight men with picks and shovels, and obtained sentries from the infantry captain in command of that particular section, who complained that it was the first time he had been on duty there. Gordon showed his moral superiority by concealing the fact that he too had never been on that ground before. He crept out alone to reconnoitre, and, going farther than was wise, found himself almost within the enemy's lines. Discovering his error in time, he returned and led his little party forward. In No Man's Land were some caves which might have contained Russians. Gordon went on, and explored them almost alone, a trying experience which he admitted he did not like. He left a couple of sentries above the entrance, and worked his way round in order to place a couple more below it. As they reached the spot two rifle shots rang out and the bullets hit the ground beside them. The sentries with Gordon retired "in a rare state of mind"; the working party simply bolted. But it soon became evident that the panic was not caused by the Russians. The shots had been fired by the two sentries above the caves, who had then run back to the trenches in such a hurry that they lost their caps. After some difficulty Gordon got his working party together again, and carried out the job with which he had been entrusted. But nothing would induce the sentries to come out a second time, for the Russians were now on the alert and keeping up a fire from a distance of 150 yards. Gordon offers no comment on the incident. It was an officer's duty to face danger. If he did so unconcernedly his men would probably follow him. Leadership and discipline were the vital factors in war. Humor also helped to keep nerves steady. When Gordon was struck in the face by stones thrown up by a shell he made the men in the trenches laugh by pretending to light his cigar at the red hair of the surgeon attending him.

So long as Gordon thought as a soldier he thought clearly. He admits to finding something "indescribably exciting in war," — a feeling which later in life he tried to stifle, — but as a rule he avoids such generalizations, contenting himself with recording the pleasure he takes in his work, and mentioning his own narrow escapes and the casualties in the corps with professional detachment. Why should death be feared when it was but the gateway to a more glorious life? At twenty-two Gordon believed that not a mouse fell into a cat's clutches except by the Will of God. In the end he came to think that every mosquito was accounted for in Heaven. "We lost one of our captains, named Craigie, by a splinter of a shell," he writes. "I am glad to say he was a serious man. The shell burst above him and, by what is called chance, struck him in the back, killing him instantly." Even the loss of a friend is weighed in the scales of futurity. "Poor Carter" (like himself, a sapper subaltern), "I had known him for years; he is to be buried to-day. We have a great deal to regret in the way of good working clergymen." So Gordon writes to his mother, while he tries to allay her anxiety for his own safety and assures her more than once that he will not run any avoidable risks. "No volunteering for me," he says, "as I have nothing to gain." In any case, he does not wish to be "lamented" after death.

He was too good a soldier to court unnecessary danger, but senior officers marked his preternatural coolness as well as his exceptional knowledge of the trenches, in which the turns of duty for the sapper officers came round with excessive frequency. General Sir Charles Staveley, at that time a Lieutenant-Colonel of infantry, afterwards wrote: —

I happened to mention to Charlie Gordon that I was field officer for the day for command in the trenches next day, and, having only just returned from sick leave, that I was ignorant of the geography of our left attack. He said at once, "Oh! come down with me to-night after dark, and I will show you over the trenches." He drew me out a very clear sketch of the lines (which I have now), and down I went accordingly. He explained every nook and corner, and took me along outside our most advanced trench, the bouquets (volleys of small shells fired from mortars) and other missiles flying about us in, to me, a very unpleasant manner, he taking the matter remarkably coolly.

Gordon hardly appears to have felt the hardships which such night duty must have entailed during a Russian winter when men were found frozen to death at their posts. "I have now been thirty-four times twenty hours in the trenches, more than a month straight on end," he writes at the beginning of August, 1855, yet his only comment is, "It gets tedious after a time, but if anything is going on one does not mind."

This "impassioned lieutenant of sappers," as Kinglake described him, saw his first big engagement in the middle of June, when the French and English planned a joint attack on

Sebastopol, which was confidently expected to end what, he says, "may be the last of modern sieges according to the old rules." It was preceded by an intensive bombardment, to which the Russians replied feebly, though Gordon reported his belief, subsequently proved to be only too correct, that the enemy were merely reserving their fire. The actual assault failed because, in Gordon's opinion, it was too timidly led. The troops were kept in the trenches when they should have gone over the top. "I am confident that if we had left the trenches in a mass, some of us would have survived and reached the Redan." Once a footing had been gained there, "the Highland Brigade and Guards would have carried all before them, and the place would have fallen." When Gordon a few years later commanded an army in war he was cautious in strategy, but bold in tactics.

He makes the same criticism of the September attack on the Redan, in which the British troops managed to set foot only to be driven back. The failure was the more galling since the French succeeded in their simultaneously delivered assault on the Malakoff. "We should have carried everything before us," he writes, "if the men had only advanced." Another attempt was planned for the next day, and Gordon was detailed as one of the Royal Engineer officers in charge of the scaling ladders for the Highland Brigade, which was to undertake the assault. But during the night he "heard terrible explosions," and, "going down to the trenches at 4 A.M.," he saw the town in flames. The rising sun revealed the last of the Russians leaving the place. Two hours after the fact of the enemy's evacuation had been established, Gordon received orders to begin a plan of the works.

As he explored the Russian positions he was impressed both by the enemy's ingenuity and by his lack of cleanliness. Litter and fleas abounded, but there was an "extraordinary rarity of knickknacks," which he wanted, not for himself, but for his parents and his sisters. The Russians had stripped the place. The ikons in the churches formed the only spoil, and these Gordon's religious scruples prevented him from buying. But he secured for his artilleryman father the lock and sight of a gun, — it used, he says, "to try and deposit its contents very often in my carcass, in which I am grateful to say it failed," — a Russian cap and other "rubbish" for his mother and sisters. "It is glorious," he writes, "going over their horrid batteries which used to bully us so much," but he chivalrously remarks what plucky troops the Russians were.

Those who believe that there is no school like that of war may find proof of it in these letters written by Gordon from the Crimea. The eager young man is always cheerful and contented, though when September comes round he confesses that he would like a week of partridge shooting. Ever frugal, he does his best to prevent his family from sending him the modest presents which their anxiety to relieve his hardships prompts, protesting that he is not utterly threadbare and destitute, as they seem to think; and he hardly ever mentions his two elder brothers, Henry and Enderby, both of whom were at the front, without also saying how comfortable they are. As for himself, he has no unsatisfied want, except for flannel shirts, which he fails to procure from England, ultimately becoming "quite tired of the question" and providing himself with a local substitute. From his sister he will accept nothing more than a pot of tooth paste. He is grateful to his mother for the present of an Etna spirit stove and a bottle of cherry brandy — these, with the new regulation caps, fit him out for the second winter, during which he is mainly engaged in destroying the docks and forts of Sebastopol. Pen and pencil have now a formidable rival in his camera, for he finds photography a splendid thing, since it is "so accurate and tells the truth better than any letter." He fraternizes, too, with the French, being particularly struck with the attainments of the French engineer noncommissioned officers, and when the fighting ceases goes for immense rides over the countryside, covering as much as fifty miles in a day.

If Gordon was astonished at the want of dash in the leadership of the British troops, he gained some amusement from the easily gained C.B.'s and brevet majorities that fell to favored officers with friends at headquarters, while men who had *earned* them (and he underlined this) got nothing. That was before Sebastopol fell. "*Remember I do not think* it is a hard case that we, the subs., do not get anything," he writes later. He assures his mother that he is not ambitious, and shows his desire to avoid such fame as the clever boy of the family acquires in the home circle of friends and acquaintances by insisting that she shall not "*publish* my remarks" nor exhibit his daubs, which are intended solely for her own amusement.

With this shyness or modesty or good sense, Gordon is obviously a keen soldier, having a professional preference for war and finding his life thoroughly congenial. When it is suggested that the Corps of Royal Engineers is to be divided into military and civilian branches, he says that he means to choose the former. He notes with pleasure how rapidly he is rising in the list of lieutenants, — there is nothing like war for quick promotion, — and the news that a Staff College is to be formed makes him anxious to join it.

To his brother officers, Graham and Wolseley, both of whom were to play a part in the story of Khartoum, Charlie Gordon appeared at this time as a singularly magnetic figure, with his crisp, curly brown hair and clear blue eyes, which seemed — as Lord Wolseley afterwards said — "to court something while at the same time they searched the inner soul." Lord Wolseley, then an infantry captain, was attached to the Royal Engineers, and thus had to serve under Gordon, his inferior in army rank, though not in that of the corps. The fact that under such circumstances they laid the foundations of a lifelong friendship, remembering each other in their daily prayers, shows that neither was of ordinary mettle. Both these able young men were alive to the defects which the Crimean War showed up only too plainly in the British Army. If Gordon had not possessed "the absolute singleness of purpose" remarked on by Wolseley, he might have played no less important a part than his friend, the future Field-Marshal, in the reorganization of the Army, which had remained unchanged since the days of the Peninsular War.

Gordon, who was never at any time influenced by conventional class distinctions, formed another friendship in the Crimea which was to have an important sequel nearly twenty years later, when he went to the Sudan. He was attracted by one Romulus Gessi, a young Italian Levantine acting as interpreter with the British troops. For Gessi, whose career Gordon afterwards believed was indissolubly linked with his own, we may believe that he felt the warm and romantic attachment which young men and boys so easily generated in his transparently honest heart.

But Gordon's character, while it made the choicer spirits among his comrades conscious of their own inferiority and shone in battle with a lustre to impress the dullest, proved too finely tempered for the world of peace. Gordon came nearest to being absorbed in his profession during the Crimean War. Had events immediately after the Peace of Paris provided him with work to exercise his intellectual powers on soldiering proper, his career might have been very different. At this time he wanted to enter the Staff Corps. But he paid the penalty of being a specialist. When the second opportunity came, after his return from China, Gordon had already begun to climb his Carmel, and regarded the Army and its failings with a detachment not altogether free from contempt.

5. A Peaceful and Primitive Interlude

His experiences, however, were useful in more ways than one. Work on the delimitation of the frontier between Russia and the principalities of Wallachia and Moldavia (soon to become Rumania) gave him his first insight into high politics. A crisis almost at once threatened over the allocation of the town of Bolgrad, and Gordon saw at close quarters the instability of international relationships, for the French, now anxious to placate their former enemy, supported Russia against the British, the Turks, and the Austrians. The young man, as he watched the play of diplomacy, admired the lucidity of Lord Clarendon's dispatches and patriotically blamed the French. He firmly believed in Lord Palmerston's strong foreign policy, and hoped that his appeal to the people on the China question would be successful. The realization of this wish, to which the humanitarian Gordon of a later period would not have subscribed, was ultimately responsible for the war against China, and for Gordon's own participation in the troubled affairs of that country.

Hate is a stronger motive than love in human affairs, and Gordon at this time had not subdued his passions to the extent of proving that he obeyed other impulses than those which direct the majority of mankind. For the Russians he soon acquired the mistrust he was never entirely to lose. Their cunning and their Punic faith were not even softened by the amiable trait of hospitality. In spite of the 30,000 rubles entertainment money allocated to the provincial government, so great a man as the Governor of Bessarabia gave no dinner party to the Commissioners ("although I should not go if there was any society," Gordon adds in a parenthesis), contenting himself with asking the French Commissioner to tea and afterwards making him pay *6s. 8d.* for the use of the cards with which they had played whist together. If Gordon disliked

Russian officers, he detested their merchants and shopkeepers for grasping profiteers who systematically robbed the members of the Commission. One of the few things that were cheap was caviare. But while he found the local wine nothing but bad vinegar, — like good Victorians, they carried their own sherry with them, which was not improved by being frozen in the bottle, — he admits to no taste for the delicacy praised by Shakespeare.

Gordon kept his eyes open in the twelve months that he spent in the plains of the Lower Danube, and mixed more with the people than his shyness should have allowed. He learned a good deal about the various nationalities in that corner of Europe, and was impressed by the ubiquity of the Jews, noting unfavorably that strictness in the religious observance of "their Sabbath on Saturday" made traveling difficult on that day. The fasts and feasts of the Orthodox Church he records with a dry disapproval, and is specially curt about Russian music, for they have not more than "two tunes which can be called really Russian." That, however, was before the days of Tchaikowsky and Rimsky-Korsakoff!

He had been hoping to get home in the summer of 1857, when the work of delimitation was finished. But in April he received orders to accompany another frontier commission, this time to Armenia. His request for an exchange was refused, and towards the end of the month he passed through Constantinople on his way to the Caucasus. At the Embassy, when he handed over the completed plans of the Bessarabian frontier, Lord Stratford de Redcliffe told him he wished they had held out for the whole of the province, an aspiration, only to be fulfilled after the World War, which Gordon notes without comment. The Great Elchi impressed him with his kindness, and Gordon dined at the Embassy — a fact he records without a groan — and found Lady Stratford sympathetic; "a very nice person" is his rather vague description. Englishmen in general lack the Frenchman's skill in the thumb-nail sketch that makes a woman live upon the page, so that he sometimes overpowers one by the scent of her perfume. Gordon's references to the women he meets are never inspired by more than a perfunctory interest. He tells his sister Helen of the beauty of Caucasian princesses; but they have dirty habits, "they prefer their nails tipped, and do not hesitate at taking a bone and gnawing it." The pretty ladies of Kutais, who dance their national dances, have also a place in the chronicle of this austere bachelor. He had long come to the conclusion that to be married is to be marred. Young men often take up this position, when they become a few years older surrendering it willingly enough to determined assault. But no batteries of bright eyes, no feminine charm, ever threatened Gordon's citadel. "Lively, volatile, and very fascinating" are the epithets he bestows on a fair fellow passenger, with whom he spent over a fortnight on the steamer taking him back to Turkey after his winter leave of 1857–58. Yet even the tedium of a sea voyage left his defenses impregnable. She remained fairy-like and agreeable, qualities which most charmers find sufficient for their purpose. Gordon, however, saw emptiness of mind under her correct conversation, and felt not in the least possessive. He is more interested in Ivan, his servant, who is a Lutheran and reads his Bible regularly. Ivan had accompanied him on leave, and in one of his letters Gordon encloses a letter from Ivan in Russian to all the servants of the Gordon household. "I declare I think Ivan has a liking for Emma," he adds; "however, I do not mean to allow it, as he belongs to me."

Chance remarks in these letters from the Armenian highlands give us glimpses of the Gordon the world was to know later. He makes acquaintance with the Wild Kurds, of whom he says, "I should not mind trusting them at all," just as later he trusted himself among the tribesmen of Darfur; and he comes across a large colony of the Daghoboorts, now better known as the Dukhobors, "a sect something like the Mormons." He obtains his first sight of the slave trade, carried on in those lawless regions to supply the demands of the harems in Stamboul. The beautiful Gourelians, who lived within Russian territory, were systematically kidnapped by their neighbors across the border. The result was constant bloodshed and suffering. Russian deserters found no better fate, and were sold into slavery — a hard lot for them, is his comment, after they had made their escape from the Russian Army. Gordon's work consisted largely in preventing the Turkish and Russian Commissioners from squabbling, and he grew tired of acting as peacemaker, a rôle for which he professed not be well adapted. Still, if he declared that he did not complain when there was no cause, he managed better than another subaltern engaged on similar work whose differences with his colleagues had to be referred home.

In spite of such annoyances, it was on the whole a congenially primitive existence, this blazing a line through immense forests and carefully setting up trigonometrical pyramids which the inhabitants as carefully destroyed, and the months it covered were perhaps the happiest he ever knew, although he describes the life as "more that of an animal than anything else." His health — then, as always, wonderful — withstood the changes in climate between the subtropical plains and the high mountains. Of these he climbed Alagoz (13,480 feet), boiling water on the top to discover its height and then sliding 3000 feet down a steep snow slope in less than two minutes. He got within a thousand feet of the summit of Ararat, being turned back by the weather, and he visited the great Etchmiazin Monastery, the Vatican of the Armenian Church, where the monks gave them "a grand dinner," and showed their relics — an arm of Saint Gregory, a finger nail of Saint Peter, and a piece of the Ark, which, says Gordon, "is necessarily of great antiquity." When he studied the question for himself later he decided against the claims of the Armenian mountain as the grounding place of that leviathan. But at this time Gordon's interest in religious questions was quiescent, his faith passive. His mind hardly seems to have wandered beyond the glare of the camp fire, and his eyes looked only to the horizons of mountains and forests.

By the autumn of 1858, when his job was finished and he prepared to return home, he had decided that he did not want to stay in England. The life of a peace-time soldier ceased to attract him. He had forgotten that he was happy at Pembroke, and he said nothing more of his ambition to fit himself by further study for the Staff commands in the new Army that was to arise on the ruins of the old which had perished in the Crimea. If possible, he said, he would like to be employed in Turkey, and one wonders what sort of career he would have carved out for himself had his wish been fulfilled. If his desire for active work was soon to be realized in a way to suit even his insatiable energy, the sedentary occupation which he feared fell for the moment to his lot. After a few months' leave he was promoted captain at the early age of twenty-six, and in May 1859 was appointed Adjutant at the Royal Engineers' headquarters in Chatham, a post regarded as a stepping-stone to the higher commands in the corps. But Gordon was looking farther afield, and when Great Britain declared war on hapless China in 1860 he volunteered for active service. There he was to find work worthy of his powers.

II

CHINA
(1860–1864)

Do not let me hear you talking together
About titles and promotions;
For a single general's reputation
Is made out of ten thousand corpses.

Ts'ao Sung (*c.* a.d. 900)

China, a country reeking of dung and death.

The Brothers Goncourt

1. Gordon's Palmerstonian View of China

As the P. and O. steamer took Gordon slowly towards Hongkong, he had plenty of time to reflect on the probability that he would be too late for the fighting. So far as he thought about the question at all, his sympathies were with Palmerston, whose "filibustering" foreign policy, as Cobden and Bright called it, appealed to the filibustering element in his own nature. But if the Chinese side of the case at this moment did not trouble him, it was China that worked his final conversion to the service of human suffering.

Gordon followed the fashion of the time in regarding the Chinese as heathen. Gonc was the respect which the eighteenth century had shown for the art and products of the Celestial Empire, when ladies in the fashionable squares of Soho and Bloomsbury sipped their China tea in Nanking ware handed them by Chinese pages as they sat in the chairs which Chippendale had made in the Chinese manner. In 1860, Englishmen wished not so much to collect objects of virtu from the Celestial Empire as to sell the cotton goods of Lancashire and the firearms from the factories of Birmingham to its peaceable and rather comic inhabitants. On this all parties were agreed, and, though voices were raised against the wrong of forcing opium on a country which, reasonably enough, did not want its people ruined by this abominable drug, men like Ruskin and Cobden, self-appointed spokesmen for the oppressed, could not bring themselves to love the Chinese. Ruskin considered their contribution to "the universal school of Gothic" — whatever he meant by the phrase — "childish and restricted," while the desire of the mandarins to hinder commercial intercourse with the outside world outraged Cobden's free-trade principles. A country which despised the civilizing influences of commercial intercourse between the nations lay beyond the benevolence of the Manchester School. "You cannot like a people who do not like you," said Cobden in the House of Commons. And Cobdenites everywhere assented to this unchristian principle.

Gordon soon ceased to share it, for he naturally came to love those he fought against. Besides, he saw the woes which in no small measure had been brought upon the people of China by the unscrupulous pressure of the Western Powers. But as yet he knew little about the intelligent and lively young Chinamen, about long-haired Taepings, the misplaced zeal of Christian missionaries, the greed of the European and American merchants, and the high-handed behavior of the officials of foreign governments. The only thing, so far as we are aware, that disturbed him on the voyage was a charge of theft brought by one of the passengers against a steward called Kirkham. Kirkham was accused of having stolen two dollars, and Gordon, alert to help young men in trouble, came to the rescue by refunding the money and arranging with the captain to take the offender as his personal servant. The experiment proved a success, Kirkham remaining in Gordon's service throughout the time he spent in China, and subsequently, on Gordon's recommendation, entering that of the King of Kings, who appointed him Generalissimo of the Abyssinian Army, afterwards sending him as a special envoy to Queen Victoria with an offer of marriage.[1] Kirkham reached Cairo safely, but

[1] The authority for this anecdote is Colonel Chaillé-Long, who records it as having been told to him by Gordon himself. The incident on the steamer is probably true. But Chaillé-Long's vivid imagination, and Gordon's own silence on the subject of this Kirkham in any extant letter from China, make its sequel highly dubious. There was a Lieutenant-Colonel J. C. Kirkham who was Adjutant-General of the Ever-Victorious Army.

there got so drunk at Shepheard's Hotel that he was handed over to the British Consul.

An otherwise uneventful journey ended with Gordon reaching Tientsin towards the end of September, 1860, nearly five weeks after the Taku Forts had been captured and three weeks after the one battle of the campaign had been fought. He felt chagrined at being "rather late for the amusement," a professional flippancy in his attitude towards war of which he soon cured himself. But even on this occasion he unselfishly tempered annoyance by the reflection that the news "won't vex my mother."

Though there was no fighting, feeling on both sides ran high. The Chinese considered that they had been wantonly attacked by these "barbarians who live in the remote parts of the earth," as an Imperial Edict put it; the French and English — for it was a joint expedition — no less firmly believed that it was their duty to teach the Chinese a lesson in civilized conduct. Gordon arrived at the moment when the dying Emperor was under the influence of the Yi concubine, a fascinating and ambitious young Manchu who had rendered the high service to her lord and master of bearing him a son and heir. Afterwards, as the Empress Dowager, Tzu Hsi, she became the ruling spirit of the government Gordon served and saved. But in her struggle to gain the supreme power she found it useful to play upon the xenophobia which the Chinese sturdily cherished against the rude foreigner, and the Emperor, speaking with her voice, offered 50 taels for the head of every black barbarian and 100 for the head of every white barbarian.

Luckily the power of the Yi concubine was counterbalanced by the sager counsels of Prince Kung, the Emperor's brother and President of the Grand Council; otherwise the party of English officers and Indian soldiers taken prisoner in violation of a flag of truce would have lost their heads. As it was, they were removed to Peking, where they suffered ill-treatment from which some died. Gordon felt the thing more keenly since one victim was an Engineer officer who had been with him in Armenia. But his hatred of cruelty did not lead him to express any desire for summary vengeance, and when this came with the sacking of the Summer Palace he stigmatized it as "wretchedly demoralizing work for an army." The Versailles of China, a museum of Chinese art, which Gordon, repeating the general opinion, valued at four million pounds, was given over to the troops to pillage and burn. "You can scarcely imagine," says Gordon, who never submitted easily to the enchantments of sense, "the beauty and magnificence of the places we burnt. It made one's heart sore to burn them; in fact, these palaces were so large, and we were so pressed for time, that we could not plunder them carefully. . . . The French" (he had not forgotten the antipathy bred in the Crimea) "have smashed everything in the most wanton way. It was a scene of utter destruction which passes my description." He records how one English officer gave sixteen shillings for a string of pearls which he sold the next day for as much as £500.

Gordon violated his principles by securing the throne in one of the audience chambers,[1] and he records that his share of the prize money was £48. But the thing pricked his conscience. He had no part in the Victorian complacency which saw nothing outrageous in such vandalism, which took pride in the fact that an English officer of rank was observed buying specimens of art from French soldiers with checks on Coutts' Bank — so high among foreigners stood the reputation of the British for integrity. A Chinese doctor of letters accounted in his diary for the "abominable behavior of the barbarians" by the supposition that the troops had got out of hand, but Gordon knew there was no such excuse. The lesson was not

[1] This is now in the Royal Engineers Museum, Chatham.

lost on him, and when he came to lead Chinese soldiers against the Taepings he sternly forbade plunder of any kind. We may also believe that, besides helping to confirm his primitive Christian attitude towards money, it opened his eyes to the heartlessness of European policy towards China, against which his own conduct as leader of the Ever-Victorious Army was a splendid protest.

2. A Second Conversion

Two years elapsed before Gordon became identified with the last concerted efforts to put an end to the civil war which is considered to have cost anything up to 150 million lives.[1] Meanwhile he was engaged on the ordinary routine work of an R.E. captain at Tientsin, which consisted chiefly in supervising the accommodation for the British army of occupation, particularly in regard to fireplaces and chimneys, matters that lay outside the Chinese philosophy. He often rode over to the Taku Forts, a distance of forty miles — sometimes, to inure his body to fatigue, doing the double journey in the day on relays of the hardy native ponies. And he found time to visit Peking, where he stayed with Sir Frederick Bruce, the British Minister, who afterwards gave him indifferent support when he commanded the Ever-Victorious Army. A trip with a brother officer to the Great Wall, accompanied only by a Chinese boy of fourteen, who filled the double rôle of servant and interpreter, impressed him with the military grandeur of China's history, as the human sights he saw everywhere, particularly in Peking and Tientsin, stirred his compassion for the poverty of the people.

Gordon's first attempt to help the poor showed him the difficulties which beset the charitable. He and others had

[1] In 1842 the population of China was reckoned at 413 millions; by 1862 it had shrunk to 267 millions.

collected a fund of some 800 dollars, but when the mandarins were asked to issue tickets to the most deserving they refused to have anything to do with this popular Victorian method of relief. There was nothing for it but to distribute the money. The valiant beggars of Tientsin, however, did little credit to the humanitarian impulses of Gordon and his fellow officers. Three thousand collected, and, in the struggle to obtain a portion of this Heaven-sent largesse, seven women and one boy were killed, a sad *dénouement* to a well-meant scheme which no doubt brought a grim satisfaction to the mandarins who had refused their sanction.

Still, Gordon was happy — happy in mind and body, he told Augusta. He liked the people and the climate, and he found the work to his taste, the only professional annoyance during this halcyon time, so far as we know, being caused by his brother Henry, who put in a word for him with his brother-in-law, General Staveley, the commanding officer of the force. Gordon went to the General, and told him he disapproved of jobbery. "It is the bother of one's life to be trying after the honors of the profession, and it has grown in late years into a regular trade — everyone uses private interest."

Not many young men of twenty-eight write like this of elder brothers who try to do them a good turn. His anger was short-lived, but he was always ready for a jest at Henry's supposed partiality for the loaves and fishes, and when, later on, he refused the money offered him by the Chinese Government, he slyly observed in a letter to his mother, "Helen will exclaim at my refusing the coin, knowing how dearly the family love it." The hit was not against his sister, who shared Charles's contempt for money, as Augusta knew when she forwarded the letter to Henry, then at the War Office. And she accordingly inserted in the margin: "Dear Henry, I am afraid this may be taken in earnest, but you remember it is Charlie's old joke."

The confederacy in piety with Augusta which was to dominate his life had not yet been fully joined. War and adventure had overlaid the shoots that sprouted in the quiet of Pembroke. Now he was visited by a mild attack of smallpox, the only illness of his adult years, and he told Augusta where his meditations had led him during the forced inactivity of the sick room. "I am glad to say that this disease has brought me back to my Saviour, and I trust in future to be a better Christian than I have been hitherto." He adds some words of praise for the chaplain, Mr. Beech, who had helped in this conversion. This he wrote in March 1862, particularly asking Augusta not to show the letter to anyone. A month later he was ordered to accompany an expedition under General Staveley which had for its object the driving of the Taepings beyond a thirty miles' radius of Shanghai, and for the next two and a half years Gordon had to carry out his resolution to live the Christian life amid the cruelties of a savage civil war, in which he was fighting to uphold what he regarded as a heathen civilization against those who acknowledged in their oblique Chinese way — as European apologists put it — the Christian God.

3. The Ignobleness of Shanghai

At Shanghai, internationalized by the Treaty of Nanking in 1842, Gordon found himself in the atmosphere of paradox and contradiction common to international mercantile communities, where the settlers have been divorced from their own national ties and enjoy privileges denied to the native inhabitants. The clear-cut divisions between friend and foe of the Crimea were no more; even the plain Palmerstonian issue of the semi-civilized yellow man against the fully civilized white man had become confused. The arrival of General Staveley's force caused the Taeping rebels to abandon their attempt to capture Shanghai, which they had besieged for six weeks during the winter of 1862. But though the people of Shanghai were determined to defend themselves against the rebels, and had actually subscribed to create a force which ultimately became the Ever-Victorious Army, a good many also sold munitions to the rebels. Shanghai acted as base of supplies to both parties, and the boom in land which occurred in the early sixties showed that the civil war was not as unprofitable as might be supposed. The moral issue in any case was far from clear. The Taepings called upon the Christian God as they battled against the forces of the Imperial Government. Missionaries preached them the Gospel, lamenting, as one English clergyman said, the errors and abominations of the movement, "yet disposed to think that Providence had a wise and gracious end to serve by it." And Liberals in England openly sympathized with a rising which they believed to be the result of the corrupt and tyrannical Imperial rule. It was monstrous, said Lord Naas in the House of Commons, that the British Government should assist reaction by giving any help to the rotten Empire of the Manchus. Years after, Wilfrid Scawen Blunt declared in similar strain that Gordon had taken in China, as at the end in the Sudan, the part of the oppressors against the oppressed.

It is not surprising, of course, to find that, where good men doubted, others less disposed to weigh causes in the moral scales took sides as self-interest prompted them. Deserters from the rebels were welcomed in the Imperial forces; deserters from the French and British troops were welcomed by the rebels; finally the American Burgevine, whom Gordon had succeeded in command of the Ever-Victorious Army, changed his allegiance in the true spirit of an Italian *condottiere* of the

Cinquecento. In such an atmosphere it was certainly not easy to live a Christian life, but, while Gordon never had any doubts as to the rightness of the Imperial cause, he kept himself free from the hate which inspired the two parties in the civil war.

4. The Younger Brother of Jesus

The Taeping Rebellion arose out of the political underworld in the turbulent area of Southern China centred in Canton. It was an attack on the traditional culture of Confucianism, clothed in a travesty of Christian theology; it marked, in fact, the beginning of the cataclysm by which the old civilization of China has been submerged in our own time. The man who started the movement, and remained at its head throughout all its vicissitudes, came from the hills south of Canton. Hung Seu-tsien, as his name was, visited that provincial capital in 1833, when he was twenty years old, and there learned something about Christianity through the tracts and Bibles which the American Baptist missionaries distributed to their converts. Hung might have inquired no further into its mysteries had his erudition been equal to his ambition. He failed in the competitive examination of 1837, a piece of ill-success which he explained by the fact that the examiners were prejudiced against him because he belonged to a despised gypsy tribe. This failure prevented him from obtaining a post in the public service, and he returned home with the disgruntled feelings common enough to disappointed examinees. Hung soon found a more exciting career than that of a mandarin. Aided by an adroit imagination and the falling sickness, he founded a religious sect, and by degrees his horizon widened until it stretched to the walls and palaces of Peking.

His doctrine, if its crudeness justified the examiners of Canton regarding Hung's intellectual capacity, proved acceptable to ignorant Southerners. As he developed into the successful evangelist, he taught that in a trance he had ascended to Heaven, where he learned that he was the younger brother of Jesus. God the Father gave him a sword and a seal — this a significant gift in Chinese eyes — and a book of celestial degrees. With these he was ordered to establish his authority upon earth. For some years he preached this gospel in circumstances no less obscure than have surrounded the founders of other religious sects. He fasted, practised austerities, and gained disciples as well as adherents. These became known as "God-worshipers," and Hung grew to be a man of some local importance.

Hung was ambitious, and in 1846 he betook himself to Canton, where he studied with an American missionary named Issachar J. Roberts. But either the laxity of Hung's morals or his curious theology prevented Mr. Roberts from making him a Baptist. Probably both reasons had something to do with the dismissal of his would-be neophyte. So Hung returned to his own hillsides and continued his mission, which by 1850 had grown sufficiently for the Imperial authorities to think him dangerous. Their attempt to arrest him caused a clash between the troops and Hung's followers. Hung, who knew that his capture would now mean the loss of his head, thereupon proclaimed his mission to be the Rule of Peace, or Taeping. And civil war now began to smoulder in the district south of Canton.

Within three years it had become a raging fire. Hung, now calling himself the Tien Wang, or Heavenly King, swept through the southern provinces, and in 1853 he established his capital at Nanking. Many believed that he would succeed in driving the Manchus from Peking. The British Government, anxious to remain neutral, sent Sir S. G. Bonham to acquaint the Tien Wang with this decision and to present him with a copy of the treaty of 1842, which it expected the Wang to observe no less scrupulously than the Imperial Government, for British trade was not to be hampered by the internal dissensions of the Chinese people.

The Tien Wang expressed disappointment when he found that the document was not, as he supposed, a formal recognition of his status as the younger brother of Jesus. But his Ministers (for the Tien Wang now remained in the seclusion of his heavenly palace) did their best to persuade the members of the mission of their common Christian fellowship and of their common hostility against the antiforeign policy of the Imperial Government. Such specious pleas were hard to reconcile with the well-stocked harems of the Tien Wang and of his Prime Minister, the Tung Wang, to whom it had been revealed in a vision that he was the Third Person of the Trinity. Nor did they tally with the jealousy shown by the Wangs towards the missionaries, who wished to purge the movement of its enormous heresies. At the same time it could not be denied that the Wangs printed the Bible, kept the Sabbath, and prayed to the Heavenly Father.

For all his liberalism in things doctrinal, Gordon never acknowledged any sort of Christian brotherhood with the Taepings. Indeed, no one in Shanghai ventured to do so after the prolonged visit which Mr. Roberts paid in 1860 to his old pupil at Nanking. Mr. Roberts's stay in the rebel capital enabled him to learn at first hand the extraordinary doctrines to which the rebels subscribed. A shocking tenet of their theology was their attribution of wives to the First and Second Persons of the Trinity. They did not do this in the case of the Third Person; but he was a nonentity, and had been figuratively under a cloud since the assassination of the Tung Wang, whose claims to this title the Younger Brother at one time was forced to admit. Finally Mr. Roberts, who had hoped that the Tien Wang's provision of eighteen chapels in every large city was the beginning of a nineteenth-century Reformation in the Far East, fell into great disfavor and narrowly escaped with his life.

But the Wangs, or Kings, — a title assumed by all the leaders of the rebellion, — if they were not good Protestants, professed to be good patriots, and loyalty to the memory of the Mings, the native dynasty which the Manchus had displaced two centuries before, was a part of their policy. They wore the Ming dress, and ceased to shave the front of their heads, from this being called the Long-hairs by their enemies — a name now applicable to all Chinamen. Whatever the Taepings' veneration for the Mings, their hatred for the Manchus was emphatically demonstrated when, on their capture of Nanking in 1853, they slaughtered the entire Manchu colony of 10,000 in the former (and present) capital of China, even to the last child in arms — a piece of savagery which was the sequel to the rebels' promise that, if the Manchus surrendered, their lives should be spared.

5. Shanghai Is Threatened

The area in which the rebellion was now localized covered the low-lying delta country on the southern bank of the Yangtze, a district dotted with walled towns and traversed by a network of canals. At its centre lay the great city of Suchow, the centre of the silk industry. Through Suchow ran the Grand Canal, a monument of the Empire's mediæval greatness and still a main artery of traffic. Over this once-smiling province, a Chinese Holland where pagodas lifted their mouldering curves on many a horizon, and graceful, unkempt bridges of stone indicated the former wealth and pontifical ease of its inhabitants, the Taepings had spread the horrors of anarchy and famine. These were only too plain to Gordon. As for the memorials of the past, no works of men's hands ever cast their spell upon him. "There is nothing of any interest in China; if you have seen one village you have seen the whole country," was his considered opinion of the capacity of the oldest civilization in the world to set its daily life in an environment of beauty.

Gordon started with a poor opinion of the Taepings' prowess. When the rebels raided the neighborhood of Shanghai he noted how the inhabitants fled in terror before them — with little enough reason, he remarked, for the "strapping fellows of peasants, running away with old women and children . . . could easily defend themselves if they had the mind." The British troops were ordered out to protect the Settlement. They let through the crowds of fugitives, carrying their chattels and driving their buffaloes before them; then they scattered the Taepings, but they did not kill many, as the rebels "beat them into fits" in getting over the country, which was everywhere intersected by ditches and swamps.

So Gordon, never very tender towards timorous civilians, nonchalantly dismisses one of the many attempts of the Taepings to secure Shanghai. When he accompanies General Staveley on his drive against the rebels, it seems, as they set out, more like a picnic or a regatta than an operation of war. Two hundred and fifty boats of every shape and size, from steamers mounting guns to "little chips like coffins" holding two men, cover the creek. A babel of sound arises from the water as the flotilla endeavors to navigate the canal towards Tsingpu, its objective. The speech of many nations answers it from the causeway, where a wonderful collection of troops is on the march: French sailors, British "Tommies," Beluchis, Chinese of General Ward's Ever-Victorious Army. The English bluejackets grumble at being left behind on their gunboats. One or two tumble overboard and swim ashore, running along the banks, dripping objects of much laughter to the Chinese spectators. That night the force bivouacs in the pleasant May weather, and the English officers enjoy an excellent alfresco dinner of roast pork, which they agree might have been dairy-fed. They wash it down with India Pale Ale. The only inconvenience is the guttering of the candles. . . . Such was Gordon's initial experience of the business that was to become stern enough even for his exacting taste.

On the following day came the opportunity for the first characteristic piece of work. Tsingpu was to be stormed, and, as Engineer officer, Gordon was responsible for the appliances to cross the moat and scale the wall. Experience had taught him the necessity of accurate preliminary observation. As he was reconnoitring the position from a boat with General Staveley, he landed to obtain a closer view of their objective. Jumping ashore and dodging the fire from the walls, Gordon rushed from one piece of cover to another until he was within fifty yards of the moat. Here behind a pagoda he started making a sketch and taking notes, while his General shouted himself hoarse in trying to get him back, for he saw that a party of rebels had emerged and was stealing round to cut the daring intruder off.

Tsingpu proved small beer after the Redan. The Armstrong guns knocked breaches in the wall with the utmost ease, tons of brickwork falling at every discharge. Then Gordon led one of the ladder parties to the walls. The rebels were not used to war carried on with such science and dash. If they still believed in their cause, to Gordon it appeared to be crumbling before his eyes.

His opinion of the rebels was not heightened at his next encounter. There was comedy in their surprising a *changmow,* as the lesser rebel leaders were called, who rushed out of a house where he had been hiding, rubbing his eyes with sleep and alarm. When the villagers saw his plight they set upon him and tore his Ming finery from his back — a ludicrous scene. Next day the rebel force advanced upon the British column with flying banners. Gordon watched them with amusement — inquiring minds, the English officers said to one another, should not be baulked. At length reserved fire turned into a volley, and the Taeping banners flew no more in the wind. This was amusing, but as Gordon thought of the *chang-mows* and their work he was not amused. "Ruthlessly cruel" is his description of these desperadoes, who carried off small boys, after murdering their parents, to train them up as rebel soldiers — the system, by the way, which Southeastern Europe knew only too well when the Osmanli Sultans recruited their Corps of Janissaries. We have a picture of Gordon, at one of these engagements round Shanghai, rescuing a little creature who in his efforts to escape had fallen into a ditch. He showed gratitude to his savior by clinging to him with "muddy paws," and so ruining Gordon's tunic. The British Army in those days still put fear into the hearts of its enemies by fighting in red, a color now even denied to most of its regiments for the softer campaigns of peace.

Terrible sights met them as they moved over the countryside, which Gordon was now surveying with a formidable escort of infantry and artillery. The dead lay about everywhere, food for the dogs and the crows. The English soldiers often shared their rations with the starving survivors. The rebels cut off heads more light-heartedly than justices of the peace put ne'er-do-wells in the stocks in eighteenth-century England. One Englishman came unexpectedly upon the scene of an execution in which the executioner, a Taeping soldier, was hacking off the victim's head with a blunt pocketknife.

Those who escaped to Shanghai often starved to death. There is a curious account in the *North China Herald* of a visit to a Buddhist temple which the editor paid one Sunday afternoon with a companion who is supposed to have been Gordon. They watched the decent ritual and the devout worshipers with satisfaction. Here was the simple piety, they decided, which forms the real stuff of religion. But when they went on to explore a neighboring temple they saw something very different — such horrors, indeed, as only China could show. At the foot of the altar, beneath a grimy Buddha, lay "a corpse full of maggots"; close by was a dead woman with her daughter dying beside her. Another party, also consisting of once well-to-do peasantry, were lying *in extremis* behind some mats which they had put up with a pathetic attempt at privacy. As the two Englishmen saw the ghastliness and breathed the pestilential stench, they contrasted it with the scene on the fashionable drive near by, where the wealthy merchants of Shanghai and their wives were taking the Sunday air. To start a relief fund was an obvious duty; and one of the first subscribers was an anonymous Gordon, donor of twenty dollars.

The main thing was to end the rebellion responsible for all this woe. He was impatient that people at home should still believe the Taepings to be fighting in a just cause, and he regretted that the British troops had been confined to the mere local operation of clearing the neighborhood of Shanghai. "It is all very well to talk of non-intervention," he writes to his mother, "and I am not particularly sensitive, nor are our soldiers generally so, but certainly we are all impressed with the utter misery and wretchedness of these poor people"; and he described the Chinese peasantry, whom he liked better than he ever did the Sudanese or the equatorial blacks, as "the most obedient, quiet, and industrious people in the world."

6. Gordon's Friend Li Hung-chang

Though the Governments of France and Great Britain did only enough to keep the Taepings out of Shanghai, the Chinese Government had stumbled on a man who was to have a decisive share in ending the rebellion. Li Hung-chang, judged by many to be the greatest man the Chinese race has produced in modern times, was in 1860 appointed Governor and Generalissimo in the province of Chekiang. With this practically absolute authority under the nominal control of the Viceroy Tseng Kuo-fan, whose right-hand man he was, he applied his great abilities to driving the Long-hairs from the face of China. Li, more liberal than most of the mandarin class, believed that the best way of achieving his ends was by European aid, a belief qualified by the suspicion that the foreign devils might have instigated the rebellion for the very purpose of being called in to suppress it, and then afterwards of presenting a thwacking bill to the Imperial Government.

As Li Hung-chang's ideas could not be realized, he supported the project of the American Frederick Townsend Ward, an adventurous spirit who saw a chance of getting rich quickly. Ward's idea was to enroll a regiment of foreigners, and to use them as a spearhead for the Imperial Chinese troops. The local native merchants, urged by Li Hung-chang and by their own fears of the Taepings, subscribed funds, and Ward, with Burgevine, another American, as second in command, found himself in the summer of 1860 at the head of a body of 300 Filipinos and Spanish half-castes, who had been enlisted in the purlieus of the port of Shanghai.

Li Hung-chang regarded with pride this motley company which was to provide the "shock troops" for his Ever-Victorious Army. Now he could smite the Long-hairs hip and thigh, more hateful to him than ever since his brother had fallen in battle against them; now he could recapture Sung-Kiang, thirty miles from Shanghai, which, so long as it remained in the rebels' hands, was a constant menace to that port.

Li Hung-chang therefore ordered an offensive; a Chinese army of 10,000 advanced against Sung-Kiang, and, thanks to the steadiness of Ward's 300, captured that place of strategic importance. The mandarins and merchants were enchanted.

These — it was before Gordon appeared on the scene — offered large rewards if Ward would go on and take Tsingpu. Ward, in too great a hurry to make his fortune, led his force, now swollen by Greek and Italian recruits, against that place, but he was decisively beaten, and Li Hung-chang's offensive would have ended in the loss of Shanghai itself had it not been for the British and French warships lying there. Ward tried to reorganize the remnant of the force, and inveigled thirty bluejackets to desert and join it. For this he found himself a prisoner in the hands of the Consuls, who would only release him if he disbanded his followers. He sent orders to Burgevine to this effect. Burgevine, no less adventurous than his chief, first tried one more assault on Tsingpu. This ended in disaster. Disbandment then became unnecessary, for the force was wiped out.

7. The Ever-Victorious Army

Ward now had another idea. The Chinese made formidable soldiers if led by Europeans. He arranged, therefore, with the local mandarins to enlist some regiments of Chinese, drill and arm them in the European fashion, and provide them with European officers. Two thousand such troops, he believed, would cut through the rebels like a knife through water. His belief was justified. Ward's irregulars were a very scourge to the Long-hairs during the critical months of 1862 and 1863, proving their metal in a hundred fights. Their *élan* equaled that of the French, perhaps because both were inspired by the hope of loot, which General Staveley forbade to the British troops. But Ward's men were wild, as dangerous to friend as to foe. In the heat of battle their shells had an unpleasant habit of dropping on either side indiscriminately, and after victory they were much too intent upon plunder to pursue the fleeing rebels. They had, in short, as Gordon saw, no idea of discipline, and their leader, a born fighter but an amateur soldier, no notion of strategy. He could win battles, but he could not win a war.

The end of Ward's career came in September 1862, while Gordon was engaged on his survey. In an attack on a town, a deserter from one of the European regiments, who was armed with a rifle and could therefore fire with some precision, shot Ward through the body. The wound proved mortal, and Li Hung-chang shed tears over the deathbed of the American who was dying so far from his family and friends; he wondered, too, where he could find another to strike the same terror into the hearts of the Long-hairs.

Ward's second-in-command, Burgevine, was the obvious choice. But this extravagant and open-handed American adventurer, optimistic, insanely ambitious, ready to promise anything to anybody, not excluding himself, was soon in difficulties. He possessed, as Gordon said, no administrative or military talent; at the same time, like many incompetent men, he was excessively jealous of his dignity, which caused him to quarrel with his second-in-command, an English captain of Marines named Holland, and, what was more serious, with Li Hung-chang. General Staveley, in answer to Li's request to remove Burgevine and appoint an English officer in his place, referred the matter home. The Chinese therefore adopted the simple expedient of starving out the American, and withheld the pay from his men. When these were on the verge of mutiny, Burgevine marched with his bodyguard from the headquarters at Sung-Kiang into Shanghai, entered the mandarin paymaster's office, and fisticuffed that notability until his face was covered with blood.

The outrage shocked even the free and easy public opinion of Shanghai. Burgevine's dismissal became a matter of course. Rumor eagerly canvassed the name of his successor. Captain Holland, who held the command temporarily, was incompetent. The local paper announced that General Staveley wished to appoint "his brother-in-law, Captain Gordon," a proposal to which, it was said, the Chinese would not listen. All January and February the appointment remained in suspense, with the chances balanced between Gordon and his friend Wolseley. Then Li Futai, as Gordon always called Li Hung-chang, received intimation from Sir Frederick Bruce and General Staveley that Gordon would be lent to the Chinese Government to take command of the Ever-Victorious Army.

The new commander differed totally from his predecessors. He set little enough store by honors. Money he did not want. True, it flattered him to be a mandarin, and he liked the deference paid by the Chinese to official rank — memories of the friendships he formed with eager Chinese youths beginning their official career remained with him all his life. Less mildly attractive was the prospect of fighting, which the filibustering Gordon loved more than anything else in the world. And the command of the Ever-Victorious Army would give him opportunity for the exercising of authority — another element in his nature that nothing ever subdued. Yet it is possible he would have refused to lead what he called his rabble of an army had he not believed that he, and he alone, could keep it together and so ensure the defeat of the Taepings. Family influences were against him. His father disliked the idea of any son of his who held the Queen's commission serving a foreign ruler; his mother did not conceal her fears that he would be killed; both wished him to have nothing to do with a cause which many people in England thought was wrong. Gordon did not lightly brush aside his parents' objections. He told them that he was undertaking a humane task, promised his mother not to act rashly, and said he would stay in China as short a time as possible. His own scruples were allayed by his determination to take nothing for himself. Gordon had already formulated his answer to Li's unasked question concerning his hire. The Chinese were heathens; he would accept from them "not even a shoe-latchet."

Gordon's plan of campaign was directed to cutting the rebels off from the Great River, the Yangtze, which was their source of supply. A flourishing trade in rice and other goods, besides munitions of war, existed between Shanghai and the districts held by the Taepings, the goods being carried on the Yangtze in junks flying foreign flags and thus claiming the privileges of extraterritoriality under the treaty of 1842. Gordon explained to Li Hung-chang his strategy, which consisted, not, as hitherto, in sporadic excursions against the rebels, but in turning their flank and rolling them away from the sea — a very different thing from driving them into it, as Li had talked of doing. And when he predicted complete success within eighteen months the mandarin, in spite of his experience of European promises, felt sanguine also. Decidedly this Englishman was a man inspiring confidence.

8. Gordon Wins His First Engagement

The force of which the Brevet Major of Engineers now found himself in command (his appointment was dated March 26, 1863) constituted no magnificent army, as he himself admitted. The officers were adventurers and desperadoes recruited in Shanghai — a more dangerous crowd of men had never been collected together, said Gordon of them afterwards; for the men were "braves," as the peaceably inclined Chinese stigmatize those whom they consider possess only the virtue of courage. Of discipline there was a minimum. "Ragged and perhaps slightly disreputable" was the flattering description of all ranks by their newly appointed G.O.C. Gordon found them seething with discontent at Burgevine's dismissal, and not in the least disposed to accept a professional soldier as their general. He paraded them on the morrow of his taking over command, and harangued them in the old Roman style. So long as they behaved themselves and carried out orders, he told them, he would see to their interests. Interpreters repeated his words, which were received with grudging assent. Little did the men of the Force know the iron will that lay under the velvet of that mild and conciliatory manner, or realize that now for the first time they were to be fashioned into a first-rate instrument of war.

As yet the Army was far from that. But Gordon had not the time to knock it into shape on the parade ground and in the training camp, even if it would have submitted to such a process.

In ten days Gordon was steaming up the Yangtze with a flotilla carrying 1200 men and artillery. His objective was Chanzu, which had come over from the rebel side early in 1863 and was now in danger of being recaptured by the Long-hairs under their best general, the Chung Wang, who had taken and destroyed its port, Fushan. By approaching Chanzu from the river, Gordon at once attacked the rebels in flank and took the first step towards cutting their communications with the outside world of Shanghai. The landing was easy, and Gordon placed his artillery among the deserted ruins, from which he began a three hours' bombardment of the rebels' stout wooden stockade (the conventional form of fieldworks for both sides). An assault then carried the enemy's position, but Taeping reënforcements from Chanzu prevented further progress, and night fell with the success of Gordon's first operation still in doubt.

The vigor and unexpectedness of his attack, however, had disheartened the rebels, and next morning they were found to be in full retreat. The Force advanced the ten miles to Chanzu along both banks, supported by the flotilla. On the way they found the charred remains of some Imperialists who had been crucified and burned — an indication of the savagery with which the war was conducted. But there was no further fighting. It had been a successful and, indeed, almost bloodless operation.

The Chanzu mandarins received Gordon in state. He was impressed by these young and polygamous ex-rebel chiefs, "very intelligent and splendidly dressed, with big pearls in their caps." The commander, who was only thirty-five,—it was a war of youth on both sides,—"looked worn to a thread with anxiety." As one reads this description the mind leaps to the careworn defender of Khartoum twenty-two years later, who was to find no Gordon to relieve him from his encircling enemies.

Gordon's original skepticism as to the military capacity of the Taepings was strengthened by the ease of his victory. But he was cautious in strategy, and before he advanced against the main rebel position, which lay along the line Taitsan-Quinsan-Suchow, more preparation was necessary. Leaving, therefore, a couple of companies at Chanzu, he led the rest back to headquarters at Sung-Kiang.

Gordon found Governor Li ready to support him in every way. The prohibition of plunder, regular pay, regular British officers in place of Burgevine's more unsatisfactory subordinates—here were three obvious and necessary, though not easily made, reforms. During the next three weeks Gordon worked with an activity which in other people would be called feverish. The Anglo-Chinese Force,[1] as it now became, was reorganized from top to bottom. The uniform, consisting of a jacket resembling that of the Zouaves and the Highlanders, knickerbockers, and boots, which made the "imitation foreign devils" particularly fearful to the rebels, was standardized and smartened up. Gordon's own bodyguard of 300 was dressed

[1] This was the official British name for it. Gordon called it the Sung-Kiang and afterwards the Quinsan Force. To the Chinese it was always known as the Ever-Victorious Army.

in blue with scarlet facings; the remainder of the 3000 troops in the Force wore green. One regiment of 650 carried rifles, the others were armed with British muskets. The artillery was strengthened and taught how to breach walls and shell enemy positions. A pontoon train, in the use of which the men were diligently exercised, was intended to give the Force the same mobility as the rebels across a country abounding in canals. Two steamers of which Gordon meant to make decisive use were mounted with guns and armored. A coolie corps of 300 and a rudimentary field hospital completed the little army when Gordon took the field on April 25, 1863, a month after he had assumed command. Swiftness of movement, superior strategy, and dashing shock tactics — by these means his 3000 Chinese were to defeat armies of their fellow countrymen ten times as numerous.

9. A Hard Fight

His intention was to attack the city of Quinsan, the rebels' arsenal and an important strategical point which, with its hill 600 feet high, dominated the surrounding country. The capture of Quinsan would cut the Taeping forces in two and give him possession of the key to Suchow. On April 27, however, news reached Gordon that the Imperialists had suffered a reverse before Taitsan, having been lured to enter the town under the pretense of its surrender and then set upon by the rebels.

Several hundred had been killed, though another of Li Hung-chang's brothers, one of the officers in command, managed to escape with an inglorious spear wound in the rump. Gordon therefore turned aside and hurried towards Taitsan, which was held by a rebel garrison of 10,000, strengthened by 2000 picked Taeping troops from the Chung Wang's army and by a number of Europeans who were in charge of the guns. The odds against Gordon were lengthened by the fact that Taitsan had been the scene of several rebel successes, the last only two months previously, when the Ever-Victorious under Holland had suffered a disastrous repulse before its walls.

The operations against that town proved Gordon's genius for leadership, and acquainted the rebels with the depressing news that the "new English piecee," whose advent they had recognized at Fushan, was now before them. His unexpected arrival on April 29, in wet weather which bogged the guns, was followed by the immediate capture of a rebel stockade a mile south of the town. There Gordon took up his position that night. On April 30, in rain which prevented active operations, he reconnoitred the defenses, and decided to attack, not from the south, as Holland had done, but from the west, where he would cut the rebel communications with Quinsan and have the advantage of the canal, on which his steamers could operate. The next morning, accordingly, operations against the west gate were begun, and the rebels, with very little resistance, were turned out of their advanced positions beyond the walls. Gordon then made preparations for the assault, the arrival during the afternoon of the steamers, which had been delayed through having to remove bridges, helping forward his plans. That night he gave orders for the 1st Regiment to move round at daybreak to the north gate, to protect his flank and to cut off one line of retreat for the rebels. The howitzers and 32-pounders were placed in position, with the special means of protection he had devised for the gunners. The pontoon train was made ready. Nothing was forgotten that forethought could suggest or mechanical inventiveness provide. And while Gordon thus completed his scheme of attack, the Taeping chief within the town anticipated the fortunes of the morrow by preparing, in case the day should be irretrievably lost, to blow himself up in his house with his wives and with the Imperial mandarins whom he held prisoners.

The issue lay for a time in doubt. Not until two o'clock in the afternoon was Gordon able to bring all his guns into action; another two and a half hours' bombardment was necessary before a practicable breach was made. At half-past four Gordon ordered the storming party forward under one of his captains. It rushed across the pontoon and scrambled up the débris of rubble and masonry. There the rebels, with the Europeans — there were always a few deserters and poor whites from Shanghai with the Taepings — at their head, met them, and for ten minutes there was desperate hand-to-hand fighting. Then the assaulting party was driven back to the ditch with heavy casualties, including the loss of its leader.

Discipline went to pieces under the cannonade, the musket fire, the obnoxious stinkpots hurled by the defenders from the walls. In the confusion one of the steamers fell into the hands of the rebels. Gordon ordered a more intensive bombardment; the storming party was re-formed, and reënforcements were thrown across the pontoon, while the howitzers shelled the rebels massed behind the walls. Gordon, as he stood in the middle of the mêlée, his cane in his hand, cool and apparently unmoved, communicating his own confidence to his troops, who did not know that all the time he was silently praying for victory to the Christian God, saw the rebel resistance falter and break. At this moment a deserter from the 31st Regiment of Foot was brought before him, wounded and a prisoner. "Mr. Gordon, Mr. Gordon," he cried, "you will not let me be killed!" "Take him down to the river and shoot him," was the General's answer for all to hear. But *sotto voce* Gordon said to the man's captors, "Put him in my boat, let the doctor attend him, and send him down to Shanghai." Two Frenchmen who begged hard for mercy were not so successful, being shot out of hand by the storming party;

a couple of American and five Indian soldiers suffered the same fate. The rebel general did not have the opportunity of making the domestic end he had purposed, for he was wounded in the fighting at the breach, and escaped to fight again at Quinsan. The losses to Gordon's Force, though not severe by more recent standards, consisted of over forty killed, and one officer in every five was a casualty.

Gordon broke all the local rules of war in leading his Force immediately on Quinsan, which an Imperialist army under General Ching already partially invested. As he lay before that place and tried to concert measures with his Chinese colleague, the difficulties of his position became only too apparent. His moral isolation resembled the geographical isolation of the great hill which he saw rising from the town before him, and which made such a magnificent post of observation for the rebel Wangs. His own men in the elation of victory at Taitsan had forgotten all about his order against looting, and were loaded with "rubbish," as he put it, which they were anxious to dispose of at Sung-Kiang, where facilities had grown up for this kind of trade.

For the moment he could not punish their disobedience. But little enough store appeared to be set upon his determination to conduct the campaign against the rebels according to the dictates of civilized warfare. True, when the Bishop of Victoria accused the Imperial mandarins of having celebrated the victory at Taitsan by inflicting "death by a thousand slashes" on their prisoners, Gordon thought it necessary to intervene with a letter to the local Shanghai paper upholding the humanity of those fighting in a just cause. Yet the Chinese mentality was undoubtedly difficult to understand. When, for instance, the former civil governor of Taitsan came to Gordon's stockade before Quinsan with complaints of the conduct of the Ever-Victorious Army in the matter of looting, Gordon was in sympathy with the man, who confidently produced a letter in English from Li Hung-chang which, as the suppliant believed, backed his claims. In reality it was a request from the Governor that Gordon would "please cut off the bearer's head." If great mandarins of the yellow button behaved like this, what could one expect from the rank and file?

Gordon, therefore, yielding to the clamor of his men, marched the grumbling Force back to Sung-Kiang, which he reached on May 10, after an absence of only fifteen days, during which the fortune of war had definitely turned in favor of the Imperialists. He did so the more readily because he felt that Quinsan would not fall so easily as General Ching anticipated. The Chinese system of attacking a town consisted of a gradual approach to the walls under cover of a stockade, which the assailants continually pushed nearer. By these tactics, familiar to European warfare before the development of artillery, the "Imps," as Gordon, with his humor in abbreviation, now called them, had advanced their positions to the edge of the canal surrounding the walls. But to cross it in face of the enemy's carefully prepared fire appeared altogether too hazardous a proceeding. Not by such tactics, which had already been found expensive enough at Taitsan, would he succeed with his 3000 men in defeating the rebels' 50,000. Besides, he did not feel inclined to risk the loss of his invaluable gunboat, the paddle steamer *Hyson*, on which Ching counted to cover his storming parties. Gordon had other ideas. Where the Chinese generals reckoned war in terms of a mêlée at a stockade or in the breach of some city wall, he looked to destroy the enemy's mass of manœuvre. Not the capture of towns, but the destruction of the rebel armies was his object. And he had already realized that, while the Long-hairs fought bravely so long as they knew their line of retreat was open, they collapsed at once when this was cut off.

For the moment, however, he had to forget about Quinsan while he slaved night and day to give his Force cohesion and discipline. An army must eat before it can fight — that was his first, as it was his last, experience of war. One of the principal reasons why the spearhead of the Ever-Victorious Army failed to pierce home was that each regiment was fed, and fed badly, by its major in command. Gordon decided to put a British officer in charge of the commissariat of the Force, and gave him the rank of lieutenant-colonel. Upon this the unruly regimental C.O.'s, hard-fighting and hard-drinking Shanghai adventurers, blazed up. They declared that they too must be given a step in rank — otherwise they would serve no longer. Naturally they would march against Quinsan — they were brave men, and no one should say that they had drawn back at the moment of danger. But their resignations would take effect from the moment Quinsan fell.

Gordon did not budge an inch, for he knew that he was "the only stay in the Force," and the sooner officers and men realized the fact the better. The regimental commanders threatened mutiny, and, when Gordon would not give way, prevented their men from parading at the time for their return to the front. On the morning of departure only his own bodyguard fell in; the others hung about, unwilling accomplices of their commanding officers' disloyalty. Gordon in a cold fury soon made them understand that he meant to be obeyed, and the rest of the Force followed the example of their General's bodyguard. The majors, seeing their men march off without them, started in pursuit, and begged Gordon to reinstate them on his own terms. But it was too convenient an opportunity to get rid of troublesome subordinates, and he dismissed all except two. Under such doubtful auspices did the Anglo-Chinese Force, equivalent in numbers to a modern brigade, set out on what was to prove the most brilliant of its exploits.

10. Thirty against Ten Thousand

When he reached Quinsan, Gordon found General Ching as intent as before on an assault against the east gate of the town, though the Imperialist army had been hard pressed by the rebels and at the moment was on the defensive. On May 28, the day after his arrival, Gordon consented to use his Force against the stockades which the enemy had advanced during his absence, and he drove the *chang-mows* from these, losing one of his best officers, a British regular, in the process. This success emboldened Ching to press forward his old plan; but Gordon declared, as he studied the rebels' position, that he liked the idea less than ever, and, with the prudence that marked the strategy of this youthful leader, he decided to look for some spot where he could attack the enemy on his terms, and not on theirs.

It was not difficult to find. Quinsan depended on its communications with Suchow, twenty miles to the westward. Only one road joined the two places. This ran for the whole of its length alongside a canal; on the other side of the road lay a lake. No other line of retreat than this narrow and dangerous causeway lay open for the garrison of Quinsan. If he could cut the Quinsan-Suchow road, Quinsan must infallibly fall. With this scheme in his head, he started on May 29 in the *Hyson* to reconnoitre the enemy's position; on board with him were General Ching and Li Hung-chang, the latter anxious to share in the glory of the capture of Quinsan, and also trying to act as a buffer between his English and his Chinese subordinates.

Steaming by a wide creek which ran in a semicircle some miles from Quinsan, they came after three hours to within a thousand yards of the Suchow-Quinsan canal, where the rebels, realizing the dangerous threat to their communications, had closed the channel with lines of stakes. The *Hyson* could

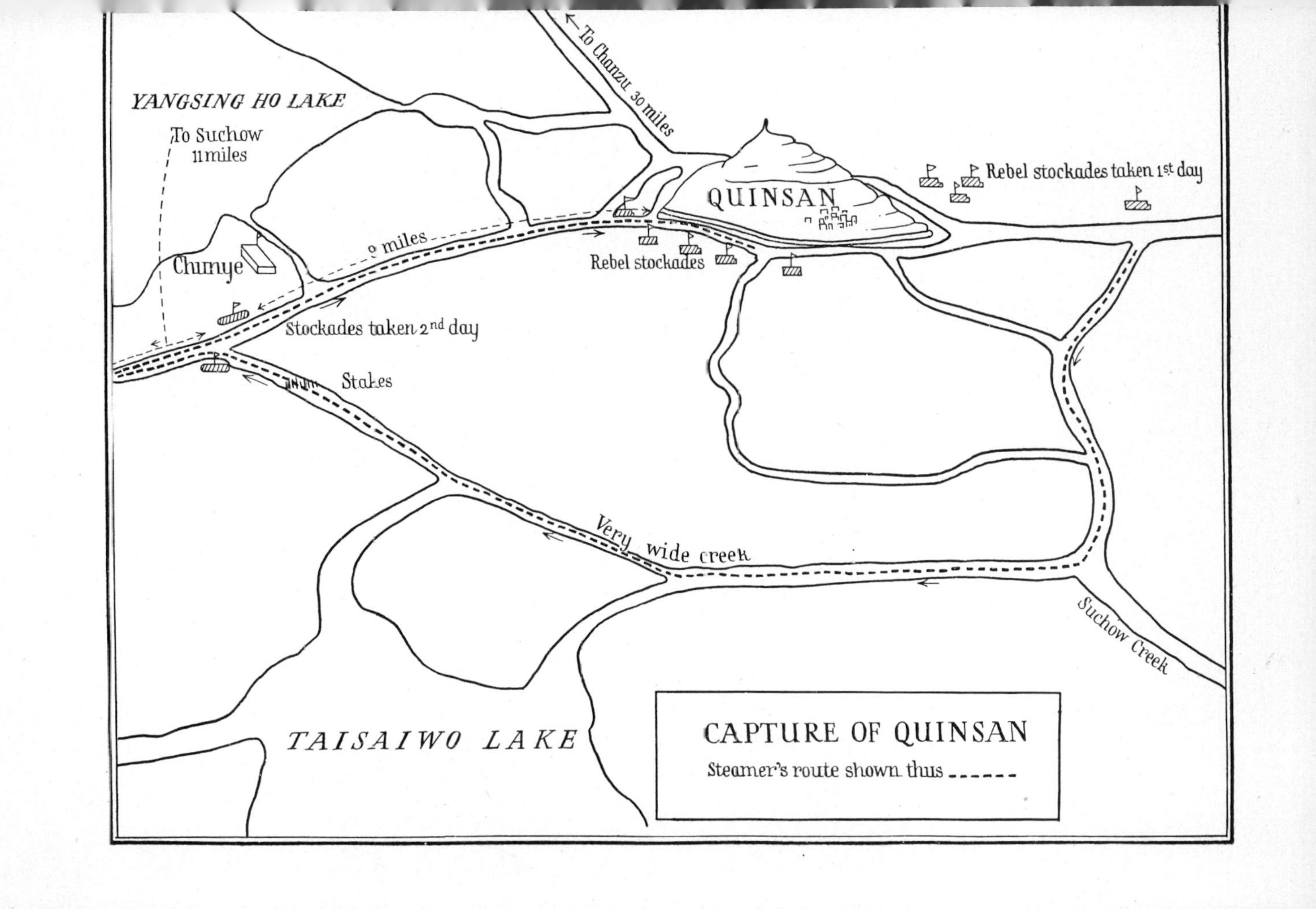

YANGSING HO LAKE
To Suchow
11 miles
To Chanzu 30 miles
QUINSAN
Rebel stockades taken 1st day
Chunye
9 miles
Rebel stockades
Stockades taken 2nd day
Stakes
Very wide creek
Suchow Creek
TAISAIWO LAKE
CAPTURE OF QUINSAN
Steamer's route shown thus - - - - - -

go no farther. But Gordon was able to observe the rebel stockades guarding the junction of the waterways at Chunye, which formed the key of the enemy's position. From the deck of the little paddle steamer they saw large bodies of *chang-mows,* including many horsemen, moving along the road that bordered the canal, the waters of which were crowded with boats. One or two of the *Hyson's* 32-pounder shells created something of a panic; the rebels had not expected such a diversion against their rear, though one is surprised that Gordon should have risked putting them on the alert by this useless demonstration of the efficacy of gunfire.

However, he had discovered what he wanted, and as the *Hyson* steamed back to headquarters he planned to strike at Chunye on the following day. Li Futai supported him against Ching, now "as surly as a bear" because his simple plan of attack against the east gate was being scrapped, and during the night the Imperial flotilla of fifty gunboats started off with orders to pull up the stakes in the channel and make the creek navigable for the *Hyson.* At dawn Gordon followed with his own flotilla, carrying the rifle regiment of his Force and artillery. He himself, as before, was with Li Hung-chang on the *Hyson,* and it pleased him to see the brave sight of the fleet of boats, with their broad lateen sails and flowing, brightly colored pennants, as they covered the waters of the creek; it was a fine thing to command men in the supreme adventure of war.

Progress was slow, but by noon they had reached the stakes, which the crews of the Imperial gunboats had been too frightened to remove. Gordon landed his infantry; the "Imps," now grown bolder, pulled up the stakes, and then the troops, supported by the *Hyson,* advanced on the stockades. Against such determined tactics the rebels put up no defense, and incontinently fled. At the entrance to the main canal Gordon ordered all the Force to pursue the enemy towards Quinsan, while he turned the *Hyson* boldly in the direction of Suchow. Owing to the number of native craft, it was impossible to go fast, but the *Hyson* managed to harass the rebels streaming in retreat along the Suchow road. The whole of that afternoon, with only some half a dozen Europeans and thirty Chinamen on board, the steamer continued its magnificently impudent pursuit. At one place Gordon landed with a handful of men and captured a stone fort. At another a large body of rebels threatened to seize the vessel, and they could only be kept off until the gun was loaded by blowing the siren — a devilish noise and obnoxious to the Long-hairs. When the skipper took 150 prisoners on board, Gordon thought it rash, for he did not see how they could be guarded; but he admired the intrepidity of four rebel chiefs, who galloped by within two yards of the *Hyson* amid a hail of bullets. One of them had his horse shot under him, but another waited and coolly took him up — "they deserved to get off" was Gordon's verdict.

At six o'clock, when within two miles of Suchow and in the heart of the Taeping country, the *Hyson* turned back. Gordon did not know what had happened to the force they had left at Chunye, nor whether the rebels had organized defensive positions on the canal bank in their rear. Nothing interrupted the return journey except the difficulties of picking their way amid the traffic, for the peaceful provincials still carried on their usual avocations so far as the Long-hairs would let them. When, at half-past ten that night, the *Hyson* approached Chunye, their ears told them that a vigorous battle was going on. Coming nearer, they found the Imperial gunboats on the point of beating a retreat. The *Hyson* blew its whistle. Its blasts, cheerful for friends as terrible for foes, and its red and green navigation lights gave the "Imps" fresh courage — much-needed courage, for the whole garrison of Quinsan, 8000 or 9000 strong, was on the road trying to force a passage to Suchow. Gordon had guessed the rebels would not fight if their retreat was cut off. Now, before the *Hyson's* 32-pounder, the columns broke and fled the way they had come. They were an easy mark, but Gordon would allow no unnecessary bloodshed as through the summer night the *Hyson* chugged its way along the canal towards Quinsan. He wanted Chinamen to love, not to kill, one another, and, looking back afterwards on that day and night of fighting, during which the *Hyson* fired between eighty and ninety rounds, he only justified it on the ground of humanity. The rebels had to be taught a lesson. If they learned it properly peace might come at once.

11. Without Fear and Without Reproach

By the following dawn Quinsan, or rather the ruins of that once prosperous town, was in the Imperialists' hands, and Gordon could take some rest after forty-eight hours of practically uninterrupted activity. His extraordinary energy was already helping to make him into the superhuman character which his fearlessness suggested.

An enigmatic personage, too — a man who did unaccountable things and had an unaccountable respect for human life, which extended even to the rebel. It was right that he should exult in the smallness of his casualties before Quinsan, — two killed and five drowned, — but we may well believe that his tenderness for the Long-hairs was incomprehensible to Li Futai. Gordon had done another extraordinary thing during the fighting; he had picked up a little naked child from the canal bank, and held him in his arms while he directed operations. "Quincey" he named the foundling, and he took pains afterwards to provide for him.[1]

Such care for the lives of others was in striking contrast to

[1] Quincey was sent to Shanghai, was adopted by an English regiment, and returned with it to England. Later on, Gordon secured him a place in the Chinese Customs under Sir Robert Hart.

the way he hazarded his own. If the Chinese soldiers were afraid to expose themselves when facing the rebels, he would seize first one and then another by the pigtail, drag them out into the open, and make them fire over his own shoulder. In the hottest moments of the action he remained unperturbed and imperturbable, a cigar — his only indulgence at this time — between his lips. His nerves and his muscles seemed both of iron. He hardly slept, never appeared to eat, and quenched his thirst in those hot summer days with drafts of tea, which he drank from the spout of a battered teapot — now a museum specimen. His abstinence became a part of the legend — but his men did not know that at night hunger would drive him to raid the commissariat, where he would suck raw eggs, to the number sometimes of a dozen, until the pangs were appeased. And, to heighten the contrast with his normal cheerfulness and affability, sadness would sometimes envelop him, or, going to another extreme of emotion, he would blaze up in furious anger.

12. Short Shrift for Mutineers

Had Gordon been able to strike immediately at Suchow, the Taepings' powers of resistance might have collapsed altogether and the rebellion been at an end. But demoralization also attacked the Imperialist forces. With Li's departure, Ching grew more surly than ever, while the Ever-Victorious in the flush of victory again resorted to mutiny. Gordon had had enough of Sung-Kiang and its disorderly ways, and he therefore established Quinsan, which also had now a more important strategical situation, as his headquarters. The decision created an uproar, and a written statement was brought to him which declared that, if he did not rescind the obnoxious order, the artillery would blow their European and Chinese officers to pieces.

Photo E.N.A.

LI HUNG-CHANG WITH HIS SUITE

Gordon acted without a moment's hesitation. Parading the N.C.O.'s, whom he suspected of being the instigators of the trouble, he demanded the names of the ringleaders. When he received no reply he told them that he would proceed to shoot one in five unless they confessed. The announcement was received with groans of disapproval, but Gordon had his own bodyguard with him on whom he could rely, while the N.C.O.'s, unsupported by the men from the ranks, were powerless. As Gordon's eye ran down the line of mutineers he noticed that one corporal was groaning louder than the rest. This evidence was enough for Gordon, who always prided himself on being quick. He rushed at the man, dragged him from the ranks, and ordered two of his bodyguard to shoot him on the spot.

Then, with this extremely disturbing example of their General's determination before them, the rest of the N.C.O.'s were marched off under arrest, to reflect that if, after an hour, they did not disclose their ringleader's name, decimation multiplied by two would still be their fate. They did not withstand such determination. The men fell in, and the N.C.O.'s judiciously put the blame upon the corporal who had already paid the penalty. But nearly two thirds of the Force decided that the military life as their General understood it was too strenuous for their taste, and melted away by desertion. Gordon repaired the loss easily by recruiting his rebel prisoners, who were excellent fighting material and were ready to serve anybody who fed and paid them regularly.

The relations between Gordon and the restless and disgruntled Ching did not improve. In that electrical atmosphere hot words easily led to blows, and at one moment Ching actually turned his guns on the Ever-Victorious. Li sent his English secretary, Halliday Macartney, to make peace, and when Ching subsequently appeared before Li with his complaints against Gordon, the Futai refused to listen to him.

For all Gordon's impetuosity of tongue and temper, Li supported him loyally, and stood out against Sir Frederick Bruce, who wished Burgevine to be reinstated in his command. Burgevine had spent the spring pleading his case in Peking, and he returned to Shanghai with the support of the British Minister. "Of General Burgevine's intelligence, tact, and good sentiments," wrote Sir Frederick Bruce, "I have formed a favorable opinion, and the fact of his being cosmopolitan, though nominally American, renders me very desirous that his restoration to command should be effected"; and the Minister inserted some reflections on the jealousy of Li Futai, who had driven Burgevine from his province. The American Minister also was naturally on his compatriot's side, but at that time the war between North and South made the United States of little account internationally.

Li Futai, however, was a better judge of men than the British Minister,[1] and Burgevine, in spite of his diplomatic backing and the ostensible sympathy of the Throne, kicked his heels in Shanghai, where he found Li determined to support Gordon. Unable to get back his command, Burgevine used his "intelligence, tact, and good sentiments" in buying munitions for the rebels, and acting as their agent in the markets of Shanghai. Li could do nothing. He could not even pay the Ever-Victorious. Gordon, as July passed and the Force, which he had forbidden to plunder, received nothing from its paymaster, fell into despondency. How under such circumstances could he prevent disaffection among officers and men? With his patience exhausted, smarting also under the reflec-

[1] Sir Frederick Bruce showed his ignorance of Chinese official psychology in demanding that the Force should be placed under the direct orders of the Central Imperial Government in Peking, an impossible request which led also to the abandonment of the scheme of an Anglo-Chinese naval force to operate on the Yangtze. Gordon incurred considerable criticism for not being a party to such a demand.

tions made upon the humanity of the troops in the local Shanghai paper, he decided to throw up his command, and on July 25 he wrote to Li Hung-chang resigning his position as commander of the Ever-Victorious Army.

The Futai's troubles had never seemed so overwhelming. All the recent successes appeared likely to count for nothing, and the devastating civil war to continue indefinitely. If Gordon left, the Ever-Victorious would collapse. That, in its turn, might mean another advance of the rebels on Shanghai. At this moment, however, an event occurred which began a new and the last chapter in the history of the Taeping Rebellion. Burgevine, with thirty-two others as desperate as himself, — "roughs," as Shanghai public opinion termed them, — seized an armed Chinese Government steamer, the *Kajow,* at Sung-Kiang, and turned its prow towards the rebel headquarters. For some time Li had suspected something of the kind to be in the wind, but Gordon — who, for one thing, found Burgevine an attractive scoundrel, and, for another, did not wish to be hard upon the man whose former post he held — promised the Futai that he would answer for his loyalty. At the moment when Burgevine joined the rebels, Gordon had just finished a forty-mile night ride from Shanghai to Quinsan, hurrying back to deal with a reverse threatening his hard-pressed troops at Kahpoo. Directly he heard of Burgevine's *coup,* all thought of resignation was at an end, and for the next three months Gordon's Force was to be engaged in incessant and often desperate fighting against troops also led by Europeans and of almost as good quality as itself.

13. Chinese Loyalty and Suspicion

The vicissitudes of the Force need no detailed recital. Gordon did not intend a direct assault upon his objective, the grizzled walls and towers of Suchow, manned by 50,000 rebels. His strategy was, as before, to nibble at the enemy's communications, until surrender became merely a matter of time. But now that the rebels had troops officered by Europeans to oppose the Ever-Victorious, and a gunboat under "a daring and capable officer," as Gordon described its skipper, Jones, to meet the *Hyson,* the morale of the two armies was much more evenly balanced. No easy victories marked this stage of the campaign. Instead of being helped by wholesale desertions from the rebels, Gordon could not trust his own troops. Burgevine's old comrades in the Ever-Victorious looked upon his latest piratical exploit with more or less unconcealed sympathy — sympathy which Gordon preferred not to censure. Always well-disposed towards open enemies, he had no feelings of animosity for the misguided Burgevine; Gordon wanted to end the war, and that consummation would not be achieved by hate.

The only way he could expect to obtain loyalty from his Force was by paying all ranks regularly. For this purpose he worried, badgered, browbeat Li Hung-chang, who made promises while he secretly groaned at being expected to fall in with such a completely un-Chinese practice.

The credit of Li Hung-chang's loyalty to Gordon stands out as all the greater in view of the tangled relations existing between the various parties. While the Ever-Victorious was fighting that autumn with varying success against the rebels round Suchow, both open and surreptitious communications were kept up between the lines. It could hardly be otherwise, when the friend of one day was the foe of the next. Gordon might shoot a mutinous corporal; he could not visit the same penalty upon a European officer whom he discovered treacherously corresponding with the enemy. All he could do was to commute the death penalty into a bargain that the officer's offense should be overlooked on condition of his leading the next forlorn hope. Gordon then forgot all about it, and the officer had to remind him when the next attack was planned. He duly carried out his bargain, only to be shot in the mouth as he stood by Gordon and to die in his General's arms.

Ching assured Li Hung-chang that Gordon himself was not to be trusted, that he had a secret understanding with the Wangs and was in communication with Burgevine, on whose head the Futai had placed a reward of 10,000 dollars. At the same time Li knew that influential Englishmen were pressing Gordon to go behind his back and to demand for the Ever-Victorious complete independence of the Futai's authority. More than this, as the operations appeared to lag, Li may well have doubted whether Gordon really wanted the rebellion to end; he had secret information [1] that Gordon was memorializing the Throne to make him Commander-in-Chief of all the Chinese armies — a project which, if it had materialized, would have constituted him dictator of the Empire.

Fantastic ambitions! Yet in the break-up of a vast empire such visions might not seem so remote. "How differently events might have turned out," said the matter-of-fact Wolseley to Gordon, when he returned home from China, "had I been sent on this mission instead of you! I should have gone there with the intention of wiping out the rebellion and of becoming Emperor of China myself." Gordon, for his part, believed that Li Hung-chang cherished similar ambitions, once telling Li that he knew he wished to overthrow the monarchy — then represented by a feeble child — and make himself Emperor of the whole Middle Kingdom. Li appears to have denied the impeachment without heat, it ran so obviously against all his conservative predilections that anger was unnecessary. But it took some strength of character on the part of the Futai not to allow his suspicion that Gordon was

[1] This refers to a project, put forward by Sir Frederick Bruce, that Gordon should remodel the Chinese Army, which in future should be removed from the authority of the provincial governors.

playing for his own hand to interfere with the support he gave him.

For Gordon did correspond with Burgevine. They were on better terms with each other than with their respective Chinese colleagues. Chaillé-Long records how Gordon told him that he was once cornered by Burgevine. "He could have bagged me and the Ever-Victorious. I wrote him to come and dine with me. After a good dinner Burgevine showed me how to get out. I gave him all the gold he wanted for his men and that night I escaped." A picturesque story, if it were true.

We know, however, for certain that Jones, of the *S.S. Kajow,* acted as intermediary. The steamer's engines had broken down, and the captain of the ex-Chinese gunboat took them to Shanghai to have them repaired. On his leisurely return to Suchow he met Gordon, who gave him a letter to Burgevine, offering him a safe-conduct for himself and the other Europeans with him if they would abandon the rebel cause. Things had gone badly in Suchow, and Burgevine's relations with the Wangs were none too harmonious, as Gordon knew. But Burgevine was a headstrong and conceited person, anxious to set his conduct in a heroic light, and not ready to admit he had lost his gambler's throw.

Besides, he might not yet have lost. All things were possible to a bold man ready to follow his star — if, in that Chinese miasma, one only knew which way it led. Burgevine answered Gordon's letter warmly. "My dear Gordon," he began, thanked him for writing and for his expressions of regard, assured him that he had not joined the rebels out of pique, and declared that five years' service in the country had made him perfectly aware that both sides were equally rotten. He added that he would gladly meet Gordon at any place that he liked to appoint. When, three days after writing this letter, Burgevine did meet Gordon at the stockades for the

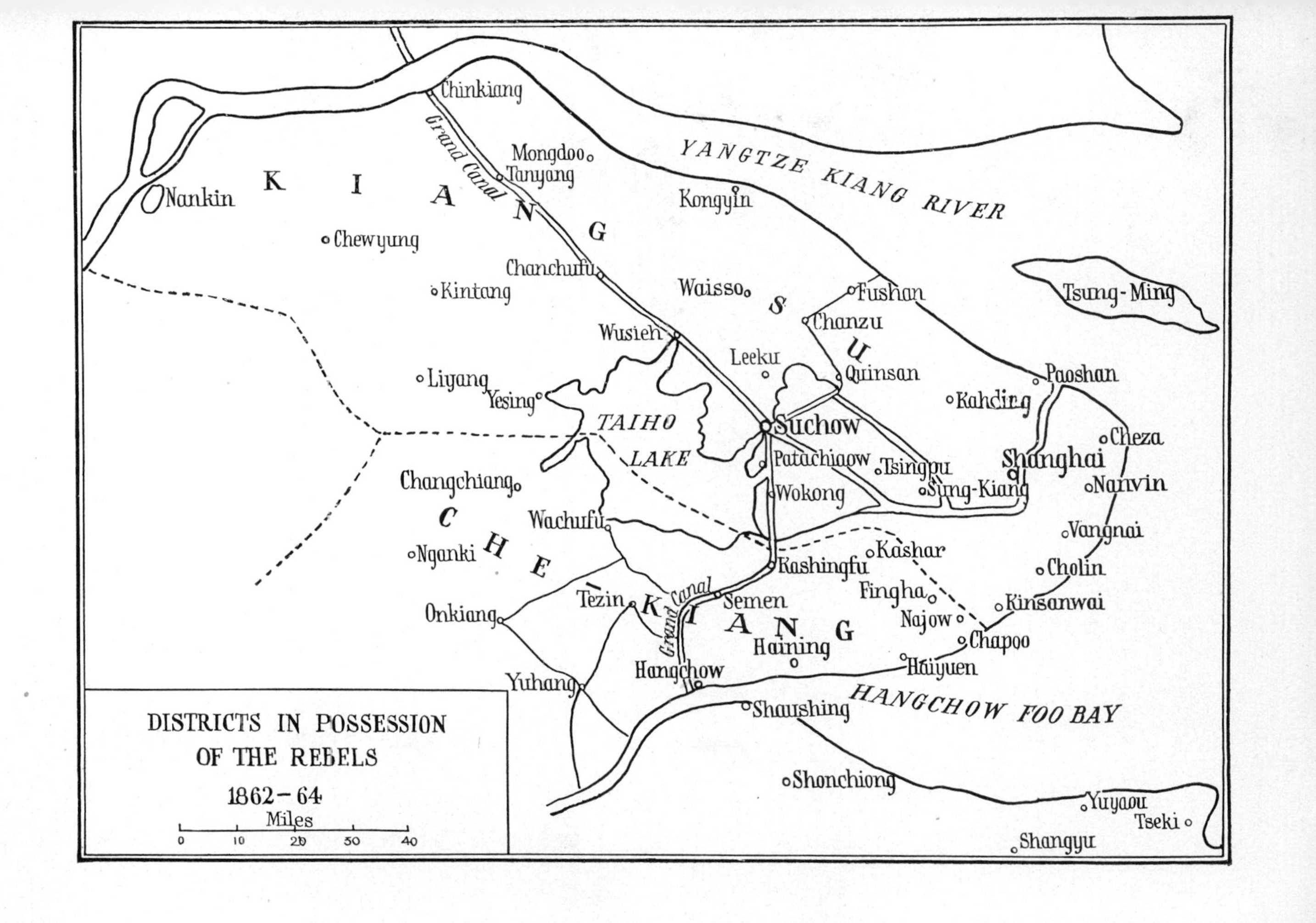
YANGTZE KIANG RIVER
KIANGSU
CHEKIANG
Nankin
Chinkiang
Grand Canal
Mongdoo
Tanyang
Kongyin
Chewyung
Chanchufu
Kintang
Waisso
Fushan
Chanzu
Tsung-Ming
Wusieh
Leeku
Quinsan
Paoshan
Liyang
Yesing
TAIHO
LAKE
Suchow
Kahding
Cheza
Shanghai
Patachiaow
Tsingpu
Sung-Kiang
Nanvin
Changchiang
Wokong
Wachufu
Vangnai
Kashar
Cholin
Nganki
Kashingfu
Fingha
Kinsanwai
Onkiang
Tezin
Semen
Najow
Chapoo
Haining
Hangchow
Haiyuen
Yuhang
Shaushing
HANGCHOW FOO BAY
Shonchiong
Yuyaou
Tseki
Shangyu
DISTRICTS IN POSSESSION
OF THE REBELS
1862–64
Miles
0
10
20
30
40

purpose of making arrangements for deserting with his European followers, other plans flitted through his mind. Surrender with a safe-conduct was a dull business — how much more attractive if he could induce Gordon, on his side, to take the same step as he proposed: let them both throw over their Chinese masters, join forces, and snap their fingers at "Imps" and Long-hairs alike. Then China would be at their feet.

Burgevine, acting thus as the devil's advocate at a second meeting, only succeeded in making Gordon angry, and he retired with smooth words which concealed a desire for revenge. This he planned to obtain by seizing Gordon at the moment he and his followers presented themselves as prisoners of war at the stockades of the Ever-Victorious Army. Such a *coup* would turn the tables upon the too-scrupulous Englishman and restore Burgevine's shaken credit with the Taeping chiefs, of whom the leader in Suchow was the young, highly educated, and liberal-minded Muh Wang. To carry out this project the connivance of Burgevine's followers was necessary. But when he broached the matter to Jones, that worthy, who shared the common admiration for Gordon, declared he would have nothing to do with so dirty a business. By way of answer Burgevine, in the true gangster spirit, fired at him point-blank with his pistol. "By God," shouted Jones, as the blood poured from his cheek, "you have shot your best friend!" "I know I have," was the answer, "and I wish to God I had killed you."

In the meantime Gordon became alarmed for the safety of the man who had such unamiable intentions towards him, particularly when one of Burgevine's officers escaped to the Imperialists' lines — "an unexpected and horrible treachery," as Burgevine described it, which nearly cost Burgevine and the other Europeans in Suchow their heads. And though Gordon did everything in his power to convince the Wangs that clemency was the best policy for everyone concerned. Ching, who was also in communication with the rebels, accompanied Gordon's letter to them by one which he professed urged Muh Wang to pardon and release Burgevine, while in reality it advised him to decapitate the lot. When the leaders were at these cross-purposes, honesty and good sense counted for little. But a pony which Gordon sent as a present to Muh Wang proved more persuasive than words, and, with the prestige Gordon enjoyed in both camps, induced the Wangs to release Burgevine, who on October 18, after six weeks' service with the Taepings, was allowed to leave Suchow. Gordon sent him down to Shanghai, where the American Consul officially tendered his thanks for the great kindness Gordon had shown to "misguided General Burgevine and his men," the majority of whom Gordon now enrolled in his own bodyguard.

14. Gordon's Methods and Personality

The negotiations about Burgevine helped to establish relations between Gordon and the Wangs which within another six weeks were to bear fruit in the surrender of Suchow. They feared, admired, and trusted Gordon. They feared him for his prowess, trusted him for his honesty, admired him as being invulnerable. A man whom death could not touch, whom no bullet could as much as scratch, must be under the protection of the Heavenly Father. Destiny clearly favored him. One story told how he stood upon the great bridge of Suchow as the bullets pattered against it. Leisurely he moved away and boarded his boat. Immediately this had passed under it, the great centre stone arch collapsed. Thus in a few moments he had twice escaped death. Such a man was better as friend than as an enemy, and only Muh Wang remained firm in his resolution to resist to the end.

One more scene of hard fighting intervened before Suchow

surrendered and the war against the Taepings reached its final phase.

Chung Wang, Generalissimo of the Taeping forces, made a last drive to save the city. He had a skill in strategy beyond that possessed by any of his enemies except Gordon, but he found against him a man as energetic and more resourceful than himself. During those critical weeks Gordon was indefatigable, never taking off his clothes and snatching when he could a few hours' sleep on board his steamer in a couple of blankets sewn up as a sack. If any alarm occurred, he was at once up and about. Often he did not sleep at all. If fieldworks had to be put up under cover of darkness, Gordon was sure to be present directing with his expert knowledge, seeing that the time-table he had ordered was adhered to — and woe betide his officers if it was not! During the day his spruce, red-coated figure seemed ubiquitous. He never stopped working — nor smoking a cheroot. Everything came under his eye; he was at once general, universal company commander, and adjutant of the Force. If Gordon wished to requisition stores from the commissariat, he would borrow some officer's notebook, tear a sheet out, and scribble on it his directions to his Commissary-General. All orders were given orally. Even battle plans were arranged by word of mouth. And if an officer did not do what Gordon told him quickly enough, Gordon carried out the order himself. Once when, during an action, his aide-de-camp, an English regular, dallied in delivering a message, making a détour to avoid dirtying his boots and uniform in a ditch, he found that Gordon had reached his objective before him. The young man was promptly returned to his regiment in Shanghai.

A sharp reverse preceded the fall of Suchow. Gordon arranged a night attack upon an outlying part of the defenses, but his plans were betrayed to the enemy, and when he led his party forward, all wearing white turbans so as to know one another in the dark, he found the rebels prepared to meet them. The Ever-Victorious carried the first breastwork, and then were held up by the desperate resistance of the defenders, headed by Muh Wang, barefooted and half-clothed, fighting with the utmost bravery amid a little band of Europeans. In the end Gordon, seeing that he could not capture the stockade, called off the attack.

15. The Fate of the Wangs of Suchow

Gordon lost no time in retrieving his defeat, and within a couple of days the city was completely invested and the Taepings' morale broken. His settled policy to soothe the animosities between the two sides in the civil war made Gordon anxious that the capitulation of the city should be unaccompanied by bloodshed. Li Hung-chang, now present in the Imperialist camp, listened favorably to his plea for moderation. Always generous towards a doughty enemy, Gordon asked that Muh Wang should be held as his special prisoner, a request which the Futai is said to have granted. In addition, both he and General Ching assured Gordon that they would deal tenderly with the Wangs in Suchow. Upon this understanding, events moved forward. Ching, accompanied by Gordon, met some of the Wangs, who agreed to surrender against promises for their personal safety, which Gordon guaranteed, but whether Li Hung-chang had ever given Gordon any definite promise that he would spare the Wangs' lives is very doubtful.

In that atmosphere of treachery and violence, however, Gordon's humanity availed little. The Wangs whom Gordon wanted to save were more bloodthirsty than their Imperialist enemies and were distrustful of one another. When Muh Wang, the most energetic of Taeping chiefs in Suchow, rose after a banquet, and made a speech insisting that the Futai's

INTERIOR OF THE WALLS OF SUCHOW
(From the "Illustrated London News," 1863)

word was not to be trusted, one of the subordinate Wangs rose and assassinated him. Not content with cutting off his head, which they sent to Li Hung-chang, these amiable Kings of Heaven decapitated the whole band of youths, to the number of thirty, whom Muh Wang, in the approved Chinese fashion, kept around his person.

In spite of this ferocity, Gordon continued to strive to prevent bloodshed, entering into negotiations with Muh Wang's successor, Lar Wang, who in other days had sworn blood-brotherhood with General Ching, at that time his fellow-rebel. Li Hung-chang at length issued a pardon to the Wangs and the majority of their followers, and the terms of the surrender on both sides were thus completed. Gordon could feel that his work was done. The strain had told upon his health and nerves. He was anxious to give up his command and return home to his complaining family, and he had already arranged in the strictest secrecy (otherwise his officers would have mutinied) that Halliday Macartney, Li's English secretary, should succeed him.

So matters stood on the afternoon before the Taepings surrendered Suchow. Gordon had issued orders that the Ever-Victorious was not to enter the city with the Imperialist troops; had they done so he knew he could not prevent them from looting. Now he went to the Futai and asked that his men should have two months' pay, as a reward for their services and as compensation for the plunder they were missing. Li's exchequer was in the usual state of deficit, but after some delay he produced half the amount demanded by Gordon. This was paid to the grumbling regiments, and on the morning of December 6 they started unwillingly for Quinsan, making a hostile demonstration as they passed the Futai's tent, where stood Gordon and another English officer to prevent any violence. Li Hung-chang was preparing to entertain the Wangs at a feast, and Gordon, who had already that morning in pique resigned his command for the second time, very unwisely refused the invitation to attend it, declaring that he had made arrangements to leave at once for Quinsan. If he had remained with the Futai and kept his bodyguard by him, the ensuing tragedy would almost certainly never have taken place.

The suspicion that all might not be well with the Wangs when the "Imps" had them in their power seems to have crossed Gordon's mind, and he actually visited Lar Wang's house to offer that leading rebel the sanctuary of his own steamer. There he met and talked with his foes of yesterday, congratulating them on their prowess and impressed by their confidence in the terms which they had made. The last Gordon saw of him and his fellow Wangs was the gaily dressed cavalcade as it moved off towards the Futai's quarters with the keys of the city, the Wangs laughing and talking among themselves, showing nothing of the humility which should accompany defeat — a fact which helped to enrage the Imperialists.

Gordon, accompanied only by his interpreter, then walked through Suchow, the Lyons of China, famous for its buildings, its bridges, and its trees, until he came to the *yamun* of Muh Wang, whom he had admired as a soldier and a brave man. It was deserted. Entering a large hall with a high, vaulted roof, in the gloom of which grotesque Chinese statues stared at him from round the walls, he found the débris of a feast. Everything had been left as it was when the scores of guests had apparently risen in their haste and fear, overturning chairs and stools. The candles were burned down in their sockets. A sickly odor of dried water lilies hung upon the air. Gordon, as he glanced round, saw one of his own officers stooping over something in the middle of the hall. It was the headless body of Muh Wang, from which he was stripping the silken robes that were stiff with gore. As Gordon came up he produced a packet from the breast pocket — the letter

Gordon had written guaranteeing the lives and property of the inhabitants if the city were surrendered. Gordon, much moved, sent his subordinate for soldiers to bury the body, remaining by it in the meantime, along with what could hardly have been very pleasant thoughts.

No clear account exists of the events of that afternoon and evening. The two first-hand authorities who have related the affair from Gordon's side disagree with each other and with Gordon himself. There is a startling discrepancy on the vital matter of the time at which the Wangs were received by the Futai. Gordon puts it at noon on December 6. According to Li Hung-chang, the feast was fixed for the evening, and the Wangs were killed at about 7 P.M. Yet Gordon tells us that he realized the Wangs had been murdered when he met the pale and frightened General Ching early in the afternoon.

In 1895, when Li Hung-chang visited England, the ex-Viceroy prepared a statement, a professed apology meant for the English public.

We were most friendly disposed when the fighting was over, and it was myself who suggested that we should have a feast in celebration. To this Chung Wang, Lar Wang, and General Ching quickly assented; and soon the banquet was set on board my private boat.

In the meantime General Gordon, who thought he had not been accorded full glory for the complete surrender of the Taepings, moved the Ever-Victorious Army away from Suchow to its old headquarters at Quinsan. This was against my orders, and also against the counsel of General Ching; but Gordon claimed there was a large amount of pay due to him and to his men. This was true, but it was also true that he had not been promised, and should not have expected, pay until the Suchow army had surrendered. He was feeling ill, and was waiting for replies to his memorials sent to the Throne. His last memorial, as I knew through Hsi Lung-ken, who wrote it, was very much against me.

When the banquet was set and we were in the midst of our joyousness, report was brought me that two large boats had pulled out from the shore and were coming directly to my boat. I went to the near side and looked. It was about the hour of the cock (7 P.M.) and I could not discern plainly, but it seemed to me as if Gordon himself captained one of the boats. I went back to the feast and told the Wangs I believed Gordon was coming. Ching turned very white and whispered to me that he was afraid — of what he did not say; but before we, Ching, Lar Wang, and myself, had time to reach that end of the boat which was pointed towards the shore, Imperial officers and soldiers clambered aboard from both sides, and began cutting down everyone they met. They killed Lar Wang by my side, and one fellow stabbed Ching, but only slightly. An officer was coming towards me with his sword, but he fell to his knees when I raised my hand.

Ching, and my other officers, succeeded in getting into one of the soldier boats with me and the pole man pushed us to the shore. Immediately I issued orders to all the troops in the city to make an attempt to capture those of the attacking party, but the feeling against the Wangs was so strong that I think but little attempt was made to carry out my orders. That night I learned that all the members of the banqueting party were decapitated and their bodies thrown into the river.[1] Among these was a great personal friend whom I loved very much, and a young nephew of mine from Wusang.

Ching's discomposure and the looting of the Imperialist troops, — itself a breach of the agreement, — if they did not convince Gordon that the worst had happened, made him seriously uneasy during the afternoon, and he rode with his interpreter to Lar Wang's house, where he had met him and the other Wangs in so friendly a fashion a few hours before. It had been looted and burned. An uncle of Lar Wang begged him to secure the safety of his nephew's wives and concubines, whom he was sheltering. Gordon, unarmed and unprotected, for a moment hesitated, but he yielded to the

[1] This is an obvious error.

Chinaman's prayers and accompanied him to his house. No sooner did he enter the courtyard than he found himself a prisoner, surrounded by excited rebel troops in truculent mood at the uncertainty about the fate of their leaders. Gordon's situation was both undignified and dangerous. Had news of the occurrences on Li Hung-chang's barge been known, his life would undoubtedly have been forfeit. As it was, the Taepings refused to allow him to go and fetch his bodyguard. He had to kick his heels as a prisoner till 2 A.M., when they permitted him to send his interpreter with a message to its commander, ordering him to seize the person of Li Hung-chang and hold him prisoner until he released the Wangs. But the interpreter was stopped by Imperialist soldiers, who seized the letter, tore it up, and turned its bearer back. An hour later Gordon persuaded the rebels to allow him to go in person. On the way he also suffered the indignity of being arrested by Ching's troops; but he managed to elude them and ultimately reached his bodyguard's quarters. The first thing he did was to send some men to look after Lar Wang's family and relations, and then, wild with rage, he planned to make the Futai answer for his outrageous conduct towards the Taepings and himself.

The strain of the fighting, followed by the events of the preceding twenty-four hours, had brought Gordon to the verge of hysteria. His native imperiousness, flattered by the part he had played in the fall of Suchow, now blazed out in a way that alarmed those who came into contact with him. Ching, wishing to break the news of the fate of the Wangs, was far too frightened to say anything about it. The Chinese general hurried from Gordon's presence and retired into the city, where he shed tears and ordered twenty Imperialist braves to be shot as a lesson in good behavior to the rest. Then he persuaded an English officer of the Ever-Victorious to go and tell Gordon what had happened. But the Englishman likewise quailed before that volcanic indignation, and he had not the courage to answer the question Gordon put to him about the Wangs, declaring that the mystery could best be resolved by Lar Wang's son, whom he was sheltering in his quarters. From this handsome youth Gordon first learned the whole truth — and then he too wept. But tears gave way to anger as, under the newly made orphan's guidance, he crossed the creek, and was shown the headless, mutilated bodies of the men for whose lives he had answered. It was a bitter moment, and he returned to his boat in a state of the wildest ferocity against the man whom he considered responsible. Arming himself with a revolver, he is said to have gone in search of Li Hung-chang, with the intention of exacting summary vengeance from the author of this outrage. But that mandarin, warned by Ching that Gordon was a man to avoid, had left his official quarters, and betaken himself to the security of some undisclosed house within the populous city of Suchow.

Again the thread of the story is tangled by contradictions. In any case, whether or not Gordon saw the Futai, he wrote him a letter to the effect that, unless he resigned his governorship at once and handed over the seals to him to put in commission until the Emperor's pleasure were known, he would launch the Ever-Victorious Army against the Imperialists. Having sent this extraordinary ultimatum, which, had it been put into effect, would have meant either war between England and China or Gordon being cashiered, he hurried to Quinsan, and prepared to carry out his threat if Li Hung-chang did not yield.

While Gordon thus betook himself to his old headquarters, meditating wild plans of vengeance, that astute mandarin was wondering how to soothe the irate barbarian, whom, for all his tempestuous character, he still admired. Li knew that Gordon was angry, but he did not realize the white heat of that rage, for when he handed Gordon's letter to Macartney to translate, his English secretary refused to do so. "This is written," said Macartney, "in a fit of indignation. You and Gordon are, and have been friends. I am the friend of both. The most friendly act I can do both of you is to decline to translate it. I will hand it back to you unread." Li acquiesced, only saying that, as he was not to know what the letter contained, he would not accept it at all. Then he arranged with Macartney that he should go at once to Quinsan, explain that he, as Futai, accepted full responsibility for what had happened, and would publish any proclamation Gordon desired, absolving him from any share in the death of the Wangs. They had been summarily executed, Macartney was to explain, because they had used defiant language, and proposed to share authority in Suchow with the Futai. For that reason Li Hung-chang had considered it unsafe to show them mercy. This face-saving explanation was probably untrue, but it excused him from the charge of weakness and of not having control over his troops, which he would have resented more than one of cruelty or treachery.

Late, therefore, on the afternoon of December 7, Halliday Macartney, who had eaten nothing all day, started off in a rowing boat for Quinsan along the canal on which Gordon and Li had fought side by side six months before, becoming as brothers in the process. Though Gordon's letter, which he carried in his pocket, indicated a state of mind not wholly rational, Macartney trusted that the hitherto unclouded cordiality of their relations and the candor of Gordon's character would bring his mission to a peaceful issue. This confidence was not to be so easily justified. He arrived in the middle of the night, a cold and famished envoy, only to learn that Gordon slept and was not to be disturbed. Coffee helped to prepare him for the painful interview. It was early dawn when Macartney was shown upstairs to a dim room where the man he had come to see sat sobbing on the edge of the bed. Without saying a word, Gordon stooped down and took something from underneath it. He held it up. "Do you see this? Do you see this?" he cried. Macartney in the semi-darkness peered at a strange-looking object. "It is the head of the Lar Wang — foully murdered," said Gordon, bursting into hysterical tears.

This morbid state of mind promised no good result to Macartney's efforts, and he withdrew. His fears were amply realized when he met Gordon, now morosely collected, at breakfast in the mess. A difficult meal can never have been taken under more difficult circumstances. The unbidden Macartney sat down beside Gordon. At the table were many officers, and some Shanghai merchants who had business dealings with the Force. For a time Gordon ignored Macartney's presence. Then he said, "You have not come for yourself. You have come on a mission from the Futai. What is it?" Macartney demurred at discussing the matter before so many people, but Gordon cut him short. "There are only friends here. I have no secrets. Speak out."

In these unpromising circumstances Macartney tried to make his friend see reason. Gordon heard with indignation and scorn that Macartney had refused to translate his letter to the Futai, and "blushed to think" that an Englishman could undertake to excuse the monstrous treachery which had been shown to the Wangs. Macartney pointed out that, whatever guilt might attach to their murder, Gordon was free from it, while the strong measures he proposed to take against the Imperialists would only react against himself. No doubt he could carry out his threats, but to put them into execution would only undo all the good he had accomplished. Besides, if he turned against the Futai, Gordon would have to pay his troops by plunder, and it was difficult to see how the Ever-Victorious could hold together for long under such circumstances, or what credit Gordon would be likely to obtain for his conduct.

Macartney spoke the truth, but Gordon, for the moment submitting to the strain of megalomania in his character, stamped his foot, and declared he would have none of Macartney's mild counsels. "Mild or not," Macartney answered, "they are the only ones your Minister [1] at Peking and our Queen will approve."

Gordon, backed by the approving silence of his officers, who wished for nothing better than fighting and loot, still would not listen, and without more ado gave orders for troops to embark on the *Hyson* and advance on Suchow. It was characteristic of the *camaraderie* which Gordon always showed in war, or an indication that he did not really intend extreme measures, that he offered Macartney a place on the steamer. But Macartney, taking an officer friend of his aside, borrowed a horse and a pair of spurs, and galloped off to warn Li Hung-chang of the apparently inevitable attack. It was never delivered. For as Gordon steamed towards Suchow the unanswerable arguments of Macartney had their effect, and, realizing the futility of violent measures, he ordered the *Hyson* to return to Quinsan.

So runs the story as told by the man [2] who knew both Gordon and Macartney. But Gordon's own official dispatch, written four days after his meeting with Macartney, throws a colder light upon his intentions when he set out from Quinsan, and indicates that, if the officers of his Force were anxious to join the rebels, Gordon was far from allowing his feelings to get the better of his judgment in the matter. "The disgust and abhorrence felt by all of them," he writes, "was, and is, so great as to lead me to fear their going over in mass to the

[1] Macartney was in the Chinese service, and therefore not answerable in any way to Sir Frederick Bruce.

[2] Demetrius C. Boulger, Gordon's friend and biographer.

rebels; but I have shown them that the sin would then be visited on the Chinese people, and not on the culprits who perpetrated it." Thus, when he started from Quinsan on December 8, he had no intention of attacking the Imperialists; his object was to recover the body of Lar Wang, and for that purpose he steamed as far as General Ching's stockade outside Suchow. He returned to Quinsan with the corpse and some of the dead Wang's family. On the following day General Brown, who had succeeded General Staveley, appeared and took the Force, at Gordon's request, under his protection, Gordon entrusting to him the solution of the various problems which now arose in consequence of the rupture between himself and Li Hung-chang.

16. Gordon Relents

General Brown's intervention did more credit to his heart than his head, and his moral indignation at the Futai's treachery blinded him to the realities of the situation. After seeing and sympathizing with Gordon at Quinsan, he went on to Suchow, where Li Hung-chang met him at the same stockade from which Gordon had recovered Lar Wang's body. The Futai immediately took upon himself full responsibility for the Wangs' fate, exonerating Gordon from any share in their death, but he attempted no justification of his own conduct, for this would have been derogatory to his dignity as Governor. Brown thereupon read the mandarin, who had some reason for considering himself a master in the art of government, a lesson in its first principles, or, as he put it, "on the impolicy of a fruitless severity which paralyzed his friends and drove the rebels to desperation when everyone had good reason to believe that they were prepared to capitulate and return to their homes in peace." The English General concluded his brief lecture by telling Li Hung-chang that he would advise the recall of Major Gordon and the disbandment of the Anglo-Chinese Force. As a slight concession Li Hung-chang, who was determined to do everything possible to conciliate Gordon, secured the General's promise that for the moment he would continue in command of the Force. In a crisis, time is always the statesman's best friend, and, when General Brown left, Li Hung-chang suddenly grasped his English interpreter's sleeve, and said, "I look to you to arrange matters and prevent a breach of friendship."

In reporting to the British Minister in Peking what he had done, General Brown recommended that the steps he had proposed to release Gordon and disband the Force should be followed by forbidding any foreigner to serve with either the Imperialists or the Taepings. The Chinese, he declared, should be left to fight out their own battles so long as they remained outside the thirty-mile radius, which he, as G.O.C. in Shanghai, would continue to protect. Set in motion by this foolish counsel, the wheels of the official machinery began to revolve, and produced on March 1, 1864, an Order in Council from the Court at Windsor which revoked the permission accorded a year previously to military officers holding Her Majesty's commission to enter the Imperial Chinese service. But by then Gordon had forgotten, or at least buried, his griefs against the Futai, and was in the middle of another campaign against the rebels.

Many motives caused him to relent. In the first place, as he sat nursing his wrath in Quinsan he was obliged to admit to himself that the Futai might be a villain, but was no fool. Gordon had hoped to end the rebellion by clemency. Yet Li's severity, far from driving the remaining Long-hairs to despair, induced, on the contrary, numerous rebels to surrender, towards all of whom the Futai scrupulously kept his word. "The Chinese," Gordon observed to his mother, "are a very odd people. They show at times the greatest and even culpable leniency, and at others are guilty of the greatest cruelties." Gordon's anger, however, was too deep not to take some time to cool, and all through December he refused to listen to the mandarins who came to explain or palliate the conduct of their official superior. When on January 1, 1864, envoys arrived with a present of 10,000 dollars from the Emperor, and with four Taeping flags, two from Li Hung-chang and two from another mandarin, Gordon refused to see them. On its being pointed out to him that this would be disrespectful to the Throne, he relented, and received the Imperial messengers at the head of his Force outside the west gate of Quinsan. But he would not take the money, nor Li's flags, though he accepted the other two, writing a note in the third person, according to the best canons of Victorian politeness, on the back of the Imperial rescript, thanking the Emperor and begging to be allowed to decline "his intended kindness."

Yet, as the days passed, Gordon began to wonder whether he had not judged the Futai over-hastily, and whether, too, he had not made a mistake in allowing General Brown to intervene in a matter which he and Li might after all have arranged between themselves. General Brown was at best a muddler, possibly a jealous intriguer — otherwise why had he sent home none of Gordon's reports since the preceding May? It was too bad, he told his mother. "I wrote them immediately after their occurrence and made capital plans to accompany them. I am very sorry about this, as the authorities will think that I have thrown them over, and I do not want them to think that, although I want to get nothing from it."

He had thrown the authorities over — this was exactly what the sympathizers with the Taepings began to say when they learned what Gordon had done. For, as January ran its course, both political and personal reasons gradually induced Gordon to resume his former friendly relations with Li Hung-chang. He chafed at inaction himself; so did the Ever-Victorious. The officers, excited by the idea of filibustering against the Imperialists, were duly sobered by the cashiering of seventeen of their number — so far as they were concerned, Gordon soon showed them that his resignation made no difference. But public opinion still remained fearful how he meant to use his redoubtable 5000, and none welcomed the possibility of his throwing in his lot with the Wangs, as Burgevine had done once and now threatened to do again — none, that is, except, on the one hand, the rowdy foreigners and low-class Chinese braves, and, on the other, the owners of house property in Shanghai, where the refugees had driven up rents to fantastic heights.

The rebels themselves were affected as they watched Gordon sulking in his tent, and plucked up heart.

Their expiring energies are again fanned into a flame. His appearance in the field will have immediate results; rowdies will commence to see that their game is hopeless and that they had better leave China; Chinese traders will again flock to Suchow, and the rebels will again lose heart. Chang-chu-fu will soon fall, and that will be followed very probably by the fall of Hangchow, and the other two or three small cities held by the rebels in Kiang-su and Che-Kiang. Whether a stand will be made at Nanking or not, Gordon thinks very problematical, but he is rather of opinion that it will not fight. The destiny of China is at the present moment in the hands of Gordon more than of any other man, and if he be encouraged to act vigorously, the knotty question of Taepingdom versus "union in the cause of law and order" will be solved before the end of May, and quiet will at length be restored to this unfortunate and sorely tried country.

In these words Robert Hart, then a young man in the Chinese Customs service, set out the political inducements which helped to bring Gordon once more into the field.

He was mollified also by the punctual and businesslike —

indeed, liberal — way in which the Futai since the fall of Suchow had paid the Force, while his conscience was clearer as to the moral responsibility for the death of the Wangs since the "bold, intelligent, and straightforward" son of Lar Wang felt confident his father had surrendered trusting not in Gordon's ability to protect him, but in his sworn brotherhood with Ching. Were that the case, Gordon had nothing to reproach himself with, and the proclamation which Li Hung-chang was ready to issue absolving him from any complicity in the course of events that day in Suchow would end the matter. So it came about that, while Sir Frederick Bruce was solemnly assuring the Imperial Government in Peking that Gordon would only continue in command of the Force on condition that he had no relations with the Futai, and in any case would do no more than provide for the safety of Shanghai, Gordon had called upon the treacherous mandarin with whom no English officer could have any dealings, and they were fast friends once more, united against the common enemy. The *volte-face* seemed perfectly natural to Gordon, but he was aware that it would not be so easily understood by others, and he wrote to Sir Frederick Bruce explaining his reason for acting against orders. The letter so well illustrates Gordon's candor that it is worth quoting in full: —

SOO-CHOW
February 6, 1864

MY DEAR SIR FREDERICK BRUCE,

In consequence of the danger which will arise by my delaying inaction with the Force any longer in a state of uncertainty, I have arranged with the Futai to issue a proclamation (which he will send to you), clearing me of any participation in the late execution of the Wangs, and have determined to act immediately.

The reasons which actuate me are as follows: I know of a certainty that Burgevine meditates a return to the rebels; that there are upwards of 300 Europeans ready to join them, of no character, and that the Futai will not accept another British officer if I leave the service, and therefore the Government may have some foreigner put in, or else the Force put under men of Ward's and Burgevine's stamp, of whose action at times we should never feel certain.

I am aware that I am open to very grave censure for the course I am about to pursue, but in the absence of advice, and knowing as I do that the Peking authorities will support the Futai in what he has done, I have made up my mind to run the risk. If I followed my own desire, I should leave now, as I have escaped unscathed, and been wonderfully successful. But the rabble called the Quinsan force is a dangerous body, and it will be my duty to see that it is dissolved as quietly as possible, and that, while in the course of dissolution, it should serve to benefit the Imperial Government.

I do not apprehend the rebellion will last six months longer if I take the field. It may take six years if I leave, and the Government does not support the Imperialists. I propose to cut through the heart of the rebellion, and to divide it into two parts by the capture of Yesing and Liyang.

If the course I am about to pursue meets your approbation, I shall be glad to hear, but if not shall expect to be well rebuked. However, I know that I am not actuated by personal considerations, but merely as I think will be most conducive to the interests of our Government.

The Futai does not want the Force to move against Nanking, I imagine, as Tseng Kuo-fan has the wish to capture it himself.

The Futai, if he is to be believed, has some extenuating circumstances in his favor for his action, and although I feel deeply on the subject, I think we can scarcely expect the same discernment that we should from an European Governor.

This letter will relieve you from any responsibility in the matter, and, thanking you very much for your kind letter, which I will answer shortly, I am, etc.

C. G. Gordon

P.S. — If you would let the matter drop, and make me responsible for my action in the matter, I think it would be more conducive to our good relations with the Peking Government than pressing them to punish or degrade the Futai.

C. G. G.

Majors do not usually write in this tone to Ministers Plenipotentiary, but then, majors with the military genius of Marlborough and the moral purpose of Lawrence or Havelock cannot be judged by conventional standards. Sir Frederick Bruce's answer admitted as much. If Gordon had taken upon himself the decision of a matter of high policy in a sense contrary to that of the British Government — well, there it was. No telegraph then existed in China, and, even if it had, it would hardly have curbed this masterful young man. Besides, Gordon's high motives, his "disinterested conduct in pecuniary questions" (how different to the normal attitude of the European in China!), and the humanity he had observed towards Burgevine — all these arguments impelled Sir Frederick to give his official blessing to the young Major of Engineers, who was respected by everyone from the Futai to the Wangs and was "universally trusted by the magistrates, elders, and population of the pacified districts." At any rate, whatever his private feelings, this was the line the British Minister followed in writing to Lord Russell, the Foreign Minister, who, under the stimulus of the indignation aroused by the Suchow affair, had already caused the Order in Council to be issued which made the course upon which Gordon was now embarking a breach of regulations.

The situation was a delicate one, and Gordon exerted himself to persuade his family that he was doing the right thing. Not without reason his mother "fretted" at the dangers which beset him in every action, and his father, now near the end of his life, hated the idea that a son of his, whose duty it was to serve the Queen, should be fighting in a cause which many Englishmen condemned. Gordon, grown to be something of a personage, became the target for criticism by those who wanted to attack the Government. His enemies in China, headed by a certain H. N. Lay, of the Customs, who was said to be anxious to have Gordon's place in command of the Ever-

Victorious, condemned the reconciliation with Li Hung-chang. Well-intentioned Members of Parliament also, who professed admiration for the Taepings, made use of the material provided by these local critics to attack Gordon in the House of Commons. Lord Naas, most prominent of them, refused to alter his tone when Gordon's brother Henry protested privately to him, and he continued to declare that, as a British officer, Gordon committed a grave error in condoning the disgraceful treachery of the Futai.

These attacks, Parliamentary and other, worried his family much more than they did Gordon. He told his mother that Lord Naas would be quickly cured of his Taeping prejudices if he came to China. "Compared with the rebels, the Imperialists are lambs," he declared — and to prove it he related how Chung Wang, though the best of the lot, had decapitated 2000 of the Lar Wang's troops who had made their escape from Suchow, but, unfortunately for themselves, had shaved their heads to help them in their flight. After things like that the Futai's conduct at Suchow, apart from the extenuating circumstances surrounding it, was clemency itself.

17. The Fortune of War Changes

When Gordon, faintly pursued by the benediction of his official superior and by the attacks of his enemies and critics, began his last series of operations against the rebels, he followed the same strategy which had already proved too much for their nerve. Attack where the enemy least expect it, make one victory the prelude to the next, be severe to your own troops and kind to the enemy's — these were the three elementary maxims of war which he followed now, as always. He moved out from Quinsan in the bitterly cold weather of a wintry February with Yesing as his objective on the far side of the Taiho Lake, some forty miles northwest of Suchow.

By obtaining possession of that tract of country, where the rebels had been in uninterrupted possession since 1860, he would cut their position in two, and render the fall of Nanking inevitable. Gordon trusted that their long immunity from attack would make the rebel strongholds in that district the easier prey. For the moment he was right.

The Long-hairs were surprised at the appearance of the "imitation foreign devils" in a country hitherto far removed from the theatre of war, and they lay low within their walls and stockades at Yesing, while Gordon, following his usual practice, carefully reconnoitred the position. He was upon a small hill when suddenly a body of enemy cavalry swept out from the town, and had Gordon, as the Chinese now firmly believed, not been invulnerable, his career would have ended then and there. Instead, it was the rebels on whom fortune frowned, and, after an attack planned as carefully as he had hazarded his own safety, Gordon could add Yesing to the list of his victories. On this occasion Li Hung-chang's threats that murder or looting would be summarily punished prevented any repetition of the disorders at Suchow, though Gordon had to shoot one of his own men before the Force, which he had forbidden to enter the town, was reduced to a suitable state of subordination.

Yesing fell on March 2. On March 9, Liyang, where the well-armed and well-provisioned garrison of 15,000 rebel troops promised a stern resistance, surrendered under Gordon's guarantee for their safety, Gordon this time saving the local Wang's mother, sister, wife, and son from the rebels, who were anxious to punish them for the sins of the rebellious Wang. As for Li Hung-chang, he busied himself with distributing the provisions stored by the rebels against a siege to the starving and cannibalistic peasants. Nothing could have been more amicable than the collaboration between the pious Englishman and the no less pious Chinaman, nothing more promising than the way the Long-hairs shaved their heads and straightway enrolled in the Imperialist ranks. At Liyang, Gordon enlisted a thousand of them in his own regiments, and formed a new corps of 1500 in which all ranks consisted of ex-rebel soldiers. It looked like the end of the Taepings, and Gordon wrote to his mother on the morrow of the capture of Liyang, predicting that the rebellion would be over in two months.

Then suddenly fortune changed, and shattered even the legend of Gordon's invulnerability. Kintang was the next city on the way to Nanking. When the Ever-Victorious appeared before its walls, better built than usual and not protected by the normal outlying stockades, the town looked strangely quiet. Gordon chose what he considered the most likely place for the assault, bombarded it for three hours, and then led the attacking party. As this landed under the walls, the rebels suddenly came to life, and opened a terrific fire. Although the men of the Ever-Victorious were used to the barbaric din of Chinese battles, to the clashing gongs and the braying of horns, they quailed under the stinkpots which rained upon them, and for a time refused to leave the boats. As the fearless Gordon encouraged them by his example, a conspicuous figure waving his Chinese battle flag, the immunity he had hitherto enjoyed — a glorious tribute indeed to the extreme wildness with which the rebels directed their aim — was on this occasion denied him, and he fell, seriously wounded in the leg. He was carried back in a half-fainting condition to the *Hyson,* and Major Brown, brother to the English General in Shanghai, took his place. But he too was hit, and Gordon, seeing from a stretcher on his steamer that the attack had failed, gave orders for it to be called off. This engagement, which in the World War would have occupied two lines in the daily bulletin, caused an immense stir. As the news passed through Shanghai it became magnified to alarming proportions, and so reached the Gordon family roof at Southampton. The Chinese showed touching solicitude, Li Hung-chang being ordered by Imperial Edict to call on Gordon every day and the same celestial authority requesting the wounded man "to wait until he shall be perfectly restored to health and strength" before going on with the war.

Unfortunately he did not follow the Emperor's advice, partly because his own repulse at Kintang was overshadowed by the sudden offensive which Chung Wang, following Gordon's strategy, undertook against the Imperialists in the country at Gordon's rear. He descended on Fushan, scene of the first engagement in which Gordon had led the Ever-Victorious, invested Kongyin, threatened Chanzu, and almost made Shanghai tremble once again. Here was an unexpected turn of affairs, and Gordon from his steamer, during the fortnight that he was incapacitated by his wound, had to arrange an immediate change in his plan of campaign. First he moved on Kongyin, then found it necessary to turn aside towards Waisso (where the rebels had established their headquarters), appearing before that place about ten days after his reverse at Kintang.

Then the Ever-Victorious Army proceeded to demonstrate with impressive thoroughness that Gordon's belief in his indispensability was completely justified. Moving by land, the infantry arrived in front of the strongly fortified stockades of Waisso, and immediately attacked before establishing any *liaison* with the artillery which Gordon had on board his flotilla. It gained sufficient success to excite the rashness of the officers; then in a counter-attack it lost its cohesion, was suddenly overcome by panic, and the crack rifle regiment of the Force broke and fled, pursued by a squadron of Taeping cavalry for three miles. In this *sauve qui peut,* which Gordon was helpless to prevent, seven European officers and more than

250 men were killed. It was a drastic lesson, only equaled by that the Force had received when Captain Holland led it against Taitsan before Gordon took command; and in the face of it Gordon decided to do nothing until his wound was completely healed.

18. The Final Victory

While Gordon, three weeks later, was making his final drive against what he called the Rebel Expeditionary Force, he heard of the Imperialist success in the southern sector of operations, news clouded by the death from wounds of General Ching — "by far the best mandarin the Imperialists had," Gordon said of him, "and, in spite of his conduct at Suchow, I am sorry for him."

But the death of one man counted for little in that holocaust. The Wangs' drive against Gordon's communications was accompanied by gruesome atrocities, and Gordon saw in every village visited by the rebels, now chiefly Cantonese and the riffraff of the South, "from ten to sixty dead, either women, — frightfully mutilated, — old men, or small children." When he was well of his wound he took his revenge for the defeat at Waisso by an impressive display of Napoleonic strategy against the rebels investing Kongying, who in their flight were turned upon by the villagers everywhere. In a single village 3000 Long-hairs were massacred; such as escaped death were stripped and left to wander naked over the country until cold and hunger did their work. As Gordon passed through this desolation he felt that he did not regret the fate of the rebels. The last six months had taught him much, and the sentiments which had warmed him towards the Wangs of Suchow had now cooled. The haunting sights of misery, the horrible, furtive looks of the starving peasantry hovering round his steamer, made him feel sick. They were more like wolves than men, he thought, without even the volition to bury their dead, who lay where they had fallen — in some cases "trodden quite flat by the passers-by," as Gordon's entirely truthful pen put it. He had no talent for description; exaggeration he abhorred. The people of Shanghai, whom he wanted to start a relief fund, he excused for not understanding the full horror of that scene of desolation — "they do not *see* these things, and to *read* that there are human beings eating human flesh produces less effect than if they saw the corpses from which that flesh is cut." In such circumstances Gordon was not the man at this eleventh hour to consider his own personal feelings or his own personal safety; "I will not be led to do what may cause great disasters for the sake of getting out of the dangers, which, in my opinion, are no greater in action than in barracks," was how this fatalist expressed it to his mother in the middle of April, 1864.

Mrs. Gordon, however, approached the end of her fretting. In another three weeks the Ever-Victorious fought its last battle. The scattering of the rebels at Kongyin was followed by another tremendous rebel defeat at Waisso, where the main Rebel Expeditionary Force was cut to pieces — "they will never try a flank march again," Gordon declared with unsuppressed professional glee. At last he and the Imperialist general, not nearly so competent a soldier as poor Mandarin Ching, invested Chanchufu, on the Grand Canal, halfway between Suchow and the Yangtze. Except Nanking, Gordon wrote, "it is the only city left of any importance, and I think, my dear mother, its fall will be the end of the rebellion." But it did not fall without the Ever-Victorious suffering one more repulse. The attack was planned on the usual principles — a bombardment, a pontoon thrown across the moat to the glacis under the breach, an assault. Once again the rebels, now hardly off for munitions, reserved their fire until the assaulting party began to cross the pontoon, and then poured upon them missiles of every conceivable kind, brickbats, fireballs, the nauseous stinkpots — prototype of our gas shells. Twice the assault faltered. Ten of the officers were killed, nineteen others wounded. They had never fought with more bravery and devotion, nor had Gordon ever exposed himself more recklessly than when he led the attacking parties. Then he was forced to withdraw and leave his pontoon train in the rebels' hands. His officers waited on him an hour later and asked to be allowed to renew the attack — a request his caution made him decline.

There was nothing for it but a siege, and Gordon proceeded to dig regular trenches, borrowing Li Hung-chang's own troops to help in the fieldworks. These were run up close to the walls, and in less than three weeks everything was ready for the final assault. On the day before it, Gordon, having some presentiment perhaps that he would be killed, wrote a longer letter home than usual.

Our grand attack will come off in a day or two. D.V. after that I shall go back to Quinsan and break up the Force. . . . I shall of course make myself quite sure that the Rebels are quashed as otherwise I should incur great responsibility, but on these subjects I act for myself, and judge for myself. This I have found to be the best way of getting on. I shall not leave things in a mess, I hope, but I think if I am spared I should be home by Christmas. The losses I have sustained this campaign have been no joke, out of 100 officers, I have had 48 killed and wounded, and out of 3500 men, nearly 1000 killed and wounded, but I have the satisfaction of knowing that as far as mortal can see six months will see the end of this rebellion, while if I had continued inactive, it might have lingered on for six years. Do not think I am ill-tempered, but I do not care one jot about my promotion,[1] or what people might say. I know I shall leave China as poor as I entered it, but with the knowledge that through my weak instrumen-

[1] Gordon had recently been promoted Brevet Lieutenant-Colonel for his services in the field.

tality upwards of 80 to 100,000 lives have been spared. I want no further satisfaction than this. I hope you do not fret about my exposure, etc., it is all nonsense what they say. I take every precaution and do not risk myself more than is absolutely necessary.

Then he goes into the military details which he loved: —

We have now within 80 yards of the wall, two 8″ howitzers, four 32- and two 24-pounders and some 12-pounders and mortars 8″ and 5½″, on our flank some 100 yards are two 8″ guns, two 24-pounder guns, and one 32-pounder and two 8″ mortars. If the Rebels can stand that I shall be astonished indeed, although they certainly did fight most bravely last time. The Rebels of this place are the "originals" of the Rebellion, and though there may be some innocent, still the mass of them are deserving the fate that awaits them.

He and Li Hung-chang would not fall out over the question whether the Wang of Chanchufu was to keep his head on his shoulders.

Two hours' fighting on the following day settled his fate and that of his followers. For a time the fortune of battle remained doubtful. The Imperialists had mounted the walls at the breach, but then met with a desperate resistance and began to falter. At this moment Gordon led his 1st Regiment, swelled by 200 volunteers from the others, into the mêlée and decided the day. His first thought after the place fell was for his mother. On a leaf torn from a notebook, belonging probably to one of his officers, upon whom he habitually relied to provide him with paper, he wrote her a few lines in pencil: —

11 *May*, '64. 4 P.M.
CHANCHUFU

MY DEAR MOTHER,

Chanchufu was carried by assault by the Quinsan Force and Imperialists at 2 P.M. this day with little loss — D.V. I go back to Quinsan on the 13th May and shall not again take the

11 May. 64. 4 PM
Chanchufu

My dear Mother.

Chanchufu was carried by assault by the Quinsan Force & Imperialists at 2 PM this day; with little loss – Dv. I go back to Quinsan on the 13th May. & shall not again take the Field, the Rebels are now done, they have only Tayan & Nankin, & the former will fall probably in a day or two, & Nankin in about two months. I am happy to say I got off safe

Your affect son

C G Gordon

GORDON'S LETTER TO HIS MOTHER AT THE END OF THE TAEPING REBELLION

Field, the Rebels are now done, they have only Tayan and Nankin, and the former will fall probably in a day or two, and Nankin in about two months. I am happy to say I got off safe.

Your affect. son,
C. G. GORDON

The brief note, with its firm handwriting and its tone of quiet assurance, shows that in the moment of victory he is carried away by no feelings of exultation. He has no wish to share in the glory of taking Nanking. His mind is already made up. He has decided on his own initiative what he will do. The Anglo-Chinese, or, as he calls it, the Quinsan Force, which Sir Frederick Bruce and General Brown considered indispensable a few months ago, is too dangerous an instrument to be kept in existence any longer. He will lead it back at once to its base, and there break it up. Again Gordon acted without reference to the British authorities. It was enough that he had made up his mind, and that his opinion was shared, if not inspired, by Li Hung-chang, no longer that "ruffian of a Futai," but a man with whom he worked in closer agreement than he did with anyone else throughout his career.

19. GORDON "DEMOBS" THE EVER-VICTORIOUS

Gordon started for Quinsan, as he had told his mother he would, on May 13, reached his headquarters on the eighteenth, and by the thirty-first not a single officer or man of the Force was left. "Sharp work," "enormous trouble," was how Gordon described this rapid "demobbing," but he had to be quick; he had to forestall, on the one hand, the British Consul in Shanghai, "who made a little row about it, but was too late and accepted the *fait accompli*," and, on the other, the possibility that the Ever-Victorious itself would object to being thus wiped out of existence. He knew that he would be censured, but did not care since the responsibility was entirely his own, and it gave him a certain malicious pleasure to pass Sir Frederick Bruce by, for he was not a man to trust — he knew that from letters of his he had seen.

Anyhow, it was certain that as the Force stood it presented a great danger for both Shanghai and the Chinese. "I can say now," he wrote on June 2, "that a more turbulent set of men who formed the officers have not often been collected together, or a more dangerous lot if they had been headed by one of their own style"; and he adds that he is seeing the Futai immediately to arrange for the permanent garrison of Shanghai — a magnificent gesture of self-confidence from a Brevet Lieutenant-Colonel of thirty-one towards a thorny problem of international politics. This question, — the safety of Shanghai, — and nothing else, kept him in China; he cannot "leave things in a mess," he tells his mother, who, poor lady, aches to see her favorite and now famous son, apparently annexed forever by China.

The Gordon whom the world knows, the soldier whose duty it is to serve the suffering and oppressed everywhere, without too punctilious a regard for officialdom, emerges clearly for the first time as the smoke of these last battles in the Yangtze delta blows away. Towards his own official superiors he begins to show a certain supercilious indifference, the result partly of his conviction that he sees things in a truer light than they, and partly of the vanity — if vanity be the proper name for it — which caused him to profess indifference to honors, let alone money. "I have declined money in any shape, and think that the Chinese Government trusts me more than any foreigner has ever been trusted," and then he copies out a translation of the memorial to the Throne by Li Hung-chang on the fall of Chanchufu which seems to reflect, in its rounded phrases, the sincerity of the original: —

> Gordon was indefatigable in devising plans, opening trenches, building batteries, laying guns, making bridges, etc., after the unsuccessful attack of the twenty-second, in which he lost a large number of men. . . .
>
> He sacrificed all personal feelings in his friendly relations and gave up everything for the object in view, the destruction of the Rebellious brood. His zeal, valor, industry, and merit are deserving of the highest commendation and gratitude. . . .
>
> He is valiant, daring, industrious, and able, has been single-minded in aiding China against the Rebels, and establishing his reputation. . . .
>
> He has since the beginning of this year consulted me in everything and respectfully obeyed me in everything, and acted in the most harmonious manner with my Generals, and Hart (Inspector of Customs) informs me that his only object has been to obtain glory and reputation and that when Your Majesty rewarded him last year with 10,000 taels he would not accept it, or had he done so would have devoted it to lessening the expenses of disbanding the Force. . . .

All these services, in Li Futai's opinion, demanded some mark of signal honor from the Celestial Throne. "I hope they will please you," Gordon says to his mother, after writing out this glowing testimonial; and then, pursuing his own thoughts, he adds, "I have never cringed or yielded in any way to them and they have respected me all the more. I feel the conviction that I have been most favored in being able to attain the position in China that I have by my own exertions." It was all true enough; he and Li Hung-chang understood one another perfectly, though the Chinaman erred in one point — he wished Gordon to receive the highest military honors with the appropriate standard and star, so that he could show them "as a testimony of his glory in his own country." But Gordon, when he had told his mother all this, made his own wishes quite clear: "I do not want anything of this published, as I think if my proceedings sank into oblivion it would be the better for everyone." Here, in all truth, was the strangeness of proportion which gives beauty to the moral, as to the physical, world.

20. Gordon's Views on the Chinese and on Europe's Duties toward Them

For the rest of the summer and autumn of 1864, Gordon stayed on in China, universally honored by the Chinese. As soon as he could escape from Quinsan he visited the camp of the Viceroy, the great Tseng Kuo-fan, Li's master in statecraft and scholarship, whose words reached the ears of Prince Kung and the Dowager Empress in far-off Peking. Now at leisure, except for the preparation of his journals and official reports, Gordon had time to think out the problems emerging from the pressure of the West upon the East in the light of his own experience. As he looked at Nanking, picturesque, enormous, desolate, "with only two or three people visible through a telescope walking about within the city," where a month later the younger brother of Jesus was to eat gold leaf and die the self-inflicted death which tradition demanded of its fallen Emperors, he contemplated the possibility of a new era for unhappy China, but only if the Chinese were helped to work out their destiny in their own way.

One can see Gordon smiling as he tells his mother of the letter of recall, the tardy result of Lord Russell's Order in Council, which had come after the Force had been entirely broken up, but the smile fades as he thinks of the way England has behaved towards China, to reappear for one wry moment when this lover of children, who could never forgive Nature for her bungling method of propagating humankind, comments on the birth of his sister Mary's child. Then his mind runs on — it was to run unceasingly for the next twenty years — and he gives a summary of the attitude which he considers the nations and Governments of Europe should adopt towards China and the Chinese: —

It is absurd to talk of Manchus and Chinese, the former are extinct and the latter are in every post, and it is equally absurd to talk of the mandarins as a class distinct from the people of the country. They are not so, but are merely the officials who hold office which every Chinese is eligible to do, without respect to birth, I will not say money, as certainly there is a certain amount of corruption in the sale of offices, but Russia is equally corrupt for that matter in her distant provinces, and it is not so very long ago that we were also tainted in the same way. What I think is this: that if we try to drive the Chinese into sudden reforms they will strike and resist with all the obstinacy of a pig, and will relapse back again into old habits when the pressure is removed. But if we lead them, we shall find them willing to a degree and most easy to manage. They like to have an option, and hate having a course struck out for them as if they were of no account in the matter. They also like to see the utility of the course proposed, and to have the reasons for that explained over and over again. They are quick in seeing advantages and disadvantages. What we have tried to do is to force them into a certain course, making them pay for the same, and thinking it was not worth while discussing the matter with them at all.

I have got on by proposing to them a course of action in such a way as to give them a certain option as to whether they will follow it or not, and have always endeavored to recommend nothing which would clash utterly with their prejudices. By this means I have led them on to change many things, which I should never have succeeded in doing if I had tried to force them to do all at once. I can say that few men have had so much faith put in them by the Chinese as myself. I always consider the great difficulties the great mandarins have to contend with. They may perfectly agree in everything that may be urged on them by us, but cannot carry it out, and we must confess it is far easier to say "Go and do this or that" than to do it. We row the poor devils if they do not make reforms in their army, but we do not consider that changes must be gradual and palatable as far as possible. My idea is that the change should be made gradually and on a small scale at first, and through the Futais, not through the Peking Government, who are a very helpless lot. There are 60,000 troops here and 40 Tetais, or Generals of Division. What a task for Tseng it would be to try and suddenly change the organization of this Force, when the troops are some six months in arrears of pay. I could say much more for the Imperialists. They have many faults, but have suffered much from Foreigners who have preyed on their country. The utter waste of money through Osborn's fleet [1] is quite painful to think of.

Gordon was under no illusions about the harm England had done in China. The Chinese, he tells his mother in confidence, "have no reason to love us, even for the assistance we have given them, for the Rebellion was our work indirectly." This he must have learned from Li Hung-chang, whose photograph, with that of the defunct Ching, he sends home to his brother Henry, asking him to have them published in the *Illustrated London News.* No more storms shook the friendship between Englishman and Chinaman; their ideas might differ, but their sentiments were the same. Each knew that he was a leader of men; each, loving the smoke and din of battle, looked beyond these to the happiness of mankind. So it was that Li won over Gordon to the Chinese point of view in politics, and may have the credit of being his master in the international liberalism from which Gordon never afterwards swerved; while Gordon began to shake Li's belief that the missionaries and the Europeans of the coast had directly instigated the Taeping Rebellion. Gordon's task was no easier since he spoke little Chinese

[1] Osborn was a captain of the Royal Navy who was lent by the British Government for the purpose of organizing an Imperial Chinese Navy to patrol the Yangtze. After the ships had been bought in England and a number of British personnel engaged, the scheme broke down owing to Osborn's insistence, inspired by Lay and backed by Sir Frederick Bruce, that he should be independent of the authority of the local Futais, a request which ran counter to all Chinese constitutional practice.

himself, and his interpreter was a "talkee-talkee-me-no-savvy-he" sort of person, expressing himself with equal vileness in Mandarin and in English. Besides being no linguist, the fellow stood in terror of the Futai, before whom he attributed to Gordon language of the extremity of abasement. But Gordon liked him, and, careless as he always was about accuracy in translation, — it had serious results later on at Khartoum, — did not seem to mind his interpreter's utter inability to understand what he said. For all that, the fact that Li Hung-chang came ultimately to admit that "thousands, perhaps millions, in China would be somewhat benefited by a knowledge of Jesus" may be traced to Gordon's efforts to impart the truth to the sympathetic Futai of Kiang-Su, who was "by far the best man in the Empire."

Much as Gordon admired Li Hung-chang, much as he loved the Chinese, he soon found the humdrum camp life irksome to his restless temperament. He was by way of organizing the nucleus of an entirely native force. As a diversion he decided to complete the ordnance survey he had begun before taking over command of the Ever-Victorious, and spent five weeks of the summer on this congenial piece of work. The British officer who accompanied him has left us a thumb-nail sketch of their being fired at from the walls of some town as they were surveying on board ship. Gordon chaffed his companion on the state of his nerves, then ordered his flag to be run up, the "Imps" being duly abashed at the identity of their visitor. He also visited the camp of the Franco-Chinese Force and drank champagne for dinner, a rare luxury. The French officers pressed Gordon to stay and help them, but he had to return to headquarters to receive the Imperial officials bringing him the Order of the Yellow Jacket, the highest honor in the Empire. The envoys, with an enormous escort, arrived in an atmosphere heavy with the fumes of saltpetre from crackers and salutes. They opened box after box. All bore the seals of the Imperial dragon, and were filled with clothes. Gordon put on one suit after another, a half-amused, half-satirical smile on his face, forcing himself to appear interested, and relieving the boredom of the five hours' ceremony by comical allusions to his appearance as he walked about the great mess tent in this finery amid grave, kowtowing Celestials. Finally he was dressed in the various uniforms of the Mandarin of the Yellow Jacket, complete with silk skirts, robes, jackets, hats, caps, fans, girdles, thumb rings of jade, and necklaces for all occasions. At this moment a fat and elderly mandarin, retreating in the course of his kowtow, took a step too far, and fell backwards into a hole filled with water, an improvised wine-cooler for the officers' mess. Gordon flushed angrily at the sudden laughter, but, when he saw the ludicrous figure of the astonished Chinaman, he too joined in, and champagne, laced with brandy, a "rajah's peg," soon restored the victim's equanimity.

October came, and Gordon prepared to return home after an absence of more than four years. He gave up the position he had made for himself in China without a pang of regret, though, as the *Times* observed (readers of Trollope's novels know what weight the "Thunderer" had), "with fewer scruples and less care for home opinions, men have carved out kingdoms and founded dynasties from opportunities less tempting than those which Colonel Gordon has neglected." The young Engineer Captain — he did not become a regimental Major *in his own corps* for another eight years — was a recognized authority on Chinese questions, and took with him a tin trunk full of letters from fellow countrymen in England who had followed his doings with interested sympathy — letters it was no good to answer unless he wrote carefully and fully, which he had not the time to do. Now he was to exchange the prestige of a victorious general in the field, the excitement of war, the interest of helping a great people in travail, for the dull round of garrison life at home. With all that, his old keenness to rise in his profession had faded away; he talked no more of Staff appointments, had forgotten the ambitions of his twenties.

The prospect was a drab one. Yet only two worldly cares bothered him, the leave-takings and his clothes. As he possessed no mufti for the voyage, he sent for a ready-made suit and a billycock from Shanghai. The shine of new clothes he detested, so he concertina'd the hat and tied the suit into a bundle and had it thrown overboard, where it lay, attached to the side of the steamer, in the waters of the creek. On the evening he left he dined as usual in the mess, but did not refer to his departure. Then he rose from the table, said good-bye as if he were merely going to Shanghai, hurriedly boarded his steamer, and shut the cabin door. The punctilious and grateful Chinese saw to it, however, that their youthful mandarin was fittingly sped, and for a mile and a half the *Hyson* passed along the beflagged banks, illuminated with lanterns and lined with troops, while volleys of artillery, crackers, booming gongs, and braying horns simulated once more the music of battle, until the vessel disappeared in the darkness, heading for Shanghai and towing in its wake the suit of clothes that "Chinese" Gordon, Mandarin of the Yellow Jacket, meant to wear on board the P. and O. boat.

He had only one desire — that his deeds in China should be forgotten.

III

THE IMITATION OF CHRIST

(1865–1873)

Verily it is misery to live upon earth: the more spiritual that a man will be the more this present life appeareth bitter: for he feeleth better and seeth more clearly the fruits of man's corruption.

For to eat, to drink, to sleep, to rest, to labour, and to be subject to the necessities of nature, is very misery and an affliction to a devout man that would fain be loose and free from sin.

THOMAS À KEMPIS, *The Imitation of Christ*

SPIRIT. *Say,*
What we possess we offer; it is thine:
Bethink ere thou dismiss us; ask again;
Kingdom, and sway, and strength, and length of days—
MANFRED. *Accursed! What have I to do with days?*
They are too long already.

BYRON, *Manfred*

1. Gordon at Gravesend

Upon the foreshore at the eastern extremity of Gravesend, where the Thames begins to broaden into an estuary, is an esplanade, complete with iron seats, a mean little bandstand, and a public lavatory for "gentlemen." The esplanade is backed by the glacis of a fort, from which it is separated by a high spiked railing. Beyond the fort, on the side away from the town, lie some prim gardens. One enters these from the esplanade. Notices warn everyone to keep off the grass. Ladies are informed that there is a "cloakroom" for their use in the gardener's cottage. Nothing could be more genteel, more in contrast to the mid-Victorian squalor still hanging over the riverside quarter of the town, than these walks where the inhabitants may rest and recreate themselves. And, most genteel of all, there stands in the middle of the gardens a Doulton ware statue of Gordon, bareheaded, wearing a braided military frockcoat, and holding the famous cane in his hand — the cane that the Chinese, with their genius for the picturesque phrase, called the wand of victory. On a grassy bank you may also see his bust ingeniously contrived in pebbles, and over it the inscription "Gordon Gardens" cut in box.

Not undeservedly is he the genius of the place. For this is the spot in England most closely identified with Gordon's memory. The fort above, New Tavern Fort, was his quarters for six years. There, freed from the excitement of war and from the spiritual snares that beset the man of action, he first seriously began the task, the impossible task, of living the Christian life. There, with *The Imitation of Christ* for his manual, the Bible for his textbook, and his sister Augusta for confidante, he attempted to reconcile the irreconcilable, to subdue the unregenerate and carnal body to the love of God.

Fort House, where he lived modestly, faces the lane bordering the fort on the side towards Gravesend. Though built towards the end of the eighteenth century, no Georgian grace hangs about its mean little front, with a wooden porch flanked by a window on either side. But what was hardly more than a cottage, intended only to accommodate some commissary of ordnance during the French Revolutionary wars, was thought inadequate to the dignity of the Lieutenant-Colonel entrusted with the command of the Thames defenses two generations later. At the back, therefore, the house was enlarged to make it fitting for a gentleman's establishment, and, with its lawn, gardens, and vinery, it would have suited the most exacting colonel's lady. To the bachelor Gordon it was unnecessarily large, and possibly it was by way of silent protest that he chose one of the older and meaner rooms for his own bedroom. However that may be, it was at Fort House that he developed the strange, almost terrible beauties of character which have surrounded his personality with the halo of saintliness. There he walked in the path traced by Thomas à Kempis, and tried to practise that "pure resignation of self" which is the highest duty of the Christian.

2. Months of Leisure

Some months elapsed between his return from China and his taking up the new appointment. In January 1865, his mother was again united with her favorite child. She had been through a trying two years, and now that Charlie, safe and sound, was once more at home her happiness might have seemed complete. Yet in every human relation there is something imperfect, and Mrs. Gordon found herself crossed by

Fort House, Gravesend

her brilliant and dutiful son in the dearest of her wishes. She desired to give expression to her maternal admiration of his greatness and his goodness — and Charlie would not allow it. Already, while still in China, he had told his mother that she must not permit herself to be bothered by the ex-officers of the Ever-Victorious who went to pay her their respects, no doubt hoping to enlist the Gordon influence on their behalf. Far from its worrying her, she loved to see anyone who could tell her about her son, not least those who had lately shared his dangers and fatigues, and had fought side by side with him in a score of battles.

In November, immediately before sailing, he wrote more insistently from Shanghai: —

MY DEAR MOTHER,

The individual is coming home, but does not wish it known, for it would be a signal for the disbanded to come to Southampton, and although the waits at Xmas are bad these others are worse.

Kind love to my father and all the family.

Believe me, my dear mother,
Your affectionate son,
C. G. GORDON

This brief and ominously impersonal letter, coming on the top of other remarks about his desire to be forgotten, was of bad augury. And Gordon soon showed that he meant every word he said. He would not be lionized even in his own family circle. The slightest breath of admiration dried up the natural gaiety of manner beneath which the Christian tradionally clothes the inherent pessimism of his faith. It was hard for his sisters, and harder still for his mother, that they could never bring out the pedestal and place him securely upon it. The only way to get him to talk about his exploits — and at the time Gordon was a hero focusing public interest in the same way as a Lindbergh or a Malcolm Campbell does to-day

— was by remaining carefully impersonal. Then "the individual" would emerge from his shell, and fight his battles over again round the drawing-room fire. But hero worship had to be conducted in silence, or else its object became tongue-tied, if he did not, as was likely, flare up in a temper. The only members of the family whom this idiosyncrasy did not worry were the younger generation. These delighted in the absence of a pedestal, and consequently with them he was on the easiest terms. Colonel Louis Gordon records his impression when, as a small boy of eight, he first saw his uncle on his return from China. He had heard his father and mother talking about him, and had gained an impression of his Uncle Charlie as a great man to be admired and feared — then this tremendous personage walked into the room with his light, easy step and friendly smile, a jolly, laughing uncle to whom any young nephew could give a playful punch and know that it would not be misunderstood. So for the young the legend of the hero faded in the equality of love — and Gordon himself rejoiced in it. His melancholy disappeared in their company, and he romped with them upon the floor in happy forgetfulness of the miseries of the world.

It *was* wicked and full of misery. After his experiences in China he hardly needed his favorite poem to remind him of it, but all the same he hung it in his bedroom at Rockstone Place, Southampton, where the family had moved when Gordon's father retired from the Army.

> Oh! ask not thou, How shall I bear
> The burden of to-morrow?
> Sufficient for the day its care,
> Its evil, and its sorrow;
> God imparteth by the way
> Strength sufficient for the day.

And his morning Bible readings with Augusta — now aged forty-five — or his evening talks with her in the kitchen, chosen because he could smoke there as much as he pleased, helped to keep his mind taut upon the vanity of the world.

Gordon was the perfect type of the man of action, and quickly grew bored if he had no one to command and nothing to contend with except his own sinful nature. As the summer of 1865 wore on, he found the want of occupation irksome. The two years' leave due to him by the generous regulations of the time seemed an impossible eternity of leisure. The ordinary diversions of life meant nothing to him. He played no games. A social engagement hung over his head like the sword of Damocles. Women made him feel awkward and shy. In congenial masculine society he talked well, even brilliantly, on the affairs of the nation and the world, but this he could hardly find in Southampton. His elder brother, Henry, a man of his own calibre, was at work in the Arsenal at Woolwich; his father was ailing, and he was soon to stand by his death-bed, an experience which caused him to follow still more strenuously the Christian example. "If thou have seen any man die think that thou thyself shall go the same way," said the book which he knew by heart. Gordon was too familiar with death to require any reminder of its omnipresence, but the event, for all that, was one of the profound impressions of his life.

Apart, therefore, from acting, in his own words, as his mother's A.D.C., going out for drives with her, sitting with her, talking or reading to her, and no doubt helping her to hunt for her spectacles, there remained Augusta. With her he felt at his ease. She was the only woman to whom he could unburden himself on the one engrossing question. Both drew their religious views from the same wellspring of evangelical Protestantism, though in her case the pure water of truth was unsweetened by any sense of humor and its cold purity undefiled by any contact with the world. Gordon knew her failing, and once, in answer to her complaint that she had little time to read, pointed out that she was free from household cares between six and eight in the morning. But Augusta did not take the suggestion playfully, and her brother, always a little in awe of his much older sister, had to pacify her by admitting that his remark was hard. She, for her part, would have liked him to show more worldly ambition; on this point she was in league with Henry, who could have brought influence to bear at the War Office and put Charlie on the straight path of professional advancement. But the only thing that would have driven Gordon to modify his self-effacing attitude was a wife and family, and here Augusta's precepts and example undoubtedly strengthened his own fear of marriage; as the intimacy between them grew, his antipathy to what the Prayer Book calls an honorable estate became almost morbid. One wonders whether Gordon would have reacted differently to the world about him, whether he would not have followed the time-honored custom of his profession and used his months of recreation after the dangers of war in embarking on the hazards of matrimony, had Augusta's own energies been directed into the normal channels of marriage and maternity. This period of leave at home was certainly the golden moment, and there must have been plenty of stylish evangelical young women in Southampton ready to seize it had the opportunity arisen.

That it never did may well be in some sort due to the dragonish Augusta, who could be jealous even of her own sisters.

So, when Gordon went to Gravesend in September 1865, it was with all his natural shyness in feminine society strengthened by his sister's influence. Being thus portcullised and moated against the love of woman did not perhaps tend to make him happier, but it enabled him, in his solitary citadel, to keep his eyes more securely fixed on the ideal held up in *The Imitation of Christ*.

3. The Thames Defenses

It showed some lack of humor on the part of the War Office that a soldier who had just brilliantly proved mobility to be the supreme factor in war should be entrusted with the supervision of the defenses then being built at the entrance to the Thames. Money for these had been voted by Parliament in one of the panics which recurred at regular intervals during the reign of Queen Victoria, the alarm on this occasion being a reaction to the aggressive foreign policy of Lord Palmerston's last Ministry. Five forts were to be built, two on the Essex shore at Tilbury and Coalhouse, and three on the Kentish shore. Gordon had no sooner got to work than his professional eye saw that the whole project was useless. An invading force had only to land lower down the river, and the two forts on the Essex marshes would be untenable against its artillery on the hills half a mile in their rear. The forts on the Gravesend side at Cliffe and Shornmead could be turned into islands by cutting the river bank above them. All these were fortifications worthy of the Chinese, and no more able to put up any serious defense. The money spent upon them would be entirely thrown away. Gordon passed on the information to his superiors, but as these did not listen he had to go on wasting public money. All he could do was to see that it was wasted as efficiently as possible.

The young Lieutenant-Colonel commanding the Royal Engineers at Gravesend combined the energy of youth with the severity of age. He was a hard taskmaster. When his night working parties in China had seemed to dawdle, he used to tell their officers that, if they did not keep up to his timetable, they would have to finish by daylight under the enemy's fire. He could not hold this threat over his men now, but he managed all the same to reduce those who came under his eye to a more or less limp condition by the time he had finished with them.

It is clear that his belief in speed remained as strong as ever, and he had a faith in the value of minutes which would have appealed to any American leader of industry, though this may have been shaken by the course of events since 1929. The solid pair-oared rowing boat provided for his official use was much too slow, so he changed it for a light four-oared gig. This always lay at the Hard below the New Tavern Fort, and directly he stepped into it he expected the Thames watermen who manned it to push off with the smartness of a man-of-war's crew. No matter what the state of the wind or tide, they had to pull with all their strength. Any slackening — and it was a long row down to Coalhouse Fort on the other bank — would draw from him, "A little faster, boys, a little faster!" until, by the time they reached their objective, they were seriously distressed. Gordon, intent only upon the business in hand, would jump ashore and run rather than walk round the fortifications. Stolid contractors, elderly foremen, even his own junior officers, had hard work to keep up with him as he climbed over earthworks, inspected the layout of gun emplacements and embrasures, and saw that the magazines were being built with the proper thickness of brick. He knew it was all useless. But he exacted, just the same, this daily kinetic sacrifice on the altar of energy, and fought his armchair critics at the War Office, if, as not infrequently happened, they found fault with his work, not less determinedly than he had battled against the Taepings.

When in his office, occupied with plans, correspondence, or the routine of administration, he held a similar rule. No genial, lotus-eating atmosphere, such as lay over official departments in the eighteen-sixties, spread its pleasant relaxation over New Tavern Fort. Gordon did not knock off for a sandwich, a glass of sherry, and a gossip in the middle of the morning. For food he had a contemptuous regard, partly the result of his religious convictions and partly of his belief that he suffered from angina pectoris, which was best treated by semi-starvation.[1] But, though he agreed with Thomas à Kempis that to eat was "very misery," this necessity of nature, especially when he had scamped his breakfast, became by noon too imperious to be neglected, and to satisfy it he would have recourse to the provisions he kept in the recesses of the drawer of his office table. He munched while he worked, carefully brushing off the crumbs and putting the loaf of bread back in its place when anyone called to see him. Smoking was his one self-indulgence. Thus from eight o'clock in the morning till two in the afternoon Gordon was the perfect martinet. No general of twice his age could have been a stricter disciplinarian and more scrupulously served or feared by his subordinates. But that was only for six hours of the twenty-four. For the rest of the time he was a very different man.

In China there had been no hour of the day or night at which he did not work. Like Napoleon, he would often call some of his officers to him at three or four in the morning, and it went hard with those who were slow to wake. Now he rigidly divided his day. Before eight and after two he was unapproachable on any official business. The story goes how one morning at New Tavern Fort the men were held up by some point which he alone could decide. It was before eight o'clock, but they saw Gordon's bedroom window was open — a sign that he was out of bed, as in those days everyone slept with his windows closed. The contractor's manager, after some hesitation, — for he knew the Colonel's rule, — went and knocked at his door. It opened a little way, and disclosed the face of the Gordon who made men fear him.

[1] Much later the symptoms were diagnosed as coming from the liver.

"Presently, presently," he said irritably, as he shut the door, and the crestfallen manager perforce retired. But when the Colonel emerged punctually as the clock struck eight, with his usual springing step, nothing showed that his religious exercises had been interfered with.

4. The Christian Life

When his daily work was done Gordon had all the rest of the day to devote to the contemplation of the mysteries of Christianity and to the analysis of his own feelings. He performed the social duties expected of him, visiting his brother officers and their families, but there was "no one to talk to in Gravesend," he said. He did not find another Captain Drew among the officers of the corps under his command with whom he could exchange ideas on the engrossing subject — and nothing else really interested him. As a mid-Victorian it would not have occurred to him to cultivate his own garden; besides, he did not care for flowers, "preferring the human face divine," as he put it, and whenever he had vegetables he gave them away. He was apt with brush and pencil. Those were the days when Ruskin was preaching that gospel of art and religion which, in the end, fell under the influence of the humanitarians among whom Gordon was a pioneer. But it passed him by. When of an afternoon he used to walk over to the church at Chalk — for he no longer kept a horse and trap — he did not think of sketching its picturesque fourteenth-century tower, or of investigating its chancel for fourteenth-century brasses. Instead he would loiter in the churchyard, indifferent to the beauties of man's and nature's handiwork, gaining no pleasure from the view of the river and the ships on its broad waters that brought the products of the world to London. He would simply "kick the stones about and think of his father."

Boredom had something to do with his unhappiness, for the residuum of his thoughts was always tinctured with the bitterness that his talents were not appreciated, and in consequence his besetting sins, as he told Augusta, were envy and backbiting. From this torture of inaction he was to find escape by taking on himself the rôle of Good Samaritan. In the meantime he went on his walks with his pockets full of tracts. When he climbed over a stile he would place one on the top bar with a stone upon it to prevent its blowing away; one on the text "And many among them shall stumble" appealed to his sense of humor as being particularly useful at such places. Others he would leave by the side of the path. No place was unsuitable. Later, after he had begun his work with boys, he used, when he went to London, to watch for any of them working on the line, and would throw them "some tracts and little books" from the window of the carriage as it jolted through the Northfleet cuttings.

All this was sowing the seed — much of it would be lost, but some would fall on good ground. Sin was the root of all evil, and sin came from unbelief. Unbelief, in fact, was the only sin — and it was a Christian's duty to combat it by every weapon in his power. What could be a more obvious one than the handbill which the Victorians habitually used as an advertising medium? The Colonel's subalterns used to follow his progress across the countryside through telescopes, but, even if they were amused at his salvationist tendencies, Chinese Gordon's exploits set him above ridicule. Not that he would have minded, for when, a few years later, his friend and neighbor Mrs. Freese discovered that he used to sit up at night mending his boys' clothes, and Gordon told her he did not want this known, she learned that it was not because he might have been laughed at, — as she at first had supposed was his reason for wishing to keep it secret, — but because the knowledge of it would probably have caused people to praise him.

From such daily exercise he returned to his Spartan establishment at Fort House, where the furniture that struck the eye was four plain deal tables, innocent of tablecloths, on which stood his books and papers. His housekeeper, whom he ruefully called "the giantess," was the widow of one of his men in China, and she had a small boy whose neck she did not keep as clean as Gordon would have liked. She looked after Gordon so far as this was possible, for he was an unsatisfactory person, taking his meals at any time and never seeming to eat enough. The normal mechanism of domestic life, the pleasures of the table and of digestion by the fireside, meant nothing to him. For music, the common recreation of the Victorian drawing-room, he had no ear, though he was sensitive about his deficiency, when taxed with it declaring that there was too much misery in the world to go to concerts; there is no record that he ever gratified his wish to hear *Elijah* and "see a tableau of the scene on Carmel." His evangelical upbringing put the theatre altogether beyond the pale of a Christian's diversions, though it is on record that he went to *The Pirates of Penzance* — and enjoyed it. So he passed the evening reading. He had an enormous appetite for the newspapers. He read many classical authors in translations — Homer, Virgil, and particularly Plutarch, on whom, he said, every young officer should be brought up. He knew, too, the Stoic philosophy as expounded by Marcus Aurelius. But above all he read the literature of Christianity, from the Bible and the Fathers — or, at least, the Anglican Fathers — down to the sermons of the Reverend Capel Molyneux, one of which he came across by accident. "By us it must be considered His Providence," he wrote to Augusta, as he told her of this good fortune in the course of a pious letter written at the Junior United Service Club on the evils of envy. "Those I am most envious of I pray for and the feeling leaves me at once," is his conclusion.

If not widely read, Gordon knew his favorite books well. Sometimes he escaped so far from his usual orbit as to read novels — later in life he experienced an almost naïve delight in Kingsley's *Hypatia*. But, on the whole, his excursions into secular literature were infrequent. Shakespeare shed none of his magnificent sanity upon that overstrung temperament, and when he read extracts from Byron in one of Murray's Continental guides they only pleased him because he saw a likeness to himself in the dark genius of the Romantic Movement. "He was a melancholy and unhappy man," wrote Gordon, "and I am no better."

Thus thrown back on his own resources, he realized the emptiness of the pagan maxim, "Know thyself." What was the good when it merely convinced one that the flesh was ruined and incapable of improvement? The only values that counted were those of the spirit, and the only way to live in the spirit was by dying in the flesh. While this must be subdued by mortification, perseverance in prayer would enable us to realize that God was, not full of love, but love itself. So Gordon started on the road of mystical experience trodden by many before him, the road which leads to those mansions of the soul described in the mystic phraseology of Saint Teresa's *The Interior Castle*. It was the more difficult for him to find because he had not the chart of dogmatic theology by which to plot his course. He might have suffered less from depression, dryness, "the doles," as he called them, — the sin of *accidie* which has been the portion in greater or less degree of all the saints, — if he could have relied upon the intellectual discipline traditionally imposed by Catholicism on its children. But, from the spiritual summits to which Gordon climbed, the differences between one form of Christianity and another appear very small. The two cardinal points of his theology, the indwelling of God and the union with Christ, which he established during his Gravesend period, are hardly distinguishable from the mystic marriage that marks the consummation of Saint Teresa's experiences in the regions of the transcendental. Only by degrees, however, did Gordon realize what the Catholic takes for granted, that the sacrament of Communion — "the eating," as he called it, with an odd emphasis on the single kind — is the bridge between the flesh and the spirit, between the world of sense and that other world which lies beyond it. In those days Gordon still thought the sermon the most important part of church worship, and as this usually disappointed him — addresses in vague terms from the pulpit do not arrest attention, he said — he was a better Christian than Churchman. He always had, too, an unprotestant dislike for long services. In the latter part of his time at Gravesend he became friendly with the Presbyterian minister, and regularly attended the Scots chapel, but, while he occasionally communicated, he did not definitely connect himself with the Presbyterian Church or any section of professing Christians. Yet his daily prayer was no other than that habitually offered by Saint Francis — that he might have fellowship with Christ's sufferings.

Here he saw the keystone, the central idea of Christianity, which is symbolized in the Cross. The more crosses we had, Gordon told Augusta, apropos of her dislike for early rising, the more we should thrive. At the same time, while we must bear as heavy a burden as God placed upon us, it was our duty to make those of others as light as we could. When Gordon saw the poverty of the people who lived in the squalid, fever-stricken slums in the neighborhood of New Fort Tavern, his heart was filled with pity. Here was another China, and not less in need of his help. When he watched the ragged urchins who haunted the beach, many of them vagabonds sleeping in the lighters and picking up a living as best they could, he thrilled with sympathy at their forlorn youth; and Gordon, who had already begun to feel the pleasure of the mystic, — pleasure so acute that it numbs the faculties, — as, pencil in hand, he meditated upon his Bible, found an outlet for his human sympathy in the pastoral theology which he practised upon old and young, and particularly upon the young.

5. The Pleasures of Friendship

When he had been two years at Gravesend he met a lady who has given us the most vivid picture we possess of this Christian knight-errant. Mrs. Freese lived with her husband and children near Fort House. One day in the summer of 1867 she made the acquaintance of the Colonel, about whom she knew no more than that he was in command of the forts. Her first impression was one of a man boyish in appearance, and in the way he made the ordinary commonplace remarks which follow an introduction, yet "with an eye and expression that might have been a thousand years old." They soon established a point of contact in their common religious views. Mrs. Freese introduced him to the town missionary, who gave him plenty of work to do. She offered him the feminine sympathy which few even of the canonized saints of Christendom have been able to forgo. His piety was soon evident, but only by degrees did she realize the beauty of the Colonel's character. Early in their friendship he offered her a key to the gardens of his house — the key to Paradise, he called it. She gladly accepted, as much for her children's sake as her own, and they were all enchanted by the old-fashioned flowers, the beehives on the lawn, the ships on the river. But it surprised Mrs. Freese to find many old people sitting about, until her host explained that he had had numbers of keys made for the poor of the neighborhood. Their intimacy quickly ripened. Gordon, always fearful of desultory conversation, could exchange spiritual confidences with Mr. and Mrs. Freese to his heart's content, and they both willingly submitted to his liveliness and charm.

She soon discovered that he must be treated with infinite tact. It was no use, for instance, when he rose to leave, asking him to stay longer, for this only frightened him. And it was equally useless asking him to come round and see them at any particular time; if she did that, Gordon showed his horror of fixed engagements by staying away. The best means of seeing him often, she found, was by never arranging a meeting. So long as she carefully avoided the slightest formality, they remained on the best of terms, and Gordon would drop in during the afternoon or evening, coming through the garden and knocking at the window, as often as not going straight up to the nursery and giving notice of his arrival to the children by saying, "Naughty, naughty!" in mock seriousness while on the stairs. He was the more at home with Mr. and Mrs. Freese because they had not the least idea that he had any claims to distinction. One day the conversation happened to turn on the Taeping Rebellion, and Mr. Freese asked Gordon if he knew anything about China. "I am the man who put the rebellion down," he said, much to the astonishment of the unworldly pair, whose ignorance on this matter, far from offending Gordon, gave him much comfort. Still, it was necessary to be careful, for he took offense easily. Mrs. Freese's womanly instincts were hurt by the way he lived. She noticed the absence of comfort at Fort House, his self-imposed semi-starvation, the way he denied himself even fruit and vegetables in order to give them to the poor at the infirmary and workhouse. One day, when she saw his tea set out on one of the deal tables, she could not help saying that it looked uninviting. Gordon's reply was to take the little stale loaf, cram it into the slop basin, and pour upon it the contents of the teapot, remarking as he did so that in a few minutes it would be ready to eat, and that half an hour afterwards it would not in the least matter what he had eaten. To press food upon him was dangerous, and once, when she took him to task for not feeding himself properly, he said, "Mrs. Freese, I would not stand that from my own mother." A difficult, yet a fascinating person, who so captured the heart of one lady crippled from spinal affection that she moved to lodgings near Fort House, where she could see the boyishly handsome Colonel with his quick, alert manner moving about the fort and grounds.

Mrs. Freese learned how to handle him, and was repaid by receiving more of his confidence than he had ever given to anyone before. Augusta did not know so much of the human side of that strange character as did the lady who lived near by at Gravesend. Perhaps it was because she had a twinkle in her eye, perhaps because she burned no incense before him. Not that Augusta had much opportunity of showing appreciation for her distinguished brother. When he went, in 1867, to the Paris Exhibition as one of the official jurors, he did not offer to take her with him. He did not even tell her anything about the visit, except that his companions all seemed "bent on this poor fleeting world and its pleasures." It was not worth while, although the buildings were good. "You will soon see greater and greater wonders," he wrote to her, "such as human eye has not seen nor ear heard" — and more to the same effect. Did Augusta, at Southampton, feel a twinge of worldly regret as she read this? In any case, she must have been uneasy when over twenty months passed without a letter in the true religious strain, while Gordon, a remiss correspondent, was "sorely wounded by the Archers." The departure of these mysterious figurative assailants coincided with the arrival of a fourteen-year-old Jewish boy, and then Gordon made up for his silence by a tremendous epistle upon the indwelling of God, and enunciated in the purest strain of

Gnosticism — oldest of the heresies — the complete separation between the soul and the body. He drew plans to make his argument more intelligible. It was shockingly unorthodox. But Gordon ceased to consider logic when his mind moved in the plane of religious metaphysics.

To Mrs. Freese he sent letters in a different strain. Sometimes they were mere notes. One came very near enlisting her as an ally to combat the possessive Augusta. "My sister comes D.V. next Monday, and the place is to become a hermitage. I cannot help it. She likes it, so I shall tell my friends I am in New Zealand till she goes." Another is obscure: "Will you not venture down and see the devastation and the giantess. I shall not be back till very late. There are a lot of boys outside my door, like bees when they swarm." We are left in the dark as to who or what was the devastation. But there are no letters to Augusta in this free and easy style. And it was to Mrs. Freese that he confided his most serious spiritual defeat. He was less certain than Pio Nono that smoking was no vice, and at one moment determined to give it up. For a fortnight he struggled. Then he went to her. "It 's beaten me," he said — and for the moment tried no further campaign against tobacco.

When he goes away he maintains the same tone of frank intimacy. He stays in Scotland with a fellow clansman, but feels frustrated because his host dislikes tracts and prevents his talking to boys, for by now his thoughts are constantly centred upon them. "I believe there are many Kings (red-haired) about, but I cannot get at them," he tells her whimsically. Kings, Wangs, doves, or angels — whatever name he called them — were a never-failing interest. "Had a deeply interesting walk yesterday and many adventures with Royalty," is a reference to them in another letter. A visit to Warwick Castle draws from him the remark, "If you had been in my state you would not have cared about Warwick or

National Portrait Gallery

GENERAL GORDON
(From a drawing by Lady Abercromby)

Kenilworth. There were boys running about worth millions." Mrs. Freese understood his love for the young. "Where are your wings?" he would ask her children, touching them on the shoulders, and as they grew older he would give more substantial proofs of his sympathy by surreptitiously planting half-crowns in the garden, and then showing them the spot where they should dig to discover the wealth. But she sympathized, also, with the housekeeper who grumbled at having to wash Gordon's street Arabs, and she deprecated his excessive austerity. It amused her to find that the camera with which he had promised to take a photograph of herself and her children had been condemned as a snare keeping him from God. A visit to Manchester in 1867 confirmed him in his resolution to reduce his life to the barest necessities. "The poor scuttlers [1] here, male and female, fill me with sorrow. . . . It does so painfully affect me, and I do trust will make me think less of self and more of these poor people," he wrote to Augusta in the days before he knew Mrs. Freese, and he tells her to obtain a thousand copies of his favorite tract. Manchester, he says, is a grand place for tracts — they are good for opening conversation with. . . .

His sympathy impelled him to present the one possession he valued to the Lancashire Relief Fund. This was the gold medal given him by the Chinese Government, and in order that the gift should be anonymous he defaced the inscription. From that time "Give up your medal" became one of his favorite maxims, which Mrs. Freese, however, did not accept as dutifully as Augusta. One day when he expressed disapproval of her gold watch chain she replied stoutly that it was a present from her husband, and that she meant to go on wearing it. Gordon did not press his point, merely remarking, "Having given up all to God, what am I to keep back? I see

[1] A noun coined by Gordon, presumably from the verb "to scuttle" (scurry), which he usually applied only to boys.

no limit." To the mystic, whether Christian, Buddhist, or Moslem, there can be no limit, and Gordon, when he declared that it was "only the material things of life that are of no import," understood the mystic's fear of what Thomas à Kempis calls "earthly winnings."

6. The Social Worker

Upon no man of the Victorian era did the condition of the poor press more insistently. He not only pitied the children of the slums. His sensitive imagination saw all the horror of the miner's existence. No mere description of it, he says, could make us understand it.

> To hear of the work in a coal-mine, however well told, could not give us a particle of an idea of what the work there really is. To know that truly we must work not a year there, but a lifetime to know the bitterness of that labor, of hard masters, of heat and cold and dirt in the delicate fibres of the skin, of the sorrows of those around us bereaved by sudden catastrophes.

Few even among professed reformers wrote with this instinctive sympathy. Yet Gordon — like most born soldiers, keenly interested in politics — approached the problem of social inequality from a spiritual elevation which even Frederick Denison Maurice, that eminent theologian and social reformer, did not reach.

This love of his for the poor was counterbalanced by no rancor towards the rich. He looked to Christ for his example, and, since he could not see any disturbance in his Master's mind at the number of afflicted who came to Him, — "we do not find Him in any way taking the part of the poor against the rich individually," Gordon said, as with his eager pen he argued the question with Augusta, — this anthropagogue, who loved to lead his fellow men by the hand and reveled in authority, stands coldly aloof from such prophets of Socialism as Ruskin and William Morris, who, a decade later, preached their gospel to a lazily tolerant England.

Gordon was as sorry for Dives as for Lazarus. If Dives' daughters, he declared, wore the false hair of dead people, it was because not to follow the fashion would be to make themselves conspicuous, and Gordon hesitated to condemn such an exhibition of herd-consciousness when he himself admitted to being less bashful when smartly than when meanly dressed. It might even be right to pray for material benefits, so long as these were not inspired merely by carnal motives. The important thing was to preserve the spirit of subjection to God — not at all an easy thing for Gordon, who knew that God had given him great gifts, but with them a rebellious spirit, in order to humble him. The rebelliousness stirred dangerously when his wish to be included in the Abyssinian expedition of 1868 did not materialize. He had overcome his scruples sufficiently to ask for an appointment, and when one was denied him he had to shut himself up for a whole day before he could see the thing in a Christian light. This was none the easier since he had a poor opinion of the brains in the higher Army commands, an opinion strengthened by what he saw of the generalship on Aldershot field days. One of those who came under his critical eye on Laffan's Plain was his connection, General Staveley, and Gordon must have been severely tormented before he grew reconciled to the fact that his sister-in-law's brother was one of the fortunate ones chosen for active service. In such trials of the spirit the Ninety-first Psalm as he read it in his Prayer Book stood as a tower of strength: "Whoso dwelleth under the defence of the Most High shall abide under the shadow of the Almighty." And he drew comfort also from the twentieth verse of the Thirty-first Psalm: "Let the lying lips be put to silence, which cruelly, disdainfully, and despitefully speak against the righteous."

While, on the one hand, Gordon found solace for restlessness, ambition, and injured pride in the Bible, the poor, the sick, and particularly the young afforded him some prophylactic against his attacks of "the doles." In helping others to be less unhappy, he forgot, or tried to forget, that he was an unhappy man. He gave them his time, his money, everything he had. To many old people he made weekly allowances — there were no Old Age Pensions in those days — which he continued after he left Gravesend, some of them still being paid till his death. He was a constant visitor at the bedsides of the sick in the infirmary. But his ardor for service found its most congenial outlet in the work he carried on among the boys of Gravesend. Whenever he went out he might have some adventure, might find some boy whose guardian angel he could be, with whom he could satisfy his starved affections. It was a perpetual romance. This feeling for the young, half Christian and half Greek, remained with him till the end.

Life was rougher but freer for the children of the lower classes in those days before compulsory education had tamed the offending Adam in the English boy, and a port like Gravesend acted as a magnet for the more adventurous spirits. One of these,[1] who had run away from home and slept with other boys in a similar case on the bawley boats and lighters, picking up a living as best he could, remembers how his companions used to leave him on Sunday afternoon to go to Sunday school. In the end they persuaded him to accompany them, and he went intending to make himself a nuisance. He succeeded so well that the teacher of his class was in despair. It happened, however, that this gentleman was absent for two or three Sundays, and while he was away his class was taken by Gordon. There was something in the personality of the new teacher under which the boy's impishness wilted, and willy-nilly he was compelled to submit to the quietly master-

[1] Mr. W. F. Scott, of Prittlewell, Southend.

ful influence of "the Kernel," as the boys are said to have described him in their scribblings on walls. The superintendent was aware that the boy had been a sore trial to his teacher and was curious to know how Gordon fared with him. "He is the best boy in the class," said Gordon.

One Sunday Gordon said to the lad, "Come to my house to-morrow morning, and I will give you breakfast." On the strength of this attractive invitation the youngster turned up at Fort House and did justice to a square meal. After breakfast Gordon took him to a shop and purchased a complete outfit. This, when packed up, made a large parcel, which the boy carried back to Fort House. On his arrival there Gordon told him to go into the bathroom and strip. A good scrubbing in the bath was followed by his putting on all his new clothes. Then Gordon stood him in front of a mirror and asked what he saw. "You see a new boy, don't you?" he said. "Well, just as you are new outside, so I want you to be new inside." For some years after this incident the boy lived with Gordon in Fort House. In later life he became an influential citizen of Southend, where he served upon the town council for sixteen years.

Sometimes Gordon kept two or three protégés under his roof. Others used to come in the evening, when he would hold classes, teaching them how to read and write, holding their fingers while they laboriously traced up-strokes, down-strokes, and pothooks, and giving them history and geography lessons with the aid of a large map over the mantelpiece. Upon this he used to keep track with little flags of the whereabouts of those youngsters who had passed through his hands and gone to sea, the natural career for a Gravesend boy. His friends the pilots told him whenever a homeward-bound ship anchored in the Thames. If it were one of those on which any of his protégés had signed on, he went on board at once to welcome the sailor home from sea. Not infrequently he would be told that the boy had deserted at some foreign port, — Rio or Fremantle or the Cape, — and in such case Bill's or Jack's flag would be removed from the map. As his sphere of benevolence widened, he bought suits by the dozen and pairs of boots by the gross. Those who were hungry had milk and hunks of bread. Sometimes he gave them all a square meal, though they were daintier than their host, rather turning up their noses at his salt beef, the regular dinner dish. And to all he spoke of God and of the necessity of believing in Almighty Providence, these earnest talks being brought to an end with a lively hymn, followed by a shout of "A day's march nearer home!" Gordon never went to bed without rejoicing that he was "one day younger," one day nearer his birth in the next world.

Naturally he was often deceived and disappointed. When he asked a little nephew if God lived in him the boy said, "No, He lives in the sky." This Gordon adjudged incorrect, although the wisdom of five years regarded the cat with some reverence after his uncle had told him that God was everywhere and in everything around him. And, if Gordon was not altogether satisfied with his nephew's localization of the Deity, the child considered that his uncle's joining in the Lord's Prayer was rather a breach of the etiquette of Rockstone Place, for Aunt Augusta as a rule recited this amid the decorous silence of the rest of the household. What impressed him most in his uncle, however, was not his religious zeal so much as the fact that, when he was on leave at Southampton, he bought a pound's worth of stamps at a time and was said to sit up all night writing letters. To Gordon himself much of his social work seemed thankless. Many abused his good nature. Visiting one of the families in Gravesend to which he gave fifteen shillings a week, he found the front door locked. When, in answer to his repeated knockings, it was opened and he saw the table laid for tea with shrimps and hot cakes, he could only say coldly that they might at least have asked him to share the delicacies he provided, and then turn on his heel and go. Such people as these he had to cut off from his bounty. But, in a world where God's ways were not man's ways, strange things were liable to happen.

One day, for example, a ragged boy came to Fort House with a dismal tale of being a homeless orphan. Gordon treated him with his usual benevolence, fed him, clothed him, lodged him, and at last discovered that he came from Peckham. From the clergyman of the parish there Gordon learned that the boy had been lying, and took him back to his home and parents. Soon the young impostor turned up again at Gravesend, having robbed his parents before he left. Clearly he was "a very bad lad," as Gordon admitted; but when he inquired into the boy's history he found the clue that explained everything. The Sunday-school teacher who had taught him told Gordon how the boy's mother had once prayed for him when he had been very ill that "if God would only let him live she did not care what came after." She had been taken at her word, and now, thanks to her son's evil conduct, understood that before she had been in a state of rebellion against God. It seemed the more natural to Gordon, who believed that all creatures would be saved, and therefore did "not question the eternal state of the lad." This wonderful case merely showed how when we prayed we should always remain subject to God's Will, otherwise God might punish us by answering our prayers.

It was a sad world, and he longed to leave it. Like the early Christians, he thought it no time to marry "when so much sorrow and trouble were about." Augusta, alone of his brothers and sisters, followed his precept and practice in this matter, and the arrival of nephews and nieces made him pity these little pilgrims for the hard journey that lay before them. The seismic events of history moved him less than the dull pain of everyday life. He told Augusta that many (surely including himself among them) suffered mentally far more than did the soldiers in the Franco-German War. If he found exquisite pleasure in reading the Bible, or rather in "chewing the cud," as he called it, over what he read, he paid the price of mystical experience by incessant attacks of depression. He managed to conceal them in his demeanor, seeming the youngest in every company, and, so long as you did not notice that look in his eyes which Mrs. Freese remarked the first time she saw him, he would have passed for the happiest of men. Certainly you would never have thought that a deep pessimism underlay his lively exterior, or that he counted the remaining years of life with the impatience of a schoolboy ticking off the days to the end of the term. "I must write and wish you a happy Xmas," begins one letter to Augusta. "I will not say many of them, for our joy is in our Lord, and we cannot wish many years will pass before He comes to deliver us from our contemptible bodies and infirmities." Augusta's answer, like all her letters, is lost, but no doubt its tone was equally grim.

In the normal course of events he could hardly hope to go home in less than thirty years. But accidents did happen, and one day when his gig struck a pile and filled with water he thrilled at the thought that, if only it had occurred in the middle of the river instead of close to the Hard, the "very bright, happy land with beautiful sights and glories" would then and there have been his to enjoy. If the world only knew a tithe of what God has for all of us, the inhabitants of the world would run to death — he sketched this universal ecstasy of self-immolation in a letter to Augusta, remarking at the same time that the sight of shivering wretches did not show that God was not good, but simply that He was incomprehensible. In any case, the duty of the Christian was to stay at his post. If the post were dangerous, so much the better. When one of his favorite protégés, a certain Bob Weston, fell ill and the doctor feared a putrid fever, as typhus was then called, Gordon decided to put off his Christmas leave and nurse him. "A certain thought will, I doubt not, flash across your mind," he wrote apropos of this to Mrs. Freese, to whom he had also confided the thoughts suggested to his mind by the accident to his boat.

7. Happy Years of Service

So the years from 1865 to 1871 passed — happy years they seemed when he looked back on them through the kindly mist that softens the past. His only official worries came from the busybodies of the War Office who made useless suggestions. Good works kept him busy in his ample leisure. Sometimes when he had been talking too much he turned temporary recluse, and gained the solitude for which the professed mystic always yearns. Sometimes he entertained brother officers, Sir William Gordon coming on one occasion to stay with him, which necessitated borrowing wine from Mr. Freese, for Gordon had none good enough to offer to a General. From time to time he visited his brother, who lived at Woolwich Arsenal, the home of his own boyhood, where he romped in the society of his nephews and nieces. One night, coming from London, he missed the last train to Gravesend, got as far as Woolwich, and walked home from there. He told Augusta about it.

> I walked down the 16 miles in 4¼ hours and got here at 5.15 A.M. This is pleasure — the last 8 miles in the rain. However, I liked it, it is so quiet, and in passing the villages you see lights up where there is sickness and death, sorrow and crying. The weary workers at the factories wending their way at an early hour to hard labor. How any one of us can think this world a happy one is a wonder with so much sorrow.

Always the claims of the Gravesend poor kept him in a proper state of humility. He found lessons to win him from his besetting sin in all sorts of ways. Ingratitude, for instance, hurt him, and he felt annoyance at one of his boys going off without saying good-bye until he remembered how often God had helped him and he had "utterly and contemptuously forgotten to thank Him." Then he cured another boy of a bad neck only for the place to break out again when the boy's mother got him a place at ten shillings a week. Gordon was annoyed until he decided that he was more put out because his advice had not been taken than because the boy's neck was bad again. In nine cases out of ten, he declares, our motives will not bear the Scriptural anatomist's knife.

His night classes had grown so large that they had to be transferred to the Ragged School, a humble little hall in a mean alley which still stands as a poignant memorial of Gordon's work. But neither the fame of this, which had spread beyond Gravesend, nor the universal respect he won in the town itself, made any difference to his desire to remain in obscurity, and when Mr. Freese asked him to take the chair at a meeting of the local mendicity society all his old fears returned. He would not even sit on the platform. "I will see you, D.V., to-night, but mean positively to refuse to go on the stage. I cannot and will not do it — there, that is over." This brief note is clearly the aftermath of one of the nervous storms which so often used to break over him with tropical violence. But nothing clouded his intimacy with the Freeses. He loved them all, not least Miss Ada Freese, a pert young lady who one day sat on the gate of their garden, which Gordon habitually used as a short cut, and when he asked to be allowed to pass replied, "Go round the other way!" — a piece of impertinence which so tickled him that he went at once and repeated it to Ada's mother. Yet life was sometimes too difficult to make even their company endurable. He had decided that it was unchristian to keep his front door closed — it must always remain open for all who wished to enter. Mr. and Mrs. Freese, passing Fort House one day, accepted the tacit invitation and walked in. As they reached the hall they heard Gordon's footsteps in retreat to the cellar, but Mr. Freese led the way to the drawing-room and sat down. When ten minutes had passed and Gordon still remained in hiding they decided the experiment had failed. Whatever the front door said, Gordon was seeing no one that day.

They left Gravesend before he did, but returned at Gordon's suggestion to spend part of the summer of 1871 there when he was under orders to take up his new post as British member of the Danube Commission. A lucrative sinecure worth £2000 a year was the last thing to apeal to Gordon, who hated leisure as much as he loved authority, but he was due for foreign service and the appointment showed that the War Office felt well disposed towards him. It was a princely salary for an R.E. captain, still Gordon's rank in the corps. At the same time he was sorry to exchange Gravesend — dear Gravesend it now became — for Galatz, on the Lower Danube, and he did not hide his feelings from the Freeses, to whom he unburdened himself of all his troubles, including the stresses and strains of family relationships. They understood him as no one else did. When they came to see him at Fort House in the evenings and he was writing letters, they sat silent while, in that rapid hand of his, he covered sheet after sheet with his thoughts on the utter corruption of the world, on justification by faith as opposed to justification by works, on the necessity of prayer, on the keeping of the Sabbath; or it might be that he was corresponding with those who could help his boys to obtain situations in the world. In any case, the time came when he would lay his pen aside, and then they would talk by the hour as Gordon let his imagination play like summer lightning over the congenial fields of religious speculation; or they would discuss more homely matters arising out of their common interest in social work. The conversation often dipped to themselves and the people round them, and Gordon, always preferring to give rather than to take advice, might prescribe the washing tub as a remedy for the unrest that afflicted even the most domesticated females of that well-disciplined age. Yet he rather liked doing unconventional things that shocked the bourgeoisie, and was pleased at the thought of how bad they were when one Sunday morning he took Mr. and Mrs. Freese for a walk, and they met the people coming out of church.

When he was leaving, Gordon gave all the furniture at Fort House to Mrs. Freese, a present she gratefully accepted. But as the news of his departure spread, those who had benefited from his bounty begged one thing after another, and Mrs. Freese saw the contents of the house disappear stick by stick. Finally on a Sunday evening he brought round his drawing-room fender, carrying it in his arms, to the astonishment of the neighborhood, and explaining that it was the only thing he had left.

At length October arrived, and the time came for saying good-bye. He suggested to Mr. and Mrs. Freese at the last moment that they should go and see him off at Dover, and they all went down to that modest port between the chalk cliffs where so many Englishmen have said farewell — as Gordon was to say it thirteen years later — to their native land. They spent the night there, and the next day Gordon, wishing to put off the separation as long as possible, suggested that they should accompany him to Calais. He was glad, he said at luncheon before the steamer left, that he was not married, for the pain of parting from a wife would have been too great — the friendliest remark he is ever recorded to have made on the subject of matrimony. But Mrs. Freese, in spite of inspiring this tenderness towards the married state, could not be persuaded to brave the Channel, and only Mr. Freese crossed it with him, Gordon talking all the way over of their days at Gravesend and of the ties which united them. In traveling he took an unavowed delight, although it made him feel "carnal"; but by the time he reached Mayence he had mastered for the moment what he called the "gadabout spirit" in himself, and was able to regard this absence from his friends with religious equanimity. "How I like England when out of it!" he wrote to Mrs. Freese, following this grudging concession to the flesh by the reflection (the afterglow of the annoyance that changing trains causes to the most hardened travelers) that he looked forward "to a terminus where there will be no more tickets or baggage or differences of language, where there will be one kingdom, that of Christ, and no more wars." This was one of the thoughts that accompanied him as he traveled first class and in great luxury across Europe.

8. From the Danube to the Nile

The two years that he spent at Galatz did nothing to reconcile him to the world. Before he left England, the nonchalant attitude of the Foreign Office clerk whom he had interviewed about the duties attaching to the post had shown him that these were of no importance. Gordon was not the man to enjoy a sinecure, and he could not, as at Gravesend, occupy himself by looking after the young. It was pleasant to see the "poor Russian laddies delighted at the sight of the large sturgeons caught by their fathers," but the language difficulty made it impossible for him to have the adventures with "royalty" which he enjoyed at home. True, solitude was a salutary thing — it helped to bring the will into union with that of God. Gordon tried as best he could to fight the ennui of his surroundings with such thoughts as these, being helped a little by meeting with the Italian, Gessi, whom he had known in the Crimea. Gessi, who since then had followed Garibaldi to Sicily, was an adventurer and a radical after Gordon's own heart, and the friendship that now ripened between them caused Gordon to take Gessi with him to the Sudan, where he became his principal lieutenant. So close, indeed, did the ties between them grow that Gordon came to believe that their lives had been providentially linked together.

Yet his prevailing mood during this Danube period was one of boredom. He escaped from Galatz in his first summer to visit the cemeteries in the Crimea, which he found in a state of great neglect — a neglect that has never been remedied, but possibly reflects a healthier state of public opinion than the bureaucratically tidy control of the cemeteries for the fallen in the Great War. As he passed through Constantinople on his return he met at the British Embassy Nubar Pasha, the Khedive Ismail's Armenian Prime Minister. In the course of conversation Nubar asked Gordon whether he could recommend anyone of the Royal Engineers to succeed Sir Samuel Baker as Governor of the Equatorial Provinces of the Sudan, a question that was to be answered a little over twelve months later by Gordon taking the post himself. He came home to find his mother paralyzed and unable to recognize him. Death was busy in his family. While his mother lingered, it carried off his youngest brother, Freddie, causing Gordon to reproach himself for not having seen more of him since the time when they had been boys together. "Oh, when I leave this world, let me go quickly!" he wrote to Mrs. Freese as he unceasingly contemplated the state of mortality.

Directly he could leave Southampton he went to Gravesend and to Chislehurst, where the Freeses were now living, telling Mrs. Freese as they took a stroll together that he was shelved at Galatz, and wondering why the War Office had sent him there. "You are being prepared in solitude and loneliness for some great work," she answered, and if Gordon made any reply to a remark which she afterwards looked upon as prophetic she does not record it. He was at the moment much moved by the recent death of the Emperor Napoleon, a man, he said, who in the respectable world was a bad man and unprincipled, yet possessing the kind heart that excused a multitude of sins; and Gordon seized the opportunity of being at Chislehurst to leave cards at Camden Place. He did more, and, unknown to Mr. and Mrs. Freese, went down for the funeral. He wrote to explain how it was he had not seen them again, and was soon rushing across Europe as rapidly as the international expresses of that time would carry him, fast enough anyhow for him to send Mrs. Freese an impressive time-table of his journey.

Before this he had tried to dispel the monotony of Galatz by offering a secretarial post to Mr. Freese, at the time in bad health. Gordon counted on his coming out to him, and hoped too that he would bring "one of the Gravesend laddies," little Webster, for instance, or any other tractable person — underlining the word "tractable." As the idea grew in his mind, letter followed letter; he told Mr. Freese how he was to provide himself with money for the journey, decided that Webster was too small and that Bill Palmer, of Chalk, would be a better choice, arranged that the boy was to receive three pounds a month — a handsome salary for those days — and that Mrs. Freese was to move with her family to Southampton. He felt sure she had tact enough "to play the difficult game of keeping in with the various members" of his family; she would pay his mother plenty of visits and would hear a good deal on one text, "I do not like." But the carefully laid plans had all come to nothing, for Mr. Freese's health would not bear the strain. And Gordon, as he went for his solitary walks, saw little except the flocks of sheep to relieve the dreariness of the landscape, and even these reminded him that they were all sacrifices. The good shepherd was he who gave most sheep to the butcher. We lived on the pain of others.

True, death was no evil; on the contrary, it was a great boon. But the infliction of it was another matter, and the unthinking, professional enthusiasm for war that had marked Gordon in his younger days now faded as he approached middle age. Not that he was proof against its excitement. It annoyed him when he was not included in the Ashanti expedition organized in 1873. Yet, when public opinion at home asked why he was passed over, he protested against the assumption that he was the proper person to command it. Letters in the papers embarrassed him all the more as Wolseley had been chosen for the post, and he did not wish to appear in any way envious of his old friend's good fortune. Not that there was any such thing as good fortune, or bad. All came from God, and it was a Christian's duty to be case-hardened to the rubs of life. So Gordon wrote to Augusta when he was passed over. Three months later, in the midst of being wounded, not this time by his thoughts, but by "swordfish in the shape of people wanting money," he received a telegram from Nubar Pasha offering him the appointment of Governor of the Equatorial Provinces.

The proposal was very attractive — too attractive, indeed, not to suggest, as he thought over it, that he desired it for selfish reasons. The result was a terrific struggle in Gordon's mind while he tried to prepare himself against the possibility that the British Government would not sanction his appointment.[1] As a Christian who had given up everything to God, he should have been indifferent as to the issue, and he tried to persuade Augusta and himself that this was the case. A will-

[1] This is clear from the letter written to Augusta on November 9, 1873. Yet on November 8 he writes to the Adjutant-General, "I have not determined what to do, but the Government have no objection."

ing acceptance (he underlined "willing"), however outrageous some things appeared to human judgment — this, Gordon declared, he would give to anything that might be decided. At the same time he hoped and believed that his Governorship came within the scheme of Providence. He could do so much: open to civilization some of the darkest and most romantic places of still unknown Africa, and suppress the slave trade in the process; "show the Khedive and his people that gold and silver idols are not worshiped by all the world," and that he was a better man than Baker. Gordon writes from the Danube in a censorious strain, "Against me will be Baker and his adherents, Pce. of Wales,[1] etc., Geographical Society, the Anti-Slavery Society, and all those who think they ought to be chosen for the post. . . ." But he is sure of success. "I have a Bank and on that I can draw: He is richer than the Khedive, and knows more of the country than anyone; I will trust Him to help me out of money and any other difficulties." Gordon, as he surveyed the problems of the Sudan under this dangerously deceptive light, became the complete optimist, and we can see him already underestimating the forces against which he would have to work, although flashes of the truth lit his inner consciousness and in one such moment he saw the possibility of martyrdom.

But the brilliant promise of the new chapter suddenly opening before him on the whole made Thomas à Kempis's disciple the dupe of the man of action. There were always two Gordons — Mrs. Freese had seen that at once in the contrast between the tired eyes of the mystic and the carriage and speech of the boyish soldier. Could they work together to inaugurate a new era in Central Africa? Gordon believed that this was not to be achieved by fighting. "I am averse to the loss of a single life, and will endeavor to prevent any

[1] The Prince of Wales was on terms of friendship with Valentine Baker, Sir Samuel Baker's brother.

happening *if I go,*" he declared an aspiration that the history of the Sudan for the next quarter of a century was to belie in singularly grim fashion, for all the carnage that resulted from the Mahdist movement can be, from one point of view, imputed to the ideas which Gordon was the first to implant in the minds of the Sudanese. "I have laid the egg which the Mahdi has hatched. I taught the people that they had rights. Everything has sprung from that." [1] With these words he admitted his responsibility. We can acquit Gordon of sentimentality. He never believed that mankind was to be controlled by fine words, and accepted as fully as any Victorian that the Englishman's business, in the Roman poet's phrase, was to vanquish the proud and spare the conquered. In the end he was crushed, not so much for miscalculating the actions and characters of the worldly-wise, from Ismail and Nubar to Baring and Gladstone, as for his failure to understand that others could be guided by motives not less unworldly than his own. Gordon, influenced by his recollections of the Chinese, — least prone of all races to religious fanaticism, — never seems to have reckoned on the impulses of their Semitic blood that caused the Mahdi's followers to despise death just as heartily as did Gordon himself. But all this lay in the future. At the moment he remained the prey of conflicting desires, and decided that "the twisting of men carries out some particular object of God." When his suspense was over and the Sudan became a certainty, he reminded himself in his humility that God always worked by weak and small means — hence the reason for his own appointment as Governor of the Equatorial Provinces of the Sudan. He could not foresee that God was also preparing to work by a young Arab, then living as

[1] Colonel Chaillé-Long puts a different interpretation on these words, alleging that the revolt of the Mahdi was incited by the "ivory influence" at Khartoum, which Gordon offended by prohibiting any private trade in ivory.

a hermit on an island in the White Nile above Khartoum. Mohammed Ahmed was his name — his nickname, Abu Fulaja ("Father of the V-shaped Gap"), from the curious conformation of his front teeth. He was also known by the shipbuilders who lived at the little town on the mainland opposite as Zahed, the Renouncer. As a youth he had studied the Koran in Khartoum, attaching himself to a sheikh noted for his piety and learning. But the young man's soul revolted against the luxury of a party given by his master for the circumcision of a son, and he had walked out into the desert to contemplate in solitude and poverty the oneness of Allah. Now in his youthful manhood he was known throughout the neighborhood for his sanctity. This gentle yet hard young man lived on alms. Men melted at his smile, and listened enraptured while he talked of holy things. A dangerous person — cast in the same mould as Gordon himself. One of the particular objects of God was to bring them together ten years later in the clash of the irreconcilable interpretations that men place upon the divine will.

IV

EQUATORIA
(1874–1876)

1. "A Fine Post"

"I am happy and peaceful, and feel more and more that, get into what trouble I may, God will take me out of it." So Gordon described his feelings to Augusta as he passed through Paris on his way to Egypt. Troubles began almost as soon as he arrived in Cairo in February 1874. He easily succumbed to the charm of the Khedive, a type of adventurer and visionary with a dash of the scoundrel to which he was always partial. The man whom Lord Cromer described as an astute but superficial cynic seemed to Gordon clever and attractive. Ismail impressed him as being "terribly anxious to put down the slave trade"; but he detected no such zeal in the Khedive's lieutenants, and as he discussed things with them they appeared to be thinking only of money. To bandy words with such people as these was only too easy, and Gordon, after a few days in Cairo, was telling Cherif, the Minister of Justice and one of the four leading pashas in the country, that he was not a hireling. Already he contemplated resignation. His tendency to dramatize a situation, which always necessitated finding a villain of the piece, led him to attribute this rôle to Nubar Pasha, who, he suspected, was primed by Baker. On Nubar's broad Armenian shoulders, therefore, he put the blame for his disillusion. The true motive for the expedition to explore and annex the Lakes, which was the main concern of the Governor-General of Equatoria, Gordon now believed, was simply to impress Europe and divert attention from the state of affairs in Egypt.

I think the Khedive is quite innocent (or nearly so) of it, but Nubar is the chief man. . . . There has been a mutual disappointment. Nubar thought he had a rash fellow to deal with, who could be persuaded to cut a dash, etc., and found that he had one of the real Gordon race; this latter thought the thing real, and found it a sham, and felt like a Gordon who had been humbugged.

Gordon fretted in the uncongenial atmosphere of Cairo. He felt that no one liked him except the Khedive, and reacted by "treading on the corns of the swells." It was a regular hotbed of intrigue, he said, and the régime was fast moving towards a catastrophe — "things cannot last long like this; they are paying 36 per cent for money." At any rate, Gordon would not be smirched by what Renan not so long before had called *l'ignominie de certaines villes levantines dominées par l'esprit d'intrigue, livrées tout entières aux basses et subtiles pensées.* It gave him a certain pleasure to contemplate his own immunity. "Your brother's conduct is a silent reproach to the usual mode of doing things in this country and is the more cutting from its silence," he wrote to Augusta. Not that Gordon ever managed for long to practise the moral grandeur of silence. "Keep me from writing and talking and then I am humanly safe," was a self-judgment which he received with no good grace from others. When a well-meaning fellow countryman advised him to be careful not to say things that would get back to Nubar, who might in consequence do him some mischief, Gordon flared up with the assertion that there was no living man who could do him the slightest injury which he could feel.

He knew that the circle of guests who witnessed this explosion thought him queer. He *was* queer. To reason that money was trash, that all the coin one took was wrung out of poor people, that the honest man need fear no one — this was "Greek and Hebrew" to the greedy, cosmopolitan world of Cairo. Gordon started by knocking four fifths off his own salary. Sir Samuel Baker, as he noted disapprovingly, had been paid £10,000 a year; he would take no more than £2000. Nubar could hardly object to such quixotism. But when Gordon wished to follow up this example of Samurai economy by going to Suakim on an ordinary passenger vessel, with a single servant, Nubar stood out, insisting that the Governor-General of the Equator must travel in state by special steamer — the Government's dignity was worth more than the £400 Gordon's plan would save. This small difference seems to have been the exciting cause of Gordon's antipathy for the "comparatively low-born Armenian," as he described Ismail's Prime Minister, who, on his side, was thought to have been unfavorably impressed by Gordon's disregard for etiquette, when, for instance, he politely rose from his seat in the Prime Minister's divan as Nubar in a rage dismissed two Egyptian officers, young men unable to hide their dismay at being chosen as his A.D.C.'s. Hughes, of the Embassy at Constantinople, pointed out his error to Gordon, only to receive the answer, "Don't bother," which he told Augusta was curt, though effective.

The impression Gordon made, however, in those first days at Cairo was not purely one of rather eccentric other-worldliness. In China the rebels used to be his best recruits; now, acting on the same principle, he decided to take on his staff one Abu Saud, a Sudani Arab who had been notorious during Sir Samuel Baker's régime for his slave-trading operations. After a career of villainy that shocked even the hardened public opinion of Khartoum, Abu Saud was laid by the heels and sent to Cairo, where he now languished in prison. Gordon, impatient of the opinion of others and quick to act on impulse, went, when he had been only three days in Cairo, to see this very unpleasant specimen of the mercantile Arab. Abu Saud's soft and ingratiating manner and his pietistic mode of speech more than counterbalanced the authentic stamp of moral obliquity which Nature had set upon him in his squinting eyes. A single conversation persuaded Gordon that Abu Saud was an instrument sent by God to help fulfill his purpose. He pressed his idea upon the Khedive. At first Ismail was surprised, but, being well acquainted with the principle of government that sets a thief to catch a thief, he agreed to the release of the slaver who had practised murder as a side line to his business, and it was settled, though not without some misgivings on the part of official pashadom, that Abu Saud should accompany Gordon. Martin Hansal, the Austrian Consul in the Sudan, one of the few Europeans to share Gordon's fate in Khartoum eleven years later, thought it a good plan, and declared that Gordon had "a European head on an African foot." But the astonished Baker, when he heard of it, raised his voice in protest and alarm.

Anxiety to escape from Cairo and the desire to reach his province without delay caused Gordon to hurry on his preparations. He had soon chosen his staff. The American, Chaillé-Long, then serving as a Colonel in the Egyptian Army, relates how at midnight one evening he was entertaining some friends to supper after the theatre at his house in the Ezbekia — at that time the fashionable European quarter — when a note arrived from Gordon. It had the brevity of a telegram. "Will you come with me to Central Africa? Come and see me at once." Chaillé-Long went immediately to the house where Gordon was staying, to be met at the door by a short, unmilitary-looking man with laughing, sympathetic, and winsome eyes. "How are you, old fellow?" he said, holding out both his hands. "Come and take a b.-and-s. It will help us to talk about Central Africa." And Gordon led him to his room. On the table was an open Bible and a bottle of brandy, in those pre-whiskey days the English gentleman's usual drink. Gordon went at once to the point. "The Khedive," he said, "spoke to me about you to-day. You are to go with me as Chief of Staff. You will command the soldiery. I don't want the bother. H.H.[1] has given me a firman as Governor-General of Equatorial Africa. Will you go?"

Chaillé-Long asked him when he proposed to start. "Oh, to-morrow night," he answered. That was impossible, the American said. He would have to turn over his present duties to his successor, he had no outfit, he must close his house and get rid of his servants and horses. "Abandon them all," was Gordon's characteristic answer. "I have clothes and everything necessary," and he thereupon produced a pair of boots from a box full of them, pulled off Chaillé-Long's shoe, and put on one of the boots in its place. It fitted perfectly, a proof that there was no need to worry about clothes and equipment. They talked and smoked till four o'clock. Early the same morning Chaillé-Long was received by the Khedive, who explained that he had been chosen as Gordon's Chief of Staff for the special purpose of guarding the interests of Egypt in Equatorial Africa, thought to be menaced at the moment by the British Government, which had eyes on Uganda. Ismail impressed upon him the necessity of hurrying to that country and making a treaty with King Mtesa at the earliest moment.

Gordon was no doubt aware of the reasons for the choice of Chaillé-Long, and agreed with them. He held strict views on the loyalty owed by foreign officials in the Khedive's service to the master whose salt they ate, and so long as he was in the Egyptian service he was determined that the interests of Egypt should come first. Besides, he knew that government departments in Whitehall had long ears and meddlesome ways, and there is an authentic ring in his remark to Chaillé-Long that he did not want a British officer for his Chief of Staff because he might write home and make trouble. Gordon was no Imperialist in the patriotic sense of the word. His conception of the white man's burden, over which the nations were to

[1] The usual term, an abbreviation for His Highness, employed by British officials between themselves when referring to the Khedive.

quarrel bitterly for the next forty years and finally to tear one another to pieces in the Great War, anticipated the views ultimately sponsored by the League of Nations. He already saw dimly the vision of a great Central African state — under the Egyptian flag, but administered by Europeans, whose first duty would be to the natives under their care. To show his freedom from any narrow patriotism, he included no less than five different nationalities on his European staff of ten. So far as he could, he tried to choose them all from what he called the "A" class, whose reward was the interest of their occupation, men who did not "want to make a good thing of it," unlike the members of the "B" class, for whom the salary was the only attraction. In this missionary spirit Gordon prepared to lead his little band to the upper waters of the Nile and to what was then with good reason regarded as one of the unhealthiest portions of tropical Africa.

It seemed a little unreal, from his designation, which (in Arabic) ran "Governor-General of the Equator," to his uniform, which consisted of his Engineer undress with a fez instead of a cap. Naturally he was "His Excellency" — of nothing, he said, and he playfully threatened death to the young German, Friedrich Bohndorff ("Berndorff," Gordon, with his habitual carelessness about names, called him), a naturalist who volunteered to accompany Gordon as his personal servant, if he used that appellation.

Was the whole thing a joke? Gordon sometimes thought so during that fortnight, as he saw behind the scenes of what another famous Englishman called the land of *opéra bouffe,* then buzzing with the preparations for the marriage of one of Ismail's daughters. When at last he left, on February 21, taking only Chaillé-Long and the Egyptian A.D.C. with him, — the rest of his staff, including Gessi, of Crimean and Danube antecedents, who was in charge of transport and stores, were to follow later, — the musical-comedy note persisted.

They had a grand send-off, all the notabilities of Cairo going in Oriental fashion to the station to speed the parting Governor-General. The special train bravely started on its journey over the line which in those days crossed the desert to Suez. But vicissitudes soon overtook them. The permanent way was blocked by an engine that had been derailed. After a long wait they were shunted and attached to "a common train with a great many people." Then a party of Europeans riding in the desert held them up. These proved to be Count Ferdinand de Lesseps and two young ladies, — one of them his niece, — who had been out hunting and had lost their way. The Count made his apologies, explained his situation, and begged to be given a lift towards Ismailia. Gordon was soon deep in conversation with de Lesseps, while Chaillé-Long and Ibrahim Bey Tewfik, the Khedive's Chief Equerry, who was accompanying Gordon as far as Suez, talked to the young Parisiennes. As the time drew near for de Lesseps to alight, he begged Gordon to stop and spend the night with him at Ismailia. Chaillé-Long and Tewfik Bey added their persuasions in vain, and Gordon late that night reached the end of the journey begun "in glory and ended in shame." As the indefatigable diarist recorded the events of the day, he said nothing about his meeting with a Frenchman famous throughout the world, nothing about the young Frenchwomen appearing so oddly out of the desert, but he mentioned how he was touched by the depression of the faint-hearted A.D.C. upon whom Nubar's wrath had descended. "The poor A.D.C. had gone off without saying good-bye to his mother and sisters. He is an Egyptian and is very low; he is young and useless. I feel sorry for him — part of the lot of life; it is very hard, poor soul!"

At Suakim he hurried through his preparations for the desert journey to Berber, nearly 300 miles away. As a rule, twelve days were allowed for the fastest-moving caravans traversing this age-long route between the Red Sea and the Nile, but Gordon, though nothing really pressed, would not be content with the normal time-table and hustled his escort of 200 troops along at such a speed that they reached the Nile after nine days, a daily average of over thirty miles which caused both camels and men to be "extenuated with fatigue." At Berber he was entertained by the local Governor, and then feverishly pursued his journey by steamer, at one place wading in the water minus his trousers to help get the vessel off a sand bank — still a not uncommon *contretemps* of Nile travel. There was no danger of crocodiles, he told Augusta, as these never took you so long as you kept moving. So, goading on the crew to unwonted exertions, the unconventional Colonel "Do-it-yourself" reached Khartoum at daybreak on March 13, 1874, and was met in state by Ismail Pasha Ayub, the Governor-General of the Sudan. His reception by a battalion of infantry and an artillery salute pleased him, and he found no fault with the raucous Egyptian military band which mingled with the cries of the natives — very shrill and somewhat musical, he thought them. It gratified him to think that the journey had been made quicker than ever before. Khartoum, he said, was now only a month from London, for he had with him a *Pall Mall Gazette* of February 13 — the coincidence of dates, and the fact that the *Pall Mall Gazette* was largely responsible for sending Gordon on his last mission to Khartoum, being things that may please the superstitious.

Gordon's luck, however, was not yet to change. He found good news awaiting him at Khartoum, for intelligence had arrived only the day before that the efforts to break through the sudd — the negotiation of which used continually to impede navigation on the White Nile — had at last been successful. The White Nile was now open to navigation right up to Gondokoro, the capital of his province, so that Gordon, instead of having to take perhaps eighteen months to reach his headquarters by painful marches through the pestilential swamp country, would be able to travel the whole way by steamer in twenty-one days. This enormously simplified the problem of reaching the Lakes, and Gordon telegraphed to the Khedive that he hoped his Governor-General of Equatoria would be the first to navigate the waters of Lake Albert on one of the Khedive's steamers. Things promised, with God's help, to work out all right. He was in good health; rather worried by the guards turning out whenever he moved, but impressed by the hospital and the schools, where the little blacks were glad to see him. The cannibalistic habits of the rats and the loose morals of the officials showed less attractive sides of life in Khartoum. On the whole, however, he was satisfied. Difficulties met him, of course, but they could usually be resolved into the choice of alternatives, and then tossing up relieved him of much anxiety. He remembered how the Apostles had done what amounted to the same thing in the choice of a successor to Judas. And if his staff were incompetent he had one excellent officer — his name was self.

Others did not share Gordon's optimism. The "stinging decree" he issued immediately after his arrival, declaring the ivory trade a government monopoly and forbidding the levying of armed bands by private persons, was a declaration of war against the merchants who until now had been the virtual rulers of the Sudan. Gordon, in fact, had put his whole province under martial law, which, as he explained to Augusta, meant "the will of the General." While he anticipated no particular opposition, all who knew the country shook their heads, and declared that Abu Saud was far too deeply implicated with the slave merchants ever to be trusted to act against them. When his name was mentioned, people's jaws dropped. Already at Berber the Governor had spoken against him. In Khartoum everyone tried to persuade Gordon to give him up, one man warning him, much to his amusement, not to eat with Abu if he wished to avoid being poisoned. No one, Gordon noticed, spoke in his favor except poor people — a fact which favorably impressed this Christian Radical. Yet he admitted it was more from innate feeling that he was doing right than anything else that he stuck to his opinion against the almost unanimous advice of those who knew the man well. He was, in fact, listening to his inner voice, to his *daimon*, which was a poor judge of character; so far from having the least fear of Abu Saud, he determined to make him "a great man" and one of his two Deputy Governors. As he steamed southward from Khartoum with Chaillé-Long and his German servant, his spirits were almost high — an unusual thing for him. He felt that his post was a fine one which would be profitable to the Government after a time, and he was glad too that he had not many English with him, for "they would be more trouble than enough to look after."

Gordon's mood grew more sombre as the miles increased between him and Khartoum. He had nothing but his favorite pursuit of map-making to keep impatience at bay. There was little to see except animal life, particularly the storks. He might have set eyes on some of these identical birds on the Danube — and now here they were 2000 miles away, "walking about among the crocodiles." Birds, he decided, were like thoughts; when the dark times of winter came in other lands they went to Egypt, just as when we grew spiritually dull and cold our thoughts went to the things of the flesh. There was some mystery about Egypt and the Nile; in its remaining, for instance, such a hotbed of slavery — as it was fond of slaves in Pharaoh's time, so it was still. . . . They were steaming along one night under the moon, and Gordon's mind was working upon the loom of recent experience, — he was thinking about the expedition and of all that had happened since he had reached Cairo, — when peals of laughter suddenly resounded from a bush on the bank. Gordon felt annoyed, until he found it came from the storks. They seemed highly amused that anyone should go all the way to Gondokoro with the hope of doing anything. The fact made sufficient impression on him to find a place in his letters to Augusta, which professedly acted as his journal. Did he take it as an omen? He did not know, as we know now, that somewhere on an island in the vicinity was living a young sheikh, Mohammed Ahmed by name, fated one day to emerge from his retreat as the Mahdi and to set all that peaceable country aflame.

Thanks to plentiful doses of quinine and to drinking only boiled water, Gordon's health remained good as they passed through the dreaded marshes of the sudd. But the heat and the mosquitoes affected his spirits, and the farther south they got, the less satisfied did he feel. Inefficiency surrounded him in a limp personnel, beginning with Chaillé-Long, a feeble fellow who preferred talking about what he had done rather than what had to be done now. The steamer did not go nearly fast enough for Gordon's wishes, and the necessity of collecting wood for fuel en route caused long waits. Chaillé-Long tells us that Gordon one day slapped the Egyptian captain's face when goaded to desperation by the immobility of the S.S. *Bordein* (afterwards to achieve fame in the siege of Khartoum), to which they had transshipped at Fashoda. Gordon's naturally irascible temper was badly frayed by being cooped up on a small steamer in that trying climate for over three weeks, and his irritation at the slowness of the Arabs was shown by explosions of anger, as well as by its being recorded in his diary. He became, too, more condemnatory of his fellow officials, his criticisms ranging from men like Ismail Ayub Pasha and Sir Samuel Baker, whom he had seen, to the functionaries at Gondokoro whom he had not seen. He expected that his arrival in his capital would not prove an agreeable surprise to the officials of that station. The only people for whom he had sympathy were the natives. As he watched them on the banks of the river and reflected that they were now under his rule, he pitied their wretchedness. They looked thin and suffering creatures born to fear. He wondered why they had been created — it was a mystery of which God alone had the key.

Gordon's mind easily passed from the temporal to the eternal, and as he journeyed on the Nile amid the tropical heat in a small and comfortless steamer he kept his eyes on the cloud by day and the pillar by night, trusting in God, but not forgetting his quinine and mosquito net. Direction, he told Augusta, was the main point. When he reached Gondokoro and saw the seat of government of Egyptian Equatoria which Sir Samuel Baker had founded, he needed all the strength he could draw from divine philosophy to keep the needle of his compass steady. The prospect was to the last degree squalid. In the whole of his province of 120,000 square miles there were only two government posts, Gondokoro and Fatiko — two islands in the middle of a hostile population, the one with a garrison of 300 troops, the other with 200. Outside the forts no government of any kind existed, and it was impossible to go more than half a mile from either in safety, because the troops had been "fighting the poor natives and taking their cattle." The men were riddled with fever, the Arab officers were incompetent and "as brave as hares." Yet Gordon's confidence remained firm while he realized the full desolation of the picture in the centre of which God had placed him, and he did not "apprehend the least difficulty in the work"; it might be hard to gain the confidence of the natives, but what he had done in China he could do again in Africa. So long as he retained his sense of direction, all would turn out well.

He soon discovered, however, that the corruption went deeper than he had imagined. The troops, wretched as they were, had some excuse, for they never received any pay from

Khartoum, being served out instead with bottles of gin and slave girls, commodities easier to obtain than cash. There was evidence that Ayub Pasha connived at, if he did not profit by, this scandalous state of affairs, which surpassed anything done by the Imperial Government in China. Gordon did not take long to make his mind up what he should do — he would tax Ayub Pasha with the enormity to his face. So, after six days in Gondokoro, he started off again northward on his return journey of a thousand miles to Khartoum.

The genial Ayub Pasha, who at first imagined there must have been a mutiny at Gondokoro, was relieved to hear that Gordon's sudden return was simply to whip up his baggage. But he soon discovered there was more to it than that. When Gordon confronted him with his discovery, "sharp skirmishing" occurred between them, with blunt language from the Englishman and "stories" from the Turkish pasha, who told them rather from Oriental politeness than because he thought they would find credence with Gordon. Finally Gordon extracted a boatload of Austrian dollars — the current coin of the country — from Ayub Pasha, and a comforting, if useless, telegram from the Khedive stating that the Equatorial Province was to be completely independent of Khartoum. Thus provided, — and having rushed down to Berber, another 180 miles farther north, where he met the rest of his staff with the stores, bringing them all up to Khartoum, — he took his second departure from the Sudanese capital in mid-June 1874, preceded, this time, by the flotilla of steamers on which the whole transport of his province was to depend. He had been traveling incessantly since the middle of January. Now, without a moment's respite, — though not without reflecting on the utter helplessness of those around him, — he started off in the hottest season of the year upon a task that was to turn out to be a perpetual fight against men and nature.

2. A Christian Governor's Doubts and Cares

Gordon had two things to do. The more spectacular was to reach the Great Lakes and to launch upon them the steamers flying the Egyptian flag. The other was to stop the slave trade. Both equally required the establishment of a line of posts upon the Nile to ensure regular communications with Egypt. He made his first station at the junction of the Nile and the Sobat River, a strategical point on the northern frontier of his province from which he could intercept the slave caravans on their way from the interior. It was a wet and unhealthy spot, detested by the Arab troops — one of the reasons that induced Gordon to spend a couple of months there himself, for he would not ask others to undergo dangers he was unwilling to face himself. Towards his European staff he was still more accommodating. "Liberty" (*Hurriat*) was his motto. Everyone was free to leave if he wanted, a permission of which one of his German servants, terrified by the damp and desolation, availed himself after a single month had passed. "So much the better," ran Gordon's comment; "the best servant I have ever had is myself — he always does what I like."

During those weeks of July and August 1874, when Gordon became acquainted at first hand with the problem of the slave trade, his views underwent a certain change. Gordon's fascination for the biographer is the candor with which he thinks aloud. He is never at any pains to be consistent, and always says exactly what he has in his mind at the moment. Now, as he realized the apathy of the natives and their lack of the commonest human virtues, the question seemed to him much less clear-cut than it did to home-keeping supporters of the Anti-Slavery Society. He abhorred as much as ever the methods of the slavers; "it was and is," he declared, "the wholesale depopulation of districts and the numbers killed or who perish in the collection of slaves which make slavery such a curse." At the same time these uncivilized blacks could not be judged by an English moral yardstick. Slavery did not outrage their family affections, because they had none. He watched a mother give her baby in exchange for a cow which her husband had stolen — and everyone seemed perfectly happy. "A lamb taken from a flock would bleat, while here you see not the slightest vestige of feeling." Gordon was ready to rescue the child, but what was the good "when the mother did not care so much as if she had lost a handful of durra"? For a small basket of the same grain he bought a Shilluk boy from the lad's elder brother, both pressing on the bargain. It was Gordon's second experiment of the kind, and in such cases, when all parties, including the subject of sale, were agreeable, he could see no objection to it.

Helplessness and misery were on every side. When he told some slaves that the Khedive gave them their liberty, they showed no signs of pleasure; and at once there arose the difficulty of providing for them. The merchant refused to take them to Khartoum: "I give them to you," he said placidly to Gordon. The ex-slaves passively wished to stay where they were, which Gordon knew would mean their death from the natives when he left. The dilemma recurred as often as Gordon captured a convoy, and he soon learned it was much easier to capture slaves than to know what to do with them after they had been freed. Their repatriation was impossible; to leave them in a strange district was to condemn them to death. Such practical difficulties hardly occurred to the members of the Anti-Slavery Society in London.

The natives would lift a hand to kill their fellows, but not to help them. Gordon, whose love burned with as bright a flame in the African wilds as it had done at Gravesend, although not nourished now by much Bible-reading, — he had little time for that, — struggled against the apathy of the blacks. Miserable as they are, he remembers that an immortal soul dwells in each one of them; and he supposes that a poor old bag of bones, who died after he had tended her for a month, "filled her place in life as well as Queen Elizabeth." He draws a picture of another humble victim of hard circumstances — "a wretched sister of yours" is how he describes her to Mrs. Freese. One wet and windy evening he saw a woman struggling up the road from the river, "a wisp of bones" so weak that she was brought to a standstill by the wind, preferring to be soaked by the rain to being blown down, for, had this happened, she never would have had the strength to get up again. "She has not even a cotton gown on," says Gordon, writing in his hut with the rain dripping on the paper, "and I do not think her apparel would be worth 1/50th of a penny." He sent the poor creature some durra by one of his men, telling him at the same time to take her into the shelter of a hut. During a stormy night he was disturbed by crying outside the enclosure. Going to see in the morning what it was, he found the woman lying, apparently quite dead, in a pool of mud, and natives passing and repassing without taking the least notice. He ordered the corpse to be buried, and then, investigating the place where the noise during the night had come from, discovered a year-old infant, who had been left out in the grass by its mother. It was not the first time he had saved a baby from death by exposure, and, from the way this "depraved little wretch" drank a gourd of milk, Gordon saw that it intended to go through with the pilgrimage of life. Then, as his orders about removing the woman's body were still neglected, he collected a burying party, only to find that the corpse was breathing. He had the woman carried to a hut, set her by the fire, poured brandy down her throat, and washed her sightless eyes, half hoping as he did so that she "was floating down with the tide to her haven of rest." His hopes were fulfilled, and the girl, for she was only sixteen, died the next day.

The world was a sad, sad place. Yet Gordon, as he told the story to the woman who shared so many of his thoughts, was at pains to emphasize the beneficence of God. "I dare say you will see — in fact, I feel sure you will see — your black sister some day, and she will tell you about it, and how Infinite Wisdom directed the whole affair. I know this is a tough morsel to believe, but it is true." And he adds that he prefers life amid sorrows, if those sorrows are inevitable, to a life spent in inaction. Besides, wretched and starved as the blacks were, he believed there was more happiness among them than among the middle classes in England. The thought of Victorian respectability continued to irritate him amid this tropical squalor. Distance lent no enchantment to that view. Anyhow, he declared, you did not see the natives of the Sobat, despite the enormous discomfort of their lives, grunting and groaning all day long, as you saw scores and scores in England, with their wretched dinner parties and attempts at gaiety where all was hollow and miserable.

Here, amid the rains on the Sobat, the two sides of Gordon's character, the active and the contemplative, maintained their uneasy relations. For a young man the monotonous existence, he said, would have been intolerable, but it suited him now that he had passed the meridian. The secret of contentment, a lesson people never learned in England, was to be happy with what you had got. This did not prevent his being impatient when the steamers which had gone to collect wood for fuel failed to return, and he fumed at the laziness of their captains, "who like to have nothing in the world to do from one day's end to another." In the meantime Gordon, always open to new impressions, decided that the slavers were not so black as they had been painted. The head trader he kept in prison for a fortnight and then pardoned: "a first-rate man and does a lot of work" is his verdict upon him. He admired the energy of the slave-hunters, hardy, active fellows from the Northern Sudan, and with their help transferred the station to another and healthier state. Idleness was the besetting sin of the country, which, he noticed with approval, the ants did not share; watching them, he decides that "they seem to be of opinion that to be idle is to be very bad." His sympathy even extends to the rats, which also are energetic, fighting and screaming all night and running over his mosquito net. They carry off his shaving brush and soap, tear leaves out of his books, and eat the tops of his boots. But they excite no vindictiveness as in a single evening he catches seven in his cabin — he has removed his quarters to his steamer — with improvised traps made from dispatch boxes, and laughs as the tops fall on them one by one and "his friends" are taken on deck and made to swim for it.

So, with matters large and small, from capturing convoys of slaves and valuable loads of ivory to making a pair of trousers for one of the blacks, he kept his health and spirits. He did not enact his rôle of universal autocrat without many hard words and actions. Sometimes at the end of the day he thought that a quiet life in a civilized country would be preferable. But in the morning he was "all on fire again," ready to continue with the same zest as yesterday. At last, towards the end of August, 1874, he started from his station at the junction of the Nile and the Sobat, where he had spent the months of the hot weather, for Gondokoro. On the way he picked up Gessi, and found that Anson, his nephew, who had thrown up a secure but humdrum post in the Civil Service at home in order to accompany his uncle, had died of fever. "No man under forty years of age should be here, and then only those who are accustomed to these climates," was Gordon's unconsciously Hibernian comment upon this loss.

As he approached his seat of government for the second

time, he knew that trouble impended. He felt sure that Raouf Bey, the Egyptian Governor, who was one of Baker's men, would quarrel with Abu Saud, and he meant to support the latter. Things turned out as he expected. The place seemed in good order, the neighborhood quiet. Gordon attributed this to Abu Saud's influence, and definitely appointed him his deputy, or *wekil,* a position of great influence, as it made him the intermediary between Gordon and the native chiefs. Raouf had reason to be vexed that another was put over his head — even Gordon admitted as much, although he did not yet realize that the man he backed against Raouf was a first-class ruffian, and he tells Augusta that "Raouf Bey went off with great joy and contentment with your brother."

The prickings of conscience made him part mildly from Raouf, but his temper was very, very short as he wrestled with the difficulties of government. One of the first things he did was to take over Baker's old bodyguard, the "Forty Thieves" — he had learned in China the advantage to his prestige of such a personal corps. In the interval of picking up the threads of government, writing to the Khedive, looking into the financial affairs of the province, and keeping a sharp eye on Abu Saud, who very soon began to excite his suspicions, Gordon had to doctor and nurse his European staff. Only Gessi and Kemp — the English engineer in charge of the steamers — were not on the sick list. Three days after his arrival he read the funeral service over the grave of Witt, a German naturalist who had accompanied the expedition as botanist without pay on the promise that he gave half his collection to the Khedive. "De Witt, amateur with Berndorff. Dead," runs Gordon's slightly contemptuous record, but he had disliked the German anyhow, and thought him a humbug. The American officer, Campbell, and the English Russell were both down with fever. His interpreter, Linant de Bellefonds, "a traitor," with whom he had quarreled, was still more gravely ill; and Gordon was glad that they were again on good terms before the Frenchman had a relapse that proved fatal. Berndorff, as Gordon continued to call Bohndorff, his naturalist servant, was laid up. Even the wily Abu Saud went sick. No white man's life was worth a week's purchase in that deadly climate, and Gordon decided to move farther south and look for a healthier site for his capital.

A week in Gondokoro, the nights being taken up in paddling about a swamped tent with more than a chance of its coming down bodily on him as he nursed the sick, made him ready to depart "as far as the things of the world are concerned." He himself remained well. The intense satisfaction, he said, of having no fear, no uneasiness about being ill, was very great, and more than half the cause of good health. "No comfort is equal to that which he has who has God for his stay; who believes, not in words, but in fact, that all things are ordained to happen and must happen."

As he thought about the divine rule of the universe, he marveled at the intricate order of the world, the detail required for each person, each work, each rag of humanity — and all of it carried through without a mistake. Gordon knew enough about the difficult art of government to admire such virtuosity. Yet, while he believed that the phenomena of sense were simply a great puppet show, that the events of this life were in themselves of not the slightest importance, and that whether he himself lived or died mattered not at all, Gordon was not a fatalist who refused to take proper precautions for his health or personal safety. He kept well because he looked after his stomach and took quinine as well as trusted in God. "Never let your mosquito net out of your sight. It is more valuable to you than a revolver and more easily carried," was one of his orders to his staff. Gordon had a high opinion of his own medical skill; he was, he said, one of the best doctors he knew. There was, in fact, only one thing Gordon valued in the world. He cared nothing for its honors or its knickknacks, — the first were false, the others useless, — but he did look upon health as God's blessing. While he had that he was rich.

At one moment during that autumn he caught a chill, which did not improve a temper already severely enough tried by the climate and the utter helplessness of his staff. To them he gave orders that in future they were not to come near him except on duty, and if they were ill they were to keep away till they got better. He ceased using soft words to his Arab officers and men, giving them "digs" instead. Abu Saud very soon fell from grace. When their collaboration was only a few days old, Gordon noticed a leakage in the ivory paid in to Government, and suspected Abu to be the culprit. As if this were not enough, his *wekil* grew bumptious, entering his cabin without so much as "By your leave," and behaving as if he, and not Gordon, were the Governor-General. Such conduct soon resulted in an explosion, and the hitherto indispensable Arab found himself disgraced and sent back to Gondokoro from Rejaf, a few miles south of Baker's capital, where Gordon had founded a healthier station. This was not before Abu had tried to excite a mutiny among the troops. Even so, the placable Gordon relented after a few days and restored Abu to favor. Then a sudden change in the hitherto favorable attitude of the natives convinced Gordon that his *wekil* was "an arrant liar and utterly false," and he decided to ship him to Cairo. But Abu's villainy was not yet exhausted, and Gordon's career, as Baker feared, very nearly ended ingloriously through a plot hatched by Abu Saud with a native chief to assassinate him on one of his marches. Gordon's suspicions were aroused in time, and the incident showed him the necessity of always remaining on the *qui vive*. When two young R.E. officers, C. M. Watson and W. H. Chippindall, joined Gordon a few weeks later and took over the scientific work of the expedition, he warned them against what he called rash adventure. "Avoid landing in narrow places among reeds," he said, "where natives can jump on boats; and, though peaceably received, be ready for war at any time."

Gordon flattered himself that, if he had the reputation of being hard to his own men, the natives trusted him. He wished to befriend them by breaking down the feudal power of the chiefs through economic means; as the feudal system, he told Augusta, was destroyed by the rise of large towns and manufactures, so now the natives might be taught to understand their rights by the use of money. With this object he paid the men directly for their work, instead of contracting with their chiefs, and settled his accounts, not in goods, but in copper piastres. It was a start in the good work of preventing the exploitation of the poor by the rich. The chiefs, he soon found, were as bad as any Europeans in their lust for money, which with them took the form of cows. Blessed were the poor, Gordon wrote, and then showed his distrust of the rich by arresting a native chief for a financial *coup,* which consisted of appropriating cows (it was not stealing, he explained, according to native ideas), and sending him down to distant Khartoum. Yet there was the text warning us not to judge others. As Gordon thought about Christian ethics from the vantage point of his forty-odd years (thanks to his age, he believed, he now saw these things more clearly), he declared that all people were more or less rogues or swindlers, and that when the time came for us to be weighed there would be little difference between one man and another.

That autumn Gordon had time, in the intervals of administration, to reflect on the imperfectibility of humankind. God had given him "great energy and some little common sense";

He had not been so liberal to others. The officials of the Sudan Government were showing that they were hand-in-glove with the slavers. How could the Khedive expect Gordon to hang the little men in charge of the slave gangs when the real culprits were his own provincial governors and the merchants in Khartoum, who were always in Ismail's power? He replied in this strain to harsh letters from the Khedive to stop the traffic, pointing out where the blame really lay. The Khedive, he could not help thinking, already regretted having given him the post — "a quieter, easy-going, salary-drawing man" would have suited him better. Gordon felt it was no use giving his life for a service that was unwelcome to his employer; besides, he feared that the influence he was now gaining over the blacks would only make them an easier prey to his Arab successor. It was all very difficult, and the solitude and the remoteness from home did not lighten his burden. He had with him only his Arab cook and the two little Shilluk boys he had bought for durra at Sobat, little spindle-shanked creatures whom he found amusing. Beyond a few words in broken Arabic he said nothing from morning to night. The mosquitoes drove him to bed every evening at half-past six, and they would not let him get up before five. The odds against him seemed impossibly long. True, Chaillé-Long had returned from his mission to Uganda with a hopeful report on the feasibility of getting the steamers on to Lake Albert, but the American's health was for the moment shattered and he was lying dangerously ill in Khartoum. On the top of this came in news that the two young R.E. officers, who were to have looked after the steamers, had both fallen sick. From every point of view the work to which Gordon had turned a year before with high hopes seemed bound to fail, and the autumn of 1874 closed gloomily with nothing to show for the losses his expedition had suffered.

3. Gordon's Vision of an Egyptian East Africa

Undoubtedly there was some mystery about the sources of the Nile. Make what arrangements you would, they were blocked time after time — Gordon decided that some spiritual meaning must underlie this curious power of the great river to frustrate human projects. Linking up data from the Old Testament and the New, he came to the conclusion that the geographical position of Egypt and Assyria in relation to the Holy Land and the geographical position of his own province to Egypt would show some curious connection, if only he had the spirit to discern it. He regretted not having his concordance and textbook with him, for then he would have tried to work out "the mystic nature of the Nile," the Nile which nearly destroyed Moses, that "type of the law." Yet in his more optimistic moods he believed that this odd river, after jealously guarding the secret of its source for millenniums, might even now yield it up to one of his own steamers. Quite possibly God had always meant to give the solution to Egypt. Might it not be that he himself was the instrument chosen for the purpose? These were some of the thoughts running in Gordon's head as he waited for the steamers — he seemed to spend most of his time waiting — on which to navigate the 200 miles between him and Lake Albert.

But Gordon saw other visions than those framed for him in the pages of his Bible. He brought to the question of the Lakes the same strategical eye that had made him the scourge of the Long-hairs ten years before. Had they been rebel Chinese cities, he would never have made a frontal attack upon them. He would have cut them off from the sea, turned their flank, set himself astride their lines of communication. Gordon looked at the map of Africa as once he had looked at the map of the Yangtze delta, and saw the true solution of the problem confronting him. He would give up his bothering steamers and escape from the awful climate of his wretched, fever-stricken province of marsh. He would have the Khedive send 150 men from Suakim to make for Mombaz (now Mombasa) Bay, establish a base there, and then push on over the healthy highlands to the Lakes, Uganda, and the rich country of King Mtesa.

In a letter to his family, Gordon outlined the idea which makes him the Romulus of Kenya.

> I propose . . . concentrating myself in the south . . . and trying to do the only thing which will open Africa, namely, coming down on the coast at Mombaz Bay, north of Zanzibar. The navigation between this and Khartoum is a terrible affair. Firewood begins to get scarce, and every year will make it scarcer; there are innumerable shoals, etc., and you cannot make the Arab captains work. Now from Suez to Mombaz is 2900 miles; from Mombaz Bay to Mtesa is 400 miles — total 3300 miles, 300 of which are land journey. From Cairo to Khartoum is (with the desert, cataracts, etc.) a distance of 1500 miles, from Khartoum to Gondokoro 1080 miles, and from Gondokoro to Mtesa is 500 miles — total 3080 miles. Now if Victoria Lake is large, I may diminish my Mombaz Bay journey by land a good bit. Anyway it is better to open a route to the sea. Zanzibar, a large place, is near Mombaz, and I hope the Khedive will let me do it. It is the only mode of helping these countries. All the northern part of my province is marsh and desert, and useless for anyone. The rich parts are the lake districts.

In January 1875, if not before, Gordon communicated to the Khedive this Napoleonic project for rounding off the dominions of Egypt by adding to them what are now the British possessions of Kenya and Uganda. So complete was his vision that he foresaw the railway between Mombasa and the Lakes, a line not to be taken in hand for another quarter of a century. Cecil Rhodes never transported his imagination so far into the future as this. How clearly the idea took shape in Gordon's mind is evident from the fact that he even settled on the leader of the expedition. Chaillé-Long had made a success of the mission he had headed the previous year to King Mtesa of Uganda — he was the obvious member of his staff to be given this new job. An additional reason for Gordon's choice of Chaillé-Long lay in the fact that he found the American personally antipathetic. He had already pointed out to Chaillé-Long when both "were in good tempers" that they would never be able to get on with one another while they were together. Mombasa was a long way off, which made it all the clearer that he was the most suitable person to undertake this new adventure.

Chaillé-Long records how he reached Rejaf early one morning in mid-March, having traveled by moonlight from Lado. The hour was 4 A.M., but Gordon was already up, seated at the door of his hut and cleaning an elephant gun. On the table stood a bottle of quinine, a bottle of cognac, and an open Bible. Gordon offered him some of both liquids, impressing on him the importance of the quinine. Then, after talking about other things, he repeated the remark about their incompatibility of temper which he had already made in his letters home. To show that he was not "mean," he followed this up with the proposal that Chaillé-Long should return to Cairo with a dispatch for the Khedive bearing upon the Mombasa project, at the same time giving Chaillé-Long a letter he had written to him on the same subject.

This letter repeated what he had already said in his private letters home. He writes: —

It would entail small cost, viz. a steamer to Mombaz Bay, with small well-assorted quantity of stores and 200 black soldiers taken from bateaux destined for those parts. Zanzibar being near could supply any petty wants, and I should work towards the sea. Profound secrecy till complete realization of project for political reasons should H.H. approve. Wish the expedition to be considered as belonging to my government.

If lake N'zo communicates with Victoria lake & I can get to it, it is 70 miles from Mt Kenia which is 200 miles from coast, and they say the River Dana is said to be navigable for some distance from the coast. Krapf speaks of the country as healthy well cultivated & the people comparatively civilized. If we could debouch at Formosa Bay, it would be much shorter than Port Durnford or Juba River, but I fear these places are in the territory of Zanzibar. I do not want this notion which is in "nubibus" to be mentioned, for it appears that Gt. Britain does not want Egypt to debouch on the sea. There is a

PART OF A LETTER FROM GORDON TO HIS SISTER ABOUT HIS EAST AFRICAN PROJECT (JUNE 1875)

The injunction to secrecy he repeated in a letter to Nubar. He impressed the same thing on Augusta (and his brothers), "for it appears that Great Britain does not want Egypt to debouch on the sea."

Gordon, says Chaillé-Long, read the astonishment shown on his face at the audacity of the scheme, with its obvious political implications. We, who know Gordon better than Chaillé-Long ever did, may guess from his nonchalant attitude towards Sir Frederick Bruce and Lord Russell when he was in China that he would not now be disposed to pay much attention to the possible attitude of the British Diplomatic Agent in Cairo and the Foreign Secretary in London. Gordon's belief in the power of the *fait accompli* to remove the mountains that stand in the way of those who adventure in regions of high politics had been exemplified in his treatment of the Ever-Victorious during the last year of its existence.

Without delay Chaillé-Long started off on his trip northwards, and after a journey through the Sudan at the hottest time of the year he reached Cairo in June, a skeleton convincingly demonstrating the unhealthiness of the climate of Egyptian Equatoria. The Khedive received him with *éclat,* being enchanted at the additions which he fondly believed Gordon's lieutenant had made to his dominions, and then hastened his departure for Europe on sick leave, saying nothing for the moment about the Mombasa project. Only a few weeks had elapsed, and Chaillé-Long was recuperating at Plombières, when he received a peremptory dispatch from Ismail to return without delay to Egypt. There he learned from the Khedive himself that he was to be put in command of the expedition to the east coast as proposed by General Gordon. The need of secrecy was emphasized when Chaillé-Long was given sealed orders which he was not to open till he was 500 miles south of Suez. He left that port on September 19. Thus, eight months after Gordon originally broached the scheme, the Khedive Ismail, desperately embarrassed as he was for money and recently involved through his grandiose foreign policy in a serious quarrel with Abyssinia, acted upon the idea which his too farseeing Governor-General of the Equatorial Sedan read in the book of futurity. But he made one serious mistake. When Chaillé-Long opened his orders he found that he was to call at Berbera, which Admiral M'Killop, late of the Royal Navy and now in command of the Khedive's naval administration, had occupied in the Khedive's name, and that they were then to proceed together to the Juba River. Mombasa, which ought to have been their objective, was not mentioned.

In the meantime the man in whose mind this conception of opening up the centre of the still unknown continent had been formed wrestled with the difficulties of government. The immediate business in hand was to establish a line of posts up the Nile, so that when the steamers arrived these could make use of them on their way to the Lakes. As Gordon labored with a Levantine interpreter, whom he detested for his "heartlessness," supported only by entirely despicable Egyptian soldiers, both his patience and temper were strained to the utmost. "I never in my life," he says, "had less confidence in troops than I have in these." They were terrified of the natives, and interested only in their slave-wives, whom Gordon rather admired since they stuck up for their rights. Often they came and stood before him in the dusk; he would make the sign that someone had beaten them, and on their assenting he would send them to the sanctuary of his "filthy kitchen" for the night. But they would soon disappear, for husbands were as easy to find as to lose. When the same woman had behaved in this way two or three times, Gordon would remonstrate with her for her inconstancy. . . .

From telling Augusta these traits of her "black sisters" his mind runs on to the larger question of civilizing the natives.

One of the obstacles in the way, this enemy of feudalism paradoxically decides, is the lack of ambition in the native chiefs. They never think of trying to annex a neighboring tribe, and their people get on well without regular laws, living out their span in comparative quiet. He inquires of one sheikh if he has ever seen strangers or white people, to receive the answer, "Why ask such a question? All men are the same." Gordon, sensitively reacting to the mood of the moment, then sees his province as an Arcadia where vice is unknown and even the intertribal wars seldom result in bloodshed. He had painted a very different picture of the natives farther north, on the Sobat!

But this impression of primitive felicity does not prevent him from going on with the work of establishing stations, and bringing to the blacks the blessings of the civilization he derides so freely in his letters. In the course of the summer of 1875, while Ismail was arranging for the East African expedition, the previously friendly attitude of the natives changed into hostility, and resulted in one serious disaster to Gordon's forces, Ernest Linant de Bellefonds [1] and the "Forty Thieves" being surrounded and cut to pieces in the bush. Gordon took the thing calmly, and sincerely sympathized with his enemies. "They say: 'We do not want your cloth and beads. You go your way and we will go ours. We do not want to see your chief.' " They had put this over and over again to Gordon, who saw their point of view. "But we cannot leave them on our flank, and it is indispensable that they shall be subjected," he wrote — and subjected they were by the humanest of men, who happened also to be a very formidable soldier. The only malice he felt was towards his own troops. He could not help laughing at the miserable instruments given him to work with. Having nothing to do, or rather neglecting what they ought

[1] He was a brother of Gordon's interpreter who had died at Gondokoro in 1874.

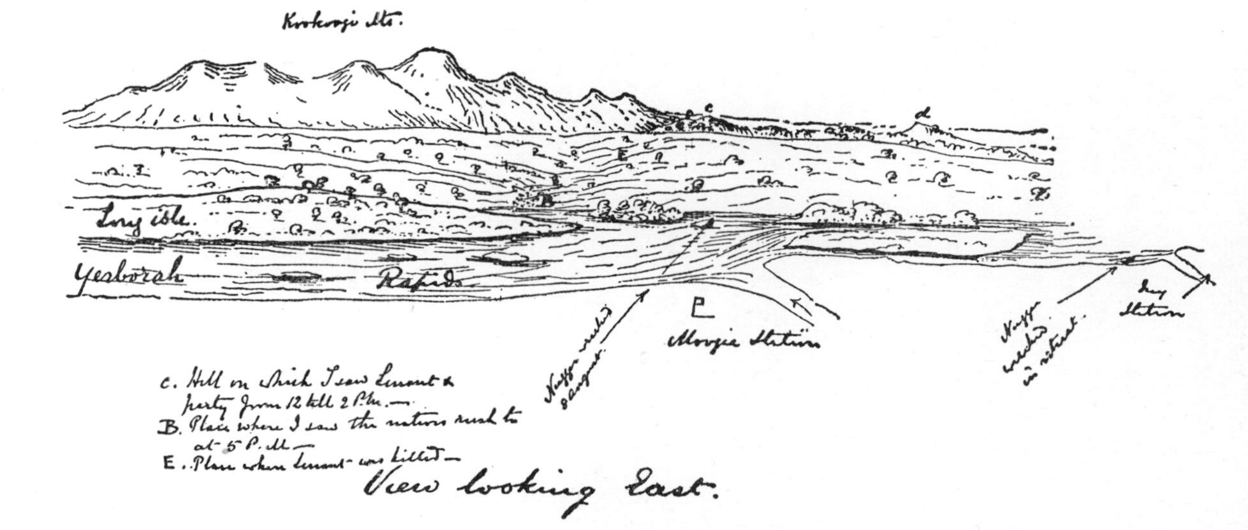

GORDON'S SKETCH OF THE REVERSE SUFFERED BY ERNEST LINANT DE BELLEFONDS AND THE "FORTY THIEVES"

(This is included in his letter to Augusta Gordon dated August 28, 1875)

to do, they sat and talked over the terrors of their position until they trembled again. As a revenge he mischievously kept the garrisons at the stations small, so that they remained thoroughly frightened and awake. But when Gordon arrived at a post they were reassured by the Pasha's presence, and the sentries slept in comfort. "I shall be glad," he says, "when I have done with these wretched scarecrows. I declare it is very unsafe — much more than even I could have expected."

From one thing that summer and autumn he was free; he drove himself so hard, being a universal handy man, that he had not time to suffer from "the doles." "He seems to think that nobody but himself can even screw a box-lid on. . . . A fearful egotist . . . but devilish kind," was the opinion of Chippindall, the R.E. officer, who had returned from his surveying farther south. He was alone with Gordon during June, and feared that the nagging he endured from his chief would end in a row. He felt he was too young to be a companion to Gordon, and he could not agree or sympathize with him in his spiritual flights. Besides, Gordon made a difficult superior officer; he would not give orders for definite things to be done, and yet if they were not done he was angry. It also embarrassed "Chipp," as Gordon called him, to be treated as an equal. "It is not right of him; he ought to keep one more at arm's length, because one is nearly certain some day or other to treat him as an equal and then there will be a row." Chippindall, unburdening himself in this way to Watson, who had already been invalided, asked his brother officer not to condemn him unheard if the row did come, and reminded him that at one moment soon after their arrival Gordon had so worried them that they had both thought of resigning. In spite of this, the fascination of Gordon's personality held the young man, and he wrote more kindly of his chief than his chief did of him. When Chippindall's health gave way, the only thing that made him regret having to go home was that he left Gordon *all alone* — he underlined the last two words.

Gordon's rows were many. None of his subordinates satisfied him — not Kemp, the stolid mechanical engineer, nor "Chipp," in spite of being a very good officer, for he was apt to be dull, to say he could not interest himself in the work; on this Gordon would ask, "Why did you come?" and the relations between the two would grow dangerously taut. Besides, the younger sapper was forgetful; one day he went on a march and actually forgot his pedometer. There was something in the country, Gordon perceived, that infected even the most highly trained Europeans with the spirit of delay. "To-morrow," *bukra,* — familiar to-day in every Arabic-speaking country, — was the universal watchword. The invaluable Gessi did not escape his chief's strictures — he interpreted his orders, Gordon said, as if he had £10 and not £40 a month. "Gessi is a perfect bee — he never sticks to one thing," runs a later criticism. As for the Egyptian officers and men, they needed watching the whole time. Yet this most punctilious of martinets, who insisted that not a screw in the magazine stores should be out of place, reminded himself as, in his own phrase, he went out to "worrit the Arabs" that it did not in the last resort matter whether they did what he told them or not. Neither he nor the Khedive was the real ruler of the province.

But Gordon, humble to God, was by no means humble to any of his fellow men. With visitors he took a high hand, only giving a passport to Burnaby, cavalryman by profession and traveler by predilection, if he promised to confine his writing in the papers to descriptions of the country and *dead objects* — a hampering restriction for picturesque journalism. Regarding Stanley, he grimly declares his intention to refuse him leave to stay in his province at all, for he objects to being "daily logged." His irritation embraces Baker, whose "led dog" he is determined not to be, the unforthcoming Khedive, who never answers his letters, and the forthcoming Royal Geographical Society, which he knew meant to "badger" him. He considers it an impertinence that an upstart society of this kind should award gold medals to people, as it undoubtedly would to him when he explored the Lakes. The thought makes his blood boil, and his mind runs over all the things he most dislikes — a visit to the Crystal Palace, a picnic, a masked ball. What more "utterly melancholy" than these? And his only regret is that, work how he may, do everything from writing orders for all his officials to cleaning a duck gun or mending his boots, he cannot keep himself fully occupied. Inaction, this one-time disciple of Thomas à Kempis confesses, is terrible to him. So he asks God for the three things, and, like a well-trained soldier, puts them down in writing: —

1. Not to be disturbed if the Khedive sends me away to-morrow.
2. Not to be disturbed if he keeps me.
3. Not to have anything of the world come between Him and me; and not to fear death, or to feel regret if it came before I have completed what I may think my programme.

He adds: —

Thank God, He gives me the most comforting assurance that nothing shall disturb me, or come between Him and me.

His programme was to reach the Lakes; these were the foci round which his thoughts unceasingly revolved all that year of 1875. By July he had worked his way to Kerri, sixty-five miles up the river south of Gondokoro, and he believed that in the next flood he would be able to navigate the remaining part of the Nile between Kerri and Lake Albert. He knew there were many rapids, but he considered it probable that none of them would be impassable to his steamers. His confidence at this time manifested itself in his truculent attitude towards the Royal Geographical Society, which reflected the struggle in his own mind between his desire to explore the sources of the Nile and the feeling that as a Christian he should put the ambition by. When he advanced south of Kerri increasing difficulties made the prospects of success more remote. Everything worked against him — the climate, the river, the natives, the very material with which he had to work. The boats were rotten; rudders dropped off in the current; even the ropes, by which each nuggar was hauled up the rapids by sixty to eighty black satin-skinned natives, as often as not broke at the critical moment. Gordon has left us many pictures of himself, but none more characteristic than his standing on the rain-soaked banks of the Nile, "praying the nuggars up" the rapids, as he used to pray for the Ever-Victorious when they wavered in the breach in China.

Though with the help of Warburg's Tincture — occasionally, when his conscience allowed him, also taking chlorodyne, "that detestable fluid" — he kept "the doles" at arm's length, a strain of discouragement runs through his letters at this time which the man of action in Gordon had never before allowed to come to the surface. He wondered what was the good of suffering as he did. His lot appeared almost intolerably hard, in a climate that was a hothouse by day and coldly humid by night, with rain that made even the vultures look ridiculous. Pour the Nile down your throat, he says, and it will not appease your thirst. Even the food disgusts him, and he makes one of the very few references in his immense correspondence to a subject which perennially interests most healthy people. "No vegetables, dry biscuits, a few bits of broiled meat and some macaroni boiled in sugar. I forgot some soup" — such is his fare, and he tells Augusta that when he comes home, as he means to do shortly, he will stay in bed all the morning and have oysters for lunch. "How I hate this country and all the work," he writes at the very time when Chaillé-Long is starting with his force from Suez on the expedition which, if successful, would immeasurably increase Gordon's responsibilities. "Without any reserve, I could at this minute pack up and go back if shame did not prevent me."

All these difficulties made him blame Augusta. Her letters, he tells her, are very poor things, "milk and watery"; and more than once he declares she and Henry are responsible for his coming to such a detestable country. "It is your and Henry's fault who persuaded me to take the post. If you were here you would speak your mind about it, for nowadays women alone dare do so."

Then he makes a wry apology for his liver, and says that Augusta must not interpret all these outbursts too literally. The only way he can let off steam is in his journal, which his letters to her are.

In fact, the Gordon strain was far from exhausted by his long battle with men and things, with "shirking Arabs only seeking a hole to hide in," with Sudanese who are no better, with boatmen who allow their boats and gear to rot and never have a knife or a bit of yarn, for he declares he has quite made up his mind to establish and equip all the stations *well* (underlined), to quell the hostile natives, to found posts right up to Lake Victoria, with a flotilla on the Victoria Nile and with a steamer which he will have put together in sections on the great lake itself. He will in this way "open the road to the interior," or, in other words, make Egypt master of Central Africa — until some grand pasha comes and lets the whole affair die out.

Certainly all is mysterious and probably useless. Yet if God's scheme is inscrutable he will not wear a "cruet-stand expression" on his face. In the meantime he has one worldly consolation: the revenue of his province is more than double the expenditure, and he holds enough ivory to pay the whole expenses of his government for the next three years. Poor elephants — many of them babies! But they make him semi-independent — a pleasant reflection. It is typical of Gordon that he admits the insufficiency of his own self-appointed salary, and yet the flattering state of his exchequer never makes it occur to him to revert to the scale of his predecessor's pay.

Gordon was wearing himself out, and knew it; the labor of the campaign against the relentless river had "taken the shine" out of him. At the beginning of October, as he looks back on the incessant trials of the previous weeks, trials which sometimes amounted to agony, he says he will never be fit for anything again. If he lives to the end of the work he will retire. But no man's life is worth a week's purchase in that deadly climate, and death, though it still passes him by, carries off in quick succession his servant and the "poor little black-eyed" Egyptian doctor, who was also acting as interpreter.

Yet the goal did not seem far off. By early October, Gordon had already pushed his advanced stations into what is now Uganda, marching from Labore to Dufile over the mountains described by Sir Samuel Baker with an enthusiasm his successor could never have felt. At Dufile, where, in Baker's words, the "grand White Nile flows in a calm, deep stream" direct to Lake Albert, only some hundred miles distant, Gordon stood beyond the last of the cataracts. If only it were possible to drag his steamers through the rapids between Labore and Dufile, — the spot intended by Baker as the starting point for the final stage of his expedition and the base for his steamers, — Gordon would be in a fair way to succeeding where his predecessor had failed. True, Baker had mentioned the Fola Falls north of Dufile, where the river boils through a narrow gorge in the mountains, but Gordon, always mistrustful of the observations of others, appears already to have seen and discounted the rapids. When he started, therefore, from Dufile to explore the river more carefully, he had hopes that he would find no insuperable obstacle barring the way to his steamers. He was soon undeceived. He had not gone far when he heard a noise like thunder. It increased as he drew near to the bank. At last the sight lay before him of the great river contracted to two narrow channels, each fifteen to twenty yards wide, and for some two miles tearing down a slope of one in six between precipitous banks.

"It is all over," he wrote, emphasizing the finality by printed letters. Any hope of getting a steamer on the lake except by the laborious method of carrying it up in sections on the backs of porters and camels had to be abandoned. It was no use dreaming of taking up "the screw steamer, or the nuggars, or indeed anything," said Gordon to his journal. Yet he gave no outward sign of his disappointment. "I bore it well," he wrote, "and for all you could see it might have been a picnic party to the Fola Falls; but it is rather sad, and it will give me a mint of trouble and delay."

Had Gordon forgotten his plan to turn the flank of the Lakes? Nine months had elapsed since he outlined it to the Khedive — and there had been no answer. In a mind so fertile in resource as Gordon's the scheme of yesterday was easily choked by the luxuriance with which new projects continually grew. Nothing could have seemed more improbable to him, faced as he was with the habitual neglect and inefficiency of the authorities in Cairo, than that the Khedive, who did not take the trouble to answer his letters, was nevertheless acting on his proposal to approach the Lakes from the east coast. Yet in fact, the day before Gordon discovered the obstacle put in his path by the Fola Falls, Chaillé-Long had taken an important step in the annexation of East Africa to the Khedive's dominions. On October 16, 1875, Egyptian troops duly landed at Kismayu, on the Juba River, and occupied its semi-derelict fort, armed with guns removed years before from a wrecked Dutch man-of-war. The Zanzibari flag was hauled down, and the Egyptian colors hoisted in its place amid the cheers for the Khedive of the Egyptian soldiers. In this classic nineteenth-century manner Egypt staked out its magnificent claim, and Chaillé-Long, choosing a suitable site a little way from the sea, settled down to await further orders from his superior officer, Gordon. "When you are safely established on the Indian Ocean, I will let you know when and where I can meet you," Gordon had said to Chaillé-Long when he bade him good-bye at Rejaf. And Chaillé-Long thought that enough. He did not worry how such communication was to be established. He trusted in Gordon. But he had made one vital error. The port for the East African hinterland was Mombasa. Such communication as Kismayu had with the interior led to Abyssinia, and was useless for the base of an expedition to the Victoria Nyanza. Chaillé-Long knew that Gordon had proposed Mombasa, but he did not appear to think that the change of plan — the reason for which he never understood — would be fatal to the project. On the contrary, he was full of hope as, with 1300 men of all arms — a much larger force than Gordon mentioned — and a small camel transport corps, he waited through October and November for the orders to join his chief, the friendliness of the natives in his immediate neighborhood appearing an additional guarantee of success.

Chaillé-Long would have better interpreted the spirit of his orders if he had gone to Mombasa. But, in that case, Gordon's reaction would almost certainly have been the same. For, if he had not forgotten about his East African plan, it was as safely pigeonholed in his mind as if it had been in any cupboard of archives in Whitehall. The truth was that the vicissitudes of that summer and autumn left him in no position to battle with the doubts and disillusionment which attacked him from every side. His *amour propre* as a soldier was outraged by the cowardice of his troops, his zeal as an administrator by the slackness and dishonesty of the pashas in Cairo and Khartoum. He had the idea that the Khedive was tired of him. In the north of his province the slavers were at their old games; in the south the natives were no longer friendly, and although he took a high hand as Governor-General to enforce his authority, seizing their cattle and killing them when necessary, the process was infinitely distasteful. He was still determined (so long as Ismail wished it) to hoist the Khedive's flag on the Lakes, but he drew no impulse from his old belief in the essential righteousness of his expedition. When his well-filled post bag arrived, containing a vast number of personal letters in addition to official correspondence, he groaned. For among them he knew he would find congratulations from philanthropists at home on his work for the "poor blacks." His answer was to tell them that he was simply leading "a pillaging horde of brigands." These well-meaning people, he said, should give up their comfortable homes, and come and see how their favorite blacks took to the processes of civilization. "We do not want your cloth; we do not want your beads: we want you to go away" — this was the cry which rang in his ears. By the middle of November, when Chaillé-Long had spent four weeks waiting at Kismayu, Gordon, "nearly dead with an attack of liver" and far from having any thought of trying to meet him, was on the verge of resigning his post. He did not see why he should go on slaving for a master who had apparently forgotten his existence.

The crisis came on November 15. Late that day a post bag arrived, and in it a letter, a very cool letter, from Ismail confirming all Gordon's suspicions about the Khedive's attitude towards him. As Gordon read the complaints he grew furious, and then and there wrote out three telegrams of resignation to be sent off in the morning. After opening a few other letters he had not the heart to go on with the rest of his mail, and he went to bed "very much out of sorts." One more chapter in his uneasy career had apparently ended.

On the following morning the station at Dufile hummed with preparations for the Governor-General's departure northwards. The loads had actually been arranged, the soldiers were in readiness for the order to march, when Gordon, who had been looking through the contents of the bag, found another packet under the Khedive's own seal. It was a very thick one — obviously an important communication. Gordon did not know that its passage through Khartoum had excited curiosity, particularly since the Khedive had ordered the Mudir of Fashoda to deliver it personally into the addressee's hands. That functionary, however, had fallen a victim to the long spears of the Shilluks, and the letter was then put into the ordinary bag along with the less urgent and less august correspondence. Now, as Gordon read it, he saw that he had entirely misjudged the master whom he served. For it told Gordon how the Khedive had gone one better than the proposal suggested by his Governor-General of the Equator, how he had actually put Admiral M'Killop with three men-of-war, to say nothing of Chaillé-Long and six hundred troops, under his orders, and sent them to Juba. All Gordon had to do, therefore, was to march upon that river and thus carry out his part of the plan.

Apart from the very civil, even fulsome tone of the letter, the fact that the Khedive had acted on his advice in this matter of high politics was proof of the esteem in which he held Gordon, who, on his side, recognizing that "the man had gone to all this expense" under the impression that Gordon would stick to him, at once destroyed his telegrams of resignation and countermanded his troops' marching orders. "So now I am in for it," he writes four days later, when he had had time to think the matter over.

But he makes no effort to carry out the Khedive's orders,

though it was clear that the *coup* could not succeed unless accomplished rapidly. On the contrary, the power of decision seems to have left him. He declares he will not even explore the Lakes; he does not mind whether there are two lakes or a million, and whether or not the Nile has a source. He does not feel in a fit state to explore anything except his way out of the province. He writes all this with the more gusto since, at the end of December, Gessi arrived at Dufile with his caravan, bearing the sections of the steamer, and it was now only a matter of weeks before it sailed on the unknown waters of Lake Albert. But on the East African scheme he is silent.

The real reason that prevented Gordon from presenting to us the piquant spectacle of a Colonel in the British Army heading an expedition which might have been a cause of war between Great Britain and Egypt was probably because he knew that its political implications made it impossible. Later on he gave military reasons for his refusal to carry it through. But if his troops were sufficiently trustworthy to enable him to fulfill his intention of hoisting the Khedive's flag on the Victoria Nyanza, which meant reckoning with Mtesa, the powerful King of Uganda, they should have been able to cross the Kenya highlands, where any opposition would be on a much smaller scale.

Whether or not Gordon held off because he foresaw what would happen, the expedition to Kismayu soon elicited the thunders of Downing Street. When the Sultan of Zanzibar realized what was happening, he appealed to the British Government to help him against "the Egyptian pirates." Lord Derby, the Foreign Secretary, at once protested to the Khedive on this infringement of Zanzibari rights; Ismail was in no position to resist, and on December 25, 1875, Chaillé-Long received orders to withdraw his troops and return to Suez immediately. It was the merit of Victorian statesmanship that it did not recognize in foreign politics the maxim that what is sauce for the goose is also sauce for the gander, or it might have been hard put to it to explain why the Egyptians should not do at Kismayu what the British had done at Aden.

Gordon, of course, did not know of these international *pourparlers* when some three weeks later he definitely stated that he had given up any idea of going to the sea with his troops. He justified himself mainly on the insufficiency of his forces. But he also adduced the impracticability of Kismayu as a base.

My proposal was that the Khedive should take Formosa Bay, or rather to the north of it, where the Dana or Ozy river debouches. It is said by Kraft to be navigable to Mount Kenia. Also I was under the impression Lake Baringo, or Ngo, joined Lake Victoria, which Stanley says it does not. The Khedive takes the exit of the Juba, whose course is from north to south, and therefore would be of no use, if navigable, to me. The Juba is much farther off, as the coast trends to the east. He sent off M'Killop and Long, and told them to wait for me. They will wait a long time, I expect.

Six or seven weeks later Gordon saw in the papers — he always read them carefully, even to the fashionable intelligence — that the Khedive had withdrawn his troops from the Juba by command of the British Government. "He is a Hindoo Prince" was his somewhat unfeeling comment on Ismail's yielding to *force majeure* exercised on him as the direct result of following Gordon's own suggestion. This was the last heard of a scheme born out of due time. But Gordon still hoped to hoist the Egyptian flag on Lake Victoria and so secure possession of it to the Khedive; "by strict international law the Lakes are his if he hoists his flag first on them," Gordon tells Augusta, adding that he fears much the Khedive will feel his forced retreat from the Zanzibari coast, "and connect it with me for proposing it."

He had other worries. He paid £30 for cognac, and the whole consignment was lost. He was furious with his brother Henry's "good-natured disposition" in helping Chippindall to return, for Gordon did not want him and ultimately sent a telegram to stop his departure. "These two, Watson and Chipp, have cost nearly £3000 between them and done nothing," he tells Augusta in February 1876. Even his inexorable sister's servant troubles leave him unmoved. "Why do you need two servants to wait on you? One would surely be enough. Learn to 'pig it' and you will be the happier." If Mary and Cook wish to leave, let them do so. For his part, he likes constant change in his establishment. Later on he apologizes for his "**X** letter." Then, after unburdening himself about a certain L. A. Lucas, a young man with £1600 a year who wanted to explore Central Africa and for whom it would have been much better "if he had been born a bricklayer's son," he declares that "after all he is only another *me*, and will be removed, when it seems good, without any action, on my part — " Gordon's pen makes the dash as he looks with approval on the punctuation of his last sentence, and there follows it in brackets, "Are my stops better? I never learnt grammar, or dancing." This, however, is the pride that apes humility, for Augusta spells "appetite" with one *p*, and he cuts out the word and sticks it on his letter in reply. "I can never let bad spelling pass," he says. When he himself writes "dreampt" he corrects it to "dreamed," but lets the former word stand in self-confession.

The thing had a moral background, since people were apt to deny their faults, which was a sin. At the same time he liked sinners better than saints. It was an odd world. He naturally had a contempt for the native witch doctors, yet when one of them put incantations upon him he felt uneasy at being thus magicked. Another delusion — one found them everywhere. The notion, for instance, that the Irish were good soldiers, or that the English were a Christian nation. The Irish were "poor fighters," and clearly the English worshiped golden idols, for he saw in the papers that Archbishop Tait had in two years bestowed patronage to the extent of £5000 a year on his own relations and only £1500 on outsiders.

In the end his thoughts always returned to Equatoria, and would be colored by his mood of the moment. He might express astonishment that Lady Baker, who had accompanied her husband, managed to stand the climate and tell Augusta the somewhat shocking news that in Equatoria she wore "bloomers" — or he might be annoyed that Baker had ever undertaken his expedition, which Gordon said the Prince of Wales had forced on the Khedive, causing him to spend £500,000. But, if Baker had been placed in Equatoria by the future King Edward VII, Gordon was very sure that he himself had been put there by God — like Bismarck, he told Augusta mischievously, knowing she was a woman without humor.

4. Gordon Leaves Equatoria

As he thought over the political future of Central Africa, he found it difficult to make up his mind. On the one hand, this region of the Lakes — and by January 1876 he was in the middle of it at Mrooli — was an impossible country. No mortal would ever civilize the myriads of natives. "They may become sharper by contact with the world, but they will ever be a lazy, unenterprising, happy lot," the energetic, enterprising, and unhappy Englishman writes in his journal, as he wonders how it is that, in spite of their numbers, they manage to get along without any law and yet have very little crime. The happy but ignoble savage is constantly the somewhat envious object of Gordon's thoughts. On the other hand, God, the real ruler of the country, was life, and true life was movement, activity, as we should see in the future world which Gordon's vision pictured kinetically pulsing through endless time; it followed that the Lakes had to be opened up to the energy of which civilization was the dynamo. This process, in its turn, created other problems. Kaba Rega, the ruler of Unyoro, was difficult and refractory, and was backed by Mtesa, who wrote a letter to "Sir Canell Gorlden" to tell him this. "I will ask you one thing but let it may please you all we Europeion for I say if I want to go to Bommbey if the governour and if the governous of Bommbey refuse me to past will I not find the orther road therefor I pray you my friends hear this my letter."

The question was not well phrased, but it was astute, and just the sort of thing to raise all Gordon's old doubts of the righteousness of civilizing the blacks. Unfortunately Mtesa followed it up with the treacherous proposal that he should ally himself with Gordon and divide Kaba Rega's dominions between them. Certainly Mtesa was a poor creature, by no means the excellent and powerful monarch described by Baker, but a bloodthirsty polygamist, a wretched general, a trimmer between Islam, Christianity, and his own magic — in short, "a native like the rest, neither better nor worse." Yet Gordon pitied him, not the least because the C.M.S. Mission at his Court was thinking more of the flag than the Bible — a deliberate and detestable confusion of the secular and spiritual. He dispatched the missionaries a note on the policy they ought to pursue "if they would benefit Mtesa in a permanent way." He does his best for the poor deluded monarch, sending him the German Dr. Schnitzer, better known as Emin Effendi, the only really efficient government servant Cairo had provided for the Equatorial Province during Gordon's governorship.

Gordon wrote to the missionaries in September 1876, shortly before he reached his farthest south at Nyamyongo, sixty miles from Lake Victoria, upon which he had hoped to unfurl the crescent and star of Egypt. He realized now that the Union Jack was a rival. He wrote in his journal: —

Every little thing helps to deepen this dislike [of the Egyptians for the English], our interference at Zanzibar, in Abyssinia, and now this Mission which, as composed (I expect by Baker), is more secular than spiritual. If this Mission does not act judiciously they will prove the ruin of Mtesa. . . . If they would benefit him and not ruin him, they should cement as close an alliance with Egypt as possible: an antagonistic attitude would be disastrous. However well-disciplined or armed Mtesa's people may become, it would be short work for Egypt to overcome Uganda.

By this time, however, Gordon's thoughts were centred no longer on Equatorial Africa. He was thinking of England, and he had already ordered his fur coat to be sent to Shepheard's Hotel, where he expected to be at Christmas. On September 15, he turned his face homeward. Success and failure had come in equal measure. If his goal, the Victoria Nyanza, had eluded him, Lake Albert had given up its secrets. True to his resolve not to give the Royal Geographical Society any excuse for offering him a medal, he had sent Gessi ahead with nuggars to explore that lake, and Gessi had reported that its southern end was a *cul-de-sac,* thus clearing up one mystery of the Nile. When Gordon subsequently steamed on the waters of the lake he experienced no thrill at doing what had never been done before. "What a wilderness this is up here," he writes, with his sensitiveness to the desolation bred by the tropics; "not a sound to be heard and all so lifeless and apparently miserable." This misery impressed itself in full measure on him while he was surveying the Victoria Nile along its innavigable portion above the Murchison Falls, making immense marches day after day in a merciless climate.

This professional pursuit, lovingly practised by him ever since the Crimea, caused him during the summer of 1876 to spend some of the most strenuous weeks of his life. "I am nearly dead," he writes on August 6. "To map the river for eight or ten miles I have had to walk in pouring rain through jungle some eighteen miles." Two days later is the following entry: "We got over fifteen miles to-day — terrible work. Such a country of ravines and gullies! As we got in, down came a deluge of rain, and we have all our things wet. Poor men, it is terrible work for them." And he adds, "I never had such fatigue. It has utterly prostrated me — a deadly coldness and emptiness of the stomach makes you feel inclined to drop. Fifteen drops of chlorodyne, however, set me up. What misery! and what for?" But in the end the work was done, and Gordon was quite sure no one would ever do it again.

Yet his health remained unimpaired, as the marches he made on his return northwards through the hostile territories of Kaba Rega, of Unyoro, sufficiently showed. Their retreat, with enemies lurking everywhere in the high grass, blowing horns and beating drums, might have been disastrous — if their only enterprising foes had not been the mosquitoes. Still Gordon was not at ease, for he had with him only a hundred soldiers, of whom thirty were mere boys, and as he thought of the plight they were in he felt a pain in the heart. But as he was reading the Psalms for the day on September 24, when the danger of attack seemed greatest, he drew comfort from the first verse: "I am well pleased that the Lord hath heard the voice of my prayer." By enormous daily marches, one being thirty-five miles, he crossed the Unyoro country, ultimately reaching Lake Albert at Chibero, halfway down the east coast, where he intended to establish an Egyptian Government station. His steamer met him there early in October, and by the end of the month he was in Khartoum. Though there he was pleased to see "English sparrows" once again, he was less sure now that he wanted to return to England for good, or even to go on leave.

In his journal he argued the pros and cons.

> Comfort-of-body — a very strong gentleman — says, "You are well; you have done enough; go home; go home, and be quiet and risk no more." Mr. Reason says, "What is the use of opening more country to such a Government? There is more now under their power than they will ever manage. Retire now, and avoid troubles with Mtesa, and the Mission." But Mr. Something (I do not know what) says, "Shut your eyes to what may happen in the future; leave that to God, and do what you think will open the country thoroughly to both Lakes. Do this, not for H.H. or for his Government, but do it blindly and in faith." An oracle also says, "Let your decision rest on the way H.H. is disposed; if he desires you to stay, then stay; but if he seems indifferent, then do not hesitate, but go away for good."

Such were the conflicting opinions that Gordon carried with him down the Nile, his suite consisting of one black boy and a lioness cub.

A chance circumstance put an end to his decision. At Korośko he heard how Ismail Pasha Saddyk, the Khedive's Minister of Finance, had recently passed in a *dahabia* with the windows railed up, on his way to exile and death, a victim of his sovereign's caprice. Gordon's pity was aroused. "How God works!" he wrote. "When I was going up to the Sudan, Ismail Pasha Saddyk was all powerful: when I am coming down, few would envy his lot." And he adds, "I have D.V. made up my mind to serve the Khedive no longer."

Such was Gordon's intention when he reached Cairo, and so he informed Cherif Pasha. But he had to take leave of the Khedive, and at this interview Ismail exerted all his personal fascination to keep Gordon in his service. Gordon pointed out the uselessness of his attempting to suppress the slave trade when the Sudan Government in Khartoum was a centre of corruption; and Ismail, lavish with promises, said that the irregularities there should cease. Upon this Gordon consented to go back, but, as he did not believe Ismail had the power to carry out his promise, he still considered himself a free man. He reached home on Christmas Eve, 1876, to be greeted by the press with a warmth that recalled the welcome he had received on his return from China. He had been away for three years — "three years without a Sunday."

V

GOVERNOR–GENERAL OF THE SUDAN
(1877–1879)

When Allah made the Sudan he laughed.
Arabic proverb

Light, sandy soil. — LORD SALISBURY

Who is the Sudan? — RUSKIN

1. Fighting the Slavers

The quiet for which Gordon had longed, the peaceful seclusion of a middle-class Victorian home in a provincial town, "the staying in bed till noon," were not to be his. He had been less than a week in England when the "pillar" that had brought him to Southampton seemed about to take a new direction. Public opinion at the moment was preoccupied with the Bulgarian question, and when the *Times*, with the superb self-confidence John Bull then felt in the native superiority of the Englishman, declared that if Gordon were made Governor of Bulgaria that province would become as peaceful as an English county, it seemed as if the most promising solution for a troublesome problem had been found. We have no record of Gordon's own feelings about this proposal, which opened up a vista of limitless possibilities; clearly it was congenial, and there can be no doubt that he would have accepted the opportunity with as much eagerness as his fatalism, now sanguine, now pessimistic, would have allowed. The suggestion of the *Times*, whether or not inspired from Downing Street, was taken up by the Foreign Secretary, and on January 11, 1877, Gordon saw Lord Derby, whose "big stick" he had disliked in Egypt. The result was so far favorable that he telegraphed to H. C. Vivian, the British Diplomatic Agent in Cairo, asking him to tell the Khedive he did not intend to return. Then obstacles arose. The Powers were jealous of an Englishman being appointed to such a post, and it was objected that a Christian could not be put over a population that was in part Moslem. The guild of royalties, too, meant to keep Bulgaria for one of themselves. So the prize eluded

Gordon, but it is impossible to believe that his impulsive temperament would have enabled him to steer his way for long through the quicksands of Balkan politics. Now, as this vision of service faded, and as he also gave up a half-formed idea of taking a position in Turkey under the reforming Grand Vizier, Midhat Pasha, he turned again to his old project of opening up East Africa, which he proposed to do with Gessi under a concession from the Sultan of Zanzibar. Once again the plan, afterwards taken up by the British East African Company, was still-born, for Ismail, determined not to let Gordon escape him, replied to his message of resignation with a telegram of friendly protest. He did not believe, said the Khedive, that a gentleman like Gordon could fail to keep a solemn promise, and he therefore confidently awaited his return to Egypt. In a quandary Gordon asked the advice of the Duke of Cambridge, who told him he was in honor bound to go. Gordon hesitated. He looked at the pillar — and the pillar stood still. Then it began to move, but not so far south as Equatoria. This was as well, for in any case Gordon did not want to go back to the Lakes. He had, in fact, decided to have the whole Sudan or nothing. He consulted his brother Henry at Woolwich. On his return he prayed. "Head to go, Tail to stay. It fell Head! ! !" The postcard to Augusta on which this is written bears the date "22.1.77." The whole Sudan or nothing — this was the promise he made to his friends Gerald Graham and Watson, with whom he dined the night before he left England, and he did not believe Ismail would ever agree to it. He had, however, written a "sharp note to the F.O." to support him in his claim. Yet he was skeptical. "I think you will see me back in six weeks," he wrote to Augusta on the day of his departure. As often happened, Gordon was wrong; he did not return till 1880.

At first it looked as if his prophecy would be realized. For two or three days his business hung fire. The Khedive and

Cherif Pasha were aloof, too busy to hear all Gordon had to say, and the influence of pashadom was obviously hostile to the finest appointment in the Government — a post carrying a salary of £12,000 a year, plus enormous opportunities of private enrichment — going to a Christian and a foreigner. As a compromise, Gordon proposed that Tewfik, the Khedive's son and heir, should be appointed Viceroy; he felt it was possibly unwise, but he did not care, "for He rules." Then the intervention of Vivian — Vivian is a stuck-up donkey, Gordon tells Augusta, that animal being expressed by the ideogram of an ass's head and a pair of very long ears — led to the Khedive deciding to give Gordon what he wanted. On February 13 he was received by Ismail, who received him "reproachfully." Gordon explained his views. He writes: —

> Then I began, and told him all; and then he gave me the Sudan, and I leave on Saturday morning. I am so very glad to get away; for I am very weary. I go up alone with an infinite Almighty God to direct and guide me, and am glad to so trust Him as to fear nothing, and indeed to feel sure of success.

With this confidence in being a divine instrument, he started out to govern an area as large as Europe west of the Rhine and south of the Alps, an area which included his former province of Equatoria. For Ismail he experienced a lively gratitude. The Khedive had made him a Marshal — "so I and the Duke of Cambridge are equals," ran Gordon's comment [1] — and sent him a uniform all covered with gold and worth £150. "He has given me all the coast of the Red Sea, even to Berbera, opposite Aden. 'Ask of me, and I will give thee to the half of my kingdom.' It is an immense command." And over all these provinces Gordon was absolute, wielding the power of life and death.

Yet he was only "very, very slightly elated by his honors

[1] Gordon seems to have forgotten that he was already a Marshal in the Chinese Army.

and powers," an elation arising not from conceit, but from the feeling that Ismail trusted him. For where others, as Gordon believed, would be crushed by the immense charge, he himself felt as if he "had naught to do with the Government." God must undertake the work, and he for the moment was simply used as His instrument. For that reason he was sure of success; in any case, the future was already mapped out in detail. "The Negro, the Arab and the Bedouin's course — their meeting with me, etc. — is decreed." With this conviction in predestination, to which every pious Moslem in his vast principality would have subscribed, Gordon began another three years' work of making others do what he wanted. It was not illogical, because he believed that he stood as the interpreter of God's Will, and that he spoke with the voice of God.

Armed with this dangerous strength, Gordon entered upon the duties of his viceroyalty. He began by a visit to Massawa, — now an Italian possession, but then a Sudan port, — where he tried, with little success, to arrange the tangled relations between Egypt and Abyssinia. Immediately news reached him that Darfur, nearly a thousand miles to the westward, was in revolt; though he did not altogether believe it, he decided to go on there from Khartoum as soon as he could. The camel was henceforth to take the place of the steamer on his incessant travels and to have a share in coloring Gordon's always sombre thoughts. Unable through his ignorance of Arabic to converse with his staff, Gordon had only his thoughts for company, and the silent, cushioned feet of his animal suggested to him that his life in those interminable and scorching deserts was a living death, and he wondered how it was that, being without ambitions, he had reached so exalted a rank. True, he was its victim. Every time he dismounted from his camel eight or ten men insisted on helping him off as if he were an invalid; in camp, sentries were all round him; when, on the

Photo E.N.A.

THE GORDON MEMORIAL AT KHARTOUM
Onslow Ford

march, he got down to walk, everyone did the same, so that, furious, he mounted again. All these small things easily annoyed him, but, while he personally found the pomp and circumstance intolerably irksome, it gave him a sardonic pleasure to call to mind many others he knew to whom all this incense would be the breath of their nostrils. And sometimes he thought with regret of Bulgaria. Regret turned to downright anger when he heard that W. G. Palgrave had been made British representative in that country — "he is," he told Augusta, "the most untruthful, intriguing fellow I ever met."

It was a kind of escape to lengthen out the stages of his journey, until these assumed almost mythical proportions — thirty, fifty miles a day, and then, in the April heats, 150 miles in sixty hours. Camels and men suffered, but Gordon always cherished a passion for speed, and now the magnitude of the country he ruled obsessed him. He must hurry on and on; with terrific exertion he calculated he might, "under God's administration," make a good province of the Sudan in two or three years; in the meantime he would not be gentle, the disease was too grave for easy remedies. So after many hundreds of miles on camel-back he reached his capital, Khartoum, and took up his quarters in the immense palace, "as large as Marlborough House and swarming with useless servants," among them a eunuch whose business (Gordon explained to Augusta) was to look after the Viceroy's harem. Gordon also found that Ayub Pasha's sister had broken all the 130 windows and cut the divans in pieces when she heard of her brother's supersession. "What a cat!" he says.

Gordon, always apt to interpret the anxiety of the natives to worship power as a personal compliment to his own integrity, believed that the inhabitants rejoiced in his arrival. They wanted justice, and were perfectly willing to take it from a Christian source — which showed how absurd was the reason for refusing to put him over the Bulgarians, of whom only one third were Moslems.[1] Still, there were solid causes for the people's joy. For one thing, he abolished the courbash, and there were no more daily floggings in Khartoum. For another, he received the ulema and the sheikhs (whom his predecessor had treated with arrogance), his visitors squatting on the divans and apparently ready to stay until the Day of Judgment. At last Gordon would rise and say in English, "Now, old bird, it is time for you to go!" which they would take as still another compliment from the Pasha who had restored the privileges Ayub had deprived them of, and they would depart highly pleased at their reception, salaaming and kissing their hands before clasping his. The many whom he could not see in person were told to put their petitions in a box at the palace gate. Honesty suddenly seemed to have become the fashion, for the clerks now brought to the Treasury the bribes offered them by petitioners. So Gordon optimistically told his sister, and felt the more convinced that a new era had begun for the unhappy Sudan. A month or two later he discovered that his Arab private secretary, whom he implicitly trusted, had been taking bribes to the extent of £3000. Yet, as he thought of the apparently hopeless tangle in which things were tied upon earth, and especially in the Sudan, his Biblical knowledge told him that the ground, and not man, had been cursed. On the contrary, man was blessed. . . .

The bashi-bazouks, the Turkish irregulars on whom the Sudan Government had hitherto relied, hardly reflected this benevolence, and Gordon was anxious to disband them, as he had disbanded the Ever-Victorious — a dangerous job, a thing that only a man who had the Almighty with him could do, and even then prudence counseled the need of dealing gently

[1] According to a reference book of about this period, 70 per cent of the population of Bulgaria were members of the Greek Church. This leaves even less than a third to be divided between Mohammedans, Jews, Roman Catholics, and smaller sects.

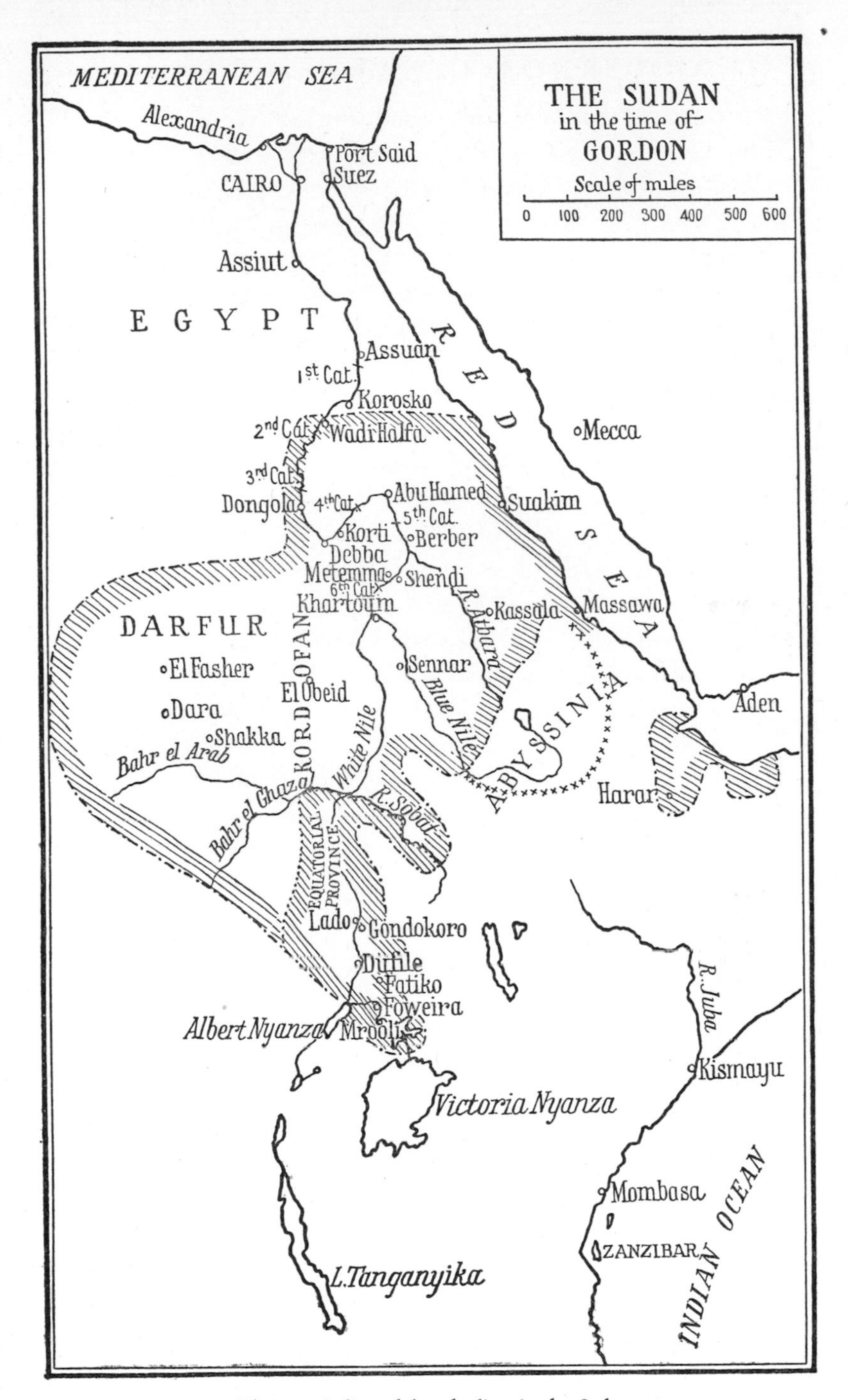

The area indicated by shading is the Sudan

with the army officers and vested interests generally. So we find Gordon, who soon quarreled with and dismissed his Egyptian deputy, Halid Pasha (he would "have no Mayor of the Palace in Khartoum"), congratulating himself in one of his quieter moods on having no Europeans in his administration, for the reason that they were too energetic and would get him into too many scrapes. Here was a change of mind indeed from the opinions he had held in Equatoria!

Undoubtedly the Governor-General's lone eminence was dangerous, and he told Vivian in Cairo that if anything happened to him the Khedive was to be defended from all blame. Good honest Ismail! From his exalted position in Khartoum, Gordon saw how impotent was the Khedive in far-off Egypt to stop the slave trade. In one of his more sanguine moments, when he had just arrived in Khartoum, he believed he had solved the ever-pressing problem. He introduced a simple plan, which required all actual slaves to be registered by the ensuing January 1 — after that date no further registration would be allowed. True, it recognized the proprietary rights of actual slave-owners, and so fell far short of the Anti-Slavery Society's programme; but Gordon did not feel very tender towards the Exeter Hall devotees, and, in any case, he considered his project, if enforced, would mean the end of slave-hunting. At the moment, however, the question took a second place, for the rumblings of the national movement, which later on engulfed the whole Sudan, were growing more ominous. At first he had not taken the Darfur news very seriously. But the information that now reached him in Khartoum left no doubt of the gravity of the situation.

Darfur was in revolt, Gordon believed, against the abominable tyranny of the Egyptian Governors and their bashi-bazouks; if the Government showed a change of heart, then the people would do likewise. But action had to be taken at once, for at the capital of Darfur, El Fasher, and other stations, 16,000 troops were surrounded. Several hundred miles of desert separated them from Khartoum and the Nile, and made their relief difficult. Worse still, a formidable body of 3000 Negro troops, belonging to Zobeir Pasha, greatest of the slave-hunters, threatened to join the insurgent Sultan. While Gordon was in Equatoria, Ismail had made Zobeir a pasha, hoping thereby to keep him quiet, if not loyal. The hope proved vain, for Zobeir's ambitions were set on the Governor-Generalship, so Ismail, playing upon his vanity, told him to come to Cairo and argue out before him his differences with Ayub Pasha. Zobeir walked into the trap and found himself a prisoner. Thus, thanks to Ismail's astuteness, Gordon had to deal, not with the lion, but with the lion's cub, Zobeir's son Soliman, a vain, if attractive, youngster whose fate became interwoven with that of Gordon.

To meet this menacing movement against the whole Egyptian régime in the Sudan, Gordon started for Darfur after a fortnight in Khartoum. With him he took 300 camelry, of whom only his bodyguard of a hundred were reliable troops: "Three hundred to relieve 16,000," ran the caption in Gordon's mind. He felt, however, the same belief in success that accompanied him in China and in Equatoria. The pitcher which goes often to the well is broken at last, and six and a half years later Gordon's luck was to change. But for the moment it held. His strength, then as always, lay in his indifference to what might befall him. He threw against fortune with the dice loaded in his favor: if he won, so much the better; if he failed, it only meant he "would have no more worries." His fatalism made him perfectly candid with himself. As he dashed off on the most famous of his exploits, he decided that his success in China and the Lakes had been due to a series of flukes. Or, rather, it simply meant that these things were part of the universal scheme. "A sack of rice," he said, "jolting on a camel would do as much as I *think* I do."

To the harried Egyptian garrisons, he appeared more like Providence. After riding "like a madman" across Kordofan he reached Foggia, the frontier post of Darfur, unheralded and alone. His camel had outpaced all his escort; the Arab sheikh acting as his guide told him he was the telegraph. Such desert travel was unheard of, and took everyone by surprise. Foggia was dozing as usual under its pitiless sun. Suddenly a speck appeared on the desert, and the next moment turned into Gordon in his coat of gold. He rode straight into the fort. The Governor, he said, "had not time to gather himself together before the enemy was upon him"; only the artillerymen had presence of mind and fired a salute. This rapidity of movement heartened friends and frightened enemies as from Foggia he moved on to relieve the beleaguered garrisons through a miserable country with wells of putrid water thirty and forty miles apart. He had still only 500 troops. The population was wholly hostile. As he advanced, the fate that later attended Hicks Pasha and his 10,000 might well have been his. An uneasy Gordon felt the same pain in the heart which he had experienced the year before under similar circumstances in the highlands of Unyoro, a pain partly physical and partly mental, inspired by the fear, not of death, but of the catastrophe that this would be for the country he governed. But all went well, and on July 13 — significant day of the month in Gordon's life — he reached Dara, where the garrison had been for half a year without news. "It was like the relief of Lucknow," he wrote in his journal. "Everything was at famine prices."

War was his *métier*. In everything else he was an amateur, with the amateur's self-conscious vanity in his cleverness; but in war he was a master, a virtuoso. The warlike natives, not aware of it and seeing the meagre relief force, again threatened the station, and forced a battle upon the reluctant Gordon. They attacked with impetuosity, and his troops wavered as the spears fell thickly upon them. One narrowly missed the white Pasha. But in the thick of the fight he calmly lit a cigarette, and then, with his bodyguard of a hundred, snatched victory from defeat. "Never in the world did I see such a thing," said one of the friendly sheikhs who was fighting on the Egyptian side.

Gordon took this campaign in his stride; he was happier on the march than in towns, with all their ceremonies and artificialities, where he was treated "like an ingot of gold." On camel-back he could think and pray secure from interruption — an immense boon. He found that, when he prayed for the chiefs he was about to see for the first time, their meeting was marked by the feeling that something had already passed between him and them. It was to prayer, prayer for his enemies, that this veteran general of forty-four attributed the success of his arms, though his distaste for war grew stronger with each year that went by. How he hated killing even mosquitoes! Yet he felt so strongly death was not an evil to man that, had he thought the shooting of any number of slave-dealers would avail in stopping the slave trade, he would have shot them without the least compunction.

The misery of the people in Darfur caused his mind to run continually on the ultimate questions of good and evil. To reconcile the infinite goodness of God with all the wretchedness around him — that was the problem. How was mankind to return to Eden? How was sin to be overcome? It became clearer if one realized that Adam was made outside the Garden, and only then put into it. True, Eve was there taken from his side, but no conception occurred in Eden, for Adam begot Cain after our grandparents had been driven out of Paradise. As a result our bodies were sinful, and the world was full of unhappiness; at the same time each one of us was the incarnation of the Godhead, and God's object in creating us and all other things was to show His manifold wisdom.

The sights Gordon continually met with in this slave hunting province demanded all the consolation he could draw from Biblical cosmogony. He read the *Iliad*, and remarked how Achilles' wrath was on account of a slave-girl he had captured. Slavery was a canker which through the ages had eaten into the heart of Egypt. Yet the Prophecy of Isaiah told him that Egypt gave asylum to Israel and to the Saviour, and for that reason it would be blessed. When he could not see any signs of this coming to pass, it struck him that no rain fell in Egypt — rain being the type of the Holy Ghost — and the country was thus spiritually parched. From every point of view the problem was baffling. His duty was to stamp out the slave trade, and he did not even know what powers he had legally to do it. The British view, as embodied in the Anglo-Egyptian Convention, signed in the summer of 1877, was that anyone engaged in the slave trade, either directly or indirectly, should be held guilty of stealing with intent to murder. For that the penalty was death. But the Khedive's decree only prohibited the sale of slaves in the Sudan after twelve years, and when Gordon asked Nubar if the sale of slaves was legal he received the answer that it was so. Thereupon Gordon pointed out that the British warships in the Red Sea were acting illegally in seizing slaves found in Egyptian ships, an observation to which no reply was given.

Morally the question was no simpler. Were the slave-owners without rights? Was he expected to shoot them all out of hand? Did not cargoes of slaves come into Bristol Harbor within living memory? And, supposing he stopped the slave razzias, slavery would still continue so long as slaves were bred from slaves. It was not even possible to distinguish the unfree from the free. When Gordon asked a man about the seven women he had with him the answer was that they were his wives. What could he do then? Risk the imputation of taking away a man's spouse? And, if he did, what was to become of the woman? One could not count on natural affection helping to solve any question that arose, for it was as absent here as on the Sobat. "I found a child whom I had seen yesterday with its mother, left by her," Gordon wrote at this time. "It was a clear case of desertion. . . . This little black creature was of no value, and no one cared for it; even the mother felt it to be a bore."

Of one thing Gordon felt sure: the Brussels Conference, called to deal with the question, would fail. God, he said, — and, with an experience of conferences far exceeding Gordon's, we may smile gloomily at his words, — had never done any of His great works by men. Or, rather, Gordon was sure of two things, the other certainty being that the climate and his responsibilities tried his temper. A bibulous Maltese major-domo gave him nothing fit to eat and got drunk on his brandy; his clerks were so lethargic that he snatched the papers from their hands, and then threw them back at them; or the people he sent for were so slow in coming that Gordon would rush to meet them. These manners became neither a Christian nor a Governor-General, but, while he deplored, he could not amend them. Indeed, as he thought of the criticisms made by members of the Anti-Slavery Society and by stay-at-home clergymen who were "bigots . . . on the churchyard or temperance," his irritation reached as far as England, and he wished such persons could have the edges knocked off by travel. Travelers, from Saint Paul downwards, — and Gordon flattered himself he was one, — were singularly open-minded.

But while Gordon, an irascible contemplative, brooded interminably and indefinitely over the things that have troubled earnest souls since the world began, another Gordon, the cool yet impetuous soldier, had only to hear that Zobeir's slave-raiders, 4000 or so men under the young Soliman, were on the move, to show at once his sureness in judgment and his speed in action. The news reached him that Dara was threatened when he was stamping out the embers of the native rebellion eighty-five miles to the northwards. He started immediately, — at dawn on Friday, August 31, — and thirty-six hours later, alone and unheralded, rode into Dara. He had left his bodyguard far behind, but seven miles from the fort a swarm of flies settled on him and his camel, an unwanted escort which annoyed them both so much that they jolted on quicker than ever. "Imagine to yourself," wrote Gordon, who took a boyish pleasure in record-breaking, "a single, dirty, red-faced man on a camel, ornamented with flies — arriving in the *diwan* all of a sudden. The people were paralyzed, and could not believe their eyes." To them he was the god from the machine.

He found that he had arrived in time. Soliman had not yet opened hostilities, and the message came from him and his chiefs that they wished to call on him that evening. Gordon, who was too tired to eat or to open his letters, answered that he would himself visit their camp on the following morning, and then turned in. His quiet sleep was not the result of any confidence in his power to defeat the slavers in the field. He had 2000 undependable troops; the slavers twice or three times as many of first-rate quality. If it came to fighting, only one issue was possible. Yet Gordon slept quietly, and when he awoke on that Sunday morning we may be sure that he prayed for Soliman, the son of Zobeir, as he habitually prayed for the shiekhs he was about to meet for the first time.

He put on his "golden armor," mounted his horse, and, with a bodyguard of fifty bashi-bazouks ("my robbers," he called them), rode off to the camp of the other robbers miles away. Soliman met him — "a nice-looking lad," he thought — and led him to his tent through lines of Negro soldiers. With approval Gordon remarked their military air, "smart dapper troops, like antelopes, fierce, unsparing, the terror of Central Africa"; he noticed, too, that the whole body of chiefs were "dumb-foundered" at his coming among them. In Soliman's tent he drank a glass of water, then, telling him to come with his family to the divan, Gordon returned to Dara. Soliman and his chiefs obeyed his order. They entered the Governor-General's quarters, seated themselves in a circle, and drank coffee. All were armed to the teeth, a gross breach of etiquette. Taking no notice of this, Gordon in broken Arabic delivered his ultimatum. They must break up their troops, and go out of business. No more slave-raiding. As for Soliman, he was to return to his old headquarters at Shakka, and there await the Governor-General's decision about his future. Gordon's sense of humor appreciated the absurdity of the scene — he pouring out a jargon of kitchen Arabic, supplemented by signs, gestures, and stern looks, to these robber chiefs on whose impassive faces he could read nothing but a stupefied astonishment. It was all the more absurd since he was in their power, and not they in his. But his anger and the prestige of his name prevented them from realizing this. He was angry not merely on the general grounds of their slave-raiding depredations. He felt it intolerable that they should have pillaged the Dara tribes while the Dara fighting men had gone with him to El Fasher as his allies; and he was furious with young Soliman in particular for his ill manners towards Gordon's sick kavass before his arrival — when the wretched fellow was unable to rise at Soliman's approach, the young man had fired three pistol shots close to his head, and nearly killed him with fright. All these griefs Gordon conveyed to Soliman with such fierceness that the young man crumpled up and protested his fidelity.

As Gordon that Sunday afternoon thought over the dramatic events through which he had just passed, he felt sorry for Soliman. He was an "attractive boy of twenty or twenty-two, clearly a spoilt child, who would be all the better for a shaking. Poor little chap! How bitter for him to be suddenly nothing [Gordon drew a line under the word] after having been accustomed to do exactly what he liked, even to killing people." Gordon's mind, forever running on the Old Testament, soon found a parallel. "And David said, 'Deal gently for my sake with the young man.' I will try to do so if I can." He was to have a good deal more trouble before he had finished with his Absalom.

For days the issue still hung in doubt. The slave camp was not broken up, and Gordon received intelligence that some of the slave chiefs were for fighting and that Soliman inclined to support them. On the Monday evening, forty-eight hours after Gordon's return, the situation was still critical, more critical than he realized. He dared not strengthen the fort for fear of frightening his "sheep soldiers," and if it came to hostilities Dara and its garrison would indubitably be wiped out. In these circumstances the friendly chiefs advised Gordon to get Soliman into his power by treachery; but, though he admitted to himself he had been too sanguine, he refused to adopt such an expedient. "If I am treacherous to Soliman," he said to his advisers, "how could *you* ever trust me?" — not a very strong argument, he realized, in that country where years of misgovernment had made men lose all sense of anything beyond their own immediate advantage. Still, the thing was morally indefensible, and Gordon would have nothing to do with it. He told himself that, in any case, God ordered all for the best.

The crisis continued unabated during the following days, while Gordon's feelings for Soliman — he did not seem to have any for himself — oscillated between admiration and pity. He admired him for the way he kept the mightiest of his slave chiefs in order, and pitied him for being the creature of his environment. But he was firm in refusing to give him any position under Government until he showed signs of grace. And Soliman, for his part, would not move until he had a command. At last, after much parleying, with Soliman's chief men showing themselves past masters in the art of trimming and quite mystifying Gordon by their skill in playing party politics, his firmness had its reward. He refused to treat with Soliman, told one of the youth's chiefs that a flogging was what the cub wanted (a statement received with Oriental acquiescence), and for the last time sent him orders to return to Shakka. That Thursday night passed painfully for Gordon, who feared an attack from the now desperate Soliman. But the following day Gordon's Absalom left "in a fearful rage," and the authority of the Governor-General was vindicated. Gordon spent the next forty-eight hours in incorporating many hundreds of the slave troops in his own army. Then, with only four companies, he started for the slave-raiders' nest at Shakka itself. It might be dangerous, but unless it was cleared out Darfur would still be at their mercy.

Everything, however, went well, for Soliman was cowed, and Gordon entered the lair of the slavers in triumphant state. Soliman made a mistake in asking Gordon to stay with him, for the sympathy the Governor-General had previously felt for the young man wilted on closer acquaintance. Soliman flinched when Gordon fired the gun which he had given to him — he was a coward. And he had no idea of business and no sense of propriety — he lolled about, yawned, fondled his naked feet, and used the language of a street boy. He cared nothing for his father, Zobeir, and was so wanting in dignity as to embrace Gordon's feet twice, when he was going to sleep, in his efforts to obtain an official post. Then he tried bribery — bribery to Gordon! Altogether an unpleasant young man, and Gordon warned him and his chiefs before banishing them to various parts of his province that any attempt to revive their slave-raiding would be punished by their death. So when, two years later, Gessi captured and shot Soliman, who had been at his old games, Gordon was unmoved. Yet the ghost of this Absalom helped to prevent Gordon from securing Zobeir for his lieutenant when he went to Khartoum for the last time — and no one, Gordon then believed, could do what Zobeir might have done.

This was the end of Gordon's adventures in wide-spreading Mohammedan Darfur. For the moment, at any rate, he had reduced it to subjection. The natives looked on his visit to Shakka as a miracle; and if Gordon was too sanguine in believing that he had definitely brought another enormous new province within the Khedive's dominions, he had, at least, temporarily asserted the power of the Sudan Government in a wild and remote country. A result of his experiences in Darfur was to make him more sympathetic to Islam. He admired the Moslem's open acknowledgment of God; the Mohammedan might "give himself a good margin in the wife line," but at any rate he never poached on others — which could not be said of "our Christian people." All of us, Gordon told his sister, were more or less pagans — he had read a striking book on the subject, *Modern Christianity a Civilized Heathenism* — and the people of England cared more for their dinners than for anything else. They condemned the slave trade, and thought they had done their duty. "It is very shocking. Will you take some more salmon?" And while his mind ran thus on comfortable England he irritably asked, "What have the F.O. to do with me or I with them? I do not want their aid. I should be unfaithful to H.H. were I to accept it." He had forgotten his appeal to the Foreign Office for support in his demand for the Governorship-General.

Troubles at the other end of the Sudan on the Abyssinian border gave him an opportunity of comparing his Bedouin Arabs of Darfur with the Christian Abyssinians, much to the disadvantage of the Abyssinians, whom he said he hated. Observation and experience naturally tempted him to comparative theology, and caused him to qualify the views he had expressed when it was a question of King Mtesa being instructed by Moslem sheikhs sent from Egypt. Allah and Jehovah — were not these but different names for the same God? Did not Christians and Moslems acknowledge the same Father? Were they not brothers, and one as good as the other? In one point the Moslems were our superiors, for they had no Pharisees with gloomy faces among them. He pushed this practical religious synthesis further by the not very clearly reasoned belief that many Jews were in some way followers of Jesus. It was on the question of the Messiah that Mrs. Freese bluntly told Gordon he was wrong in his suppositions regarding the affinity between Islam and Christianity, and Gordon, though he took contradiction hard, was forced to admit it. "Yes: you were right. They could not know Christ," were the first words he said to her as he entered her drawing-room at Chislehurst on his return home — and then he went on shaking hands and talking of other things, Mrs. Freese tells us in that intimate portrait she has drawn of the strange and vital personality who came into her quiet life.

He went on talking of other things. One marvels at the vitality of a man who, living such a life, was yet able to fill a volume with his theological speculations alone. As he dashed from one end of his viceroyalty to the other in the year 1877, trying to make the sultan's carpet of Oriental story lie flat, he covered nearly 4000 miles on camel-back — in itself an extraordinary achievement. And when on his travels he reached camp, the fuss and responsibilities of being Governor-General at once came upon him. The bigger places were illuminated in his honor, and he had to go out and see them — "a regular sacrifice." He inspected barracks, hospitals, and prisons. The poor cried after him, "We are miserable," and he could not resist telling them he was the same. The great trembled before him, and he felt a grim pleasure. He knew he was feared, thought he was respected, had the intuition he was "not overmuch liked." Petitioners he refused in a loud voice. When callers would not sit down in his presence, he sometimes dragged them to a seat, which upset them; or else he shouted at them until they forgot what they wanted to say from sheer fright. These scenes were frequent and caused amusement to the bystanders. But Gordon, if he also smiled at such things, never ceased to feel the bitter taste of life. He was far from well. He had a pain in his chest "like a crick in the neck." Wine and spirits he had given up — one of the many times in his life that he took this vow of abstinence. His meals occupied only ten minutes of the day. The food was garbage, he said, and in itself destroyed all appetite. It was, in short, a wretched globe, from the country of the blacks, which was too big for proper supervision, to Victorian England, where all was "money, money, money." English products had steadily deteriorated during the past fifteen years. "My dear Augusta, I feel sure it is nearly all over with us," said Gordon, at a time when England had hardly set its hand to the work of opening up Africa, a work which, in any case, Gordon was not at all anxious for his countrymen to undertake.

He yearned for only one thing: "I wish, I wish the King would come again and put things to rights on earth; but His coming is far off, for the whole world must long for Him ere He comes." Very few, he feared, wished this, since it was to wish for death. He himself never ceased to do so. Yet, as he pondered over it, he saw that death would not mean rest. On the contrary, a future life meant active employment, a place where there was no such thing as half-pay idleness. Carrying this pleasant train of thought farther, Gordon decided that in his own times of preëxistence he had surely been actively employed; and the essential feature of the series of incarnations through which he and all others were passing, our Victorian *malgré lui* decided, was progress, a progress towards a perfection always unattainable.

2. Gordon Dabbles in High Finance

This Christian knight, thus engrossed with the problems besetting the Sudan, the world, and himself, was on his way back to Khartoum from the Abyssinian frontier in January 1878 when he received a long telegram from the Khedive. Telegrams from the Khedive were unusual. This clearly indicated a crisis. The Khedive's creditors, it was said, were trying to interfere with his sovereign prerogatives, and since Ismail knew of no one except Gordon Pasha who could help him in his difficulties, he asked him to come at once to Cairo. The prospect was disagreeable. Not so much that Gordon feared the intrigues of the Egyptian capital, or considered himself unfitted to deal with financial questions, as that he felt he had lost, in the rough life he had been leading, all his civilized tastes. Gordon, so far as we are aware, never read Montaigne. Had he done so, he would have known that Montaigne was wrong in saying that the heart of the bravest man beat quicker in going into battle than when sitting down to dinner. Gordon feared the pleasures of the table far more than the hazard of any battlefield.

The punctilious views Gordon held on the loyalty owed by a European to an Oriental master made Ismail's request tantamount to a command, and he reluctantly prepared to obey. On his way north, suffering intensely from the cold desert winds, he began his policy of retrenchment by cutting down his salary. This he had reduced, on receiving his appointment, from £12,000 to £6000 a year. Now he decided to halve it a second time.

At Assuan he was received with much honor by the people,

though he was now outside his province. And he found a note from Lord and Lady Aberdeen, asking him to stop and visit their *dahabia* while on his way down. A cool invitation, he thought, for he knew they only wanted a tow. Still, they were Gordons too, so he stopped and went on board, asking himself "what he would be the Earl of Aberdeen for" and looking with critical eyes on the Countess, "a great fat girl."

"Did you think we were going to ask you for a tow?" they said.

Gordon's answer was blunt. "Yes, and wrote to my sister my suspicions, so I was quite prepared for your request." The Countess blushed. "Lord A.," Gordon records, "said nothing."

However, he gave them a tow, but soon chafed at the waste of time. Then, deciding he did not want any invitations for grouse-shooting or deer-stalking in the Highlands, and irritated at "butterfly people" imposing themselves on a busy man like himself, he ordered the Aberdeens' *dahabia* to be cast off, and added the Earl and Countess to the list of people he meant to avoid in Cairo — Vivian being another.

As he approached the capital, the urgency of his mission was emphasized by a telegram from the Khedive containing an invitation to dinner on his arrival. In any case, the train was not due till eight o'clock; it happened to arrive at nine. What was Gordon's astonishment to find an equerry and the Khedivial carriages at the station! In spite of his being dirty and travel-stained from 350 miles in a dusty railway carriage, he was whisked off to Abdin Palace, where Ismail was still waiting dinner. Even then the Khedive did not go to table until he had led Gordon aside and asked him to be president of an inquiry into the state of the national finances. He said that the Commissioners of the Debt had proved so hostile to him personally that he wished Gordon to object to their being on the board of inquiry. Gordon made not the least difficulty, agreeing the more readily since he thought the Commissioners had been hard on the Khedive. He was not so happy when Ismail assured him he would have the help of his private financial agents, Messrs. Walker and Pasquali, for he mistrusted persons whose names ended in *i* and *o*. At dinner he was treated with all honor, sitting on the Khedive's right hand; afterwards he found himself transported in the true style of the *Thousand and One Nights* to a gorgeous palace. It was full of candelabras, mirrors, and gentlemen to wait on him, and he was not too tired to record in his journal that its grandeurs had lodged General Grant and the Prince of Wales. If its magnificence dazzled Gordon, it did not apparently make him suspicious of the motives underlying such marked treatment, though before he went to bed he regretted his camel.

In fact, Ismail was relying on Gordon's prestige and his reputation for disinterestedness to shield him in the financial crisis that threatened his throne. Little by little the Powers had been tightening their hold on the revenues of Egypt. Owing partly to the Russo-Turkish War, which had made it necessary for the Khedive to send an expeditionary force to help his suzerain, the Sultan, and partly to a low Nile, the year 1877 had proved particularly disastrous to the finances, and it was with the greatest difficulty that enough revenue was raised to meet the claims of the secured creditors, represented by the four European Commissioners of the Debt.[1] While the unsecured creditors sued the Government in the recently established Mixed Courts, and thus directed attention to the bankrupt state of the public finances, official salaries remained unpaid, and government servants were faced with starvation.

It was under these circumstances that Captain Evelyn Baring, the English Commissioner of the Debt, had proposed

[1] The total debt was £81,000,000, on which Ismail was expected to pay no less than 7 per cent.

In October 1877 a board of inquiry into the whole field of Egyptian finance. Ismail accepted the principle of the commission, but refused to agree to Baring's proviso that the commissioners should take part in the inquiry. His suspicion that Baring was personally hostile to himself had something to do with this refusal, which he based on the ground that, as representatives of the creditors, they were interested parties. On this issue Baring decided to fight the Khedive, whom he considered to be at the root of all Egypt's financial troubles, and Ismail, realizing what his refusal entailed, had decided to enlist Gordon as his champion in the struggle against the Debt Commissioners, led by Baring and supported by their respective Foreign Offices. The paradox of two Englishmen being the protagonists in this clash between Egypt and Europe was in keeping with the serio-comic traditions of the political stage on which the drama was played. Both were professional soldiers, both had been educated at "The Shop," and no two men could have been more unlike. Where Gordon was impulsive, Baring was cautious; where Gordon, confident in the honesty of his intentions, thought to employ in high politics the methods of speed and dash which had proved so successful against semi-civilized enemies, Baring never took a step in advance until he had thoroughly consolidated the ground already won, and even then he always kept an eye on his supports. So it was that on March 8, 1878, Gordon and the future Lord Cromer fought the first round of their unequal duel.

When he awoke that morning, Gordon must have known that trouble brewed. This, at any rate, became plain when he called on Vivian and listened to his expressions of astonishment that Gordon should have consented to preside over the inquiry without the Commissioners of the Debt. Gordon, who had known Vivian "as a pretty black-eyed boy at the Royal Military Academy," where he had not been strong enough to stand the life at that rough school, answered tartly that he was free to accept or refuse, implying thereby that so long as he was in the Khedive's service he was under no obligation to consult the British Government regarding his actions — a point of view which would hardly be agreeable to the British Consul-General. After this unsatisfactory interview Gordon went to see Vivian's German colleague, possibly with the idea of obtaining diplomatic support from that quarter. If that were so, Gordon was soon undeceived, for while he was there the French and Austrian Consuls-General came in with Vivian and attacked him for having accepted the presidency of the Commission of Inquiry. When Gordon, thinking always rather of the starving Egyptian officials than of the European financiers who had lent money to the Khedive, repeated what he had told Vivian, they pointed out that Ismail risked his very throne if he persisted in keeping the Commissioners of the Debt out of the inquiry. Gordon was skeptical and scornful, and asked why in that case they did not tell the Khedive so themselves. They replied that it was his business, as His Highness's servant, to do so. "Do you authorize me to tell him your views," he asked, "with any remarks I may make as to the futility of your words?" On the strength of their affirmative, Gordon before dinner that evening passed on to the Khedive the information given him by the representatives of the European Powers. As he expected, Gordon found that "H.H. did not seem to care a bit," saying he was only afraid of England, who, he was sure, would not move. And, still unconscious how delicate was the ground on which he walked, Gordon received without cavil Ismail's orders to arrange the details of the Commission of Inquiry with de Lesseps, who was to be his colleague.

When de Lesseps came to see Gordon amid his palatial grandeurs the next morning, the comedy broadened. With him was Standen, whom Gordon had known as General

Stokes's secretary on the Danube Commission, now one of de Lesseps's colleagues in the Suez Canal Company's administration.

Long residence in Egypt, the Latin temperament, and a young wife made the French *vicomte* indisposed to take the vicissitudes of local politics too seriously. Gordon, slightly contemptuous of "old Lesseps" on moral grounds, had already learned that the Frenchman did not mean to set himself against "the European concert," and the atmosphere on Gordon's side was strained from the start. De Lesseps began by saying that the Commissioners of the Debt must sit upon the board of inquiry. Gordon, whose French was by no means polished, rejoined that it was a *sine qua non* they should not be members, at which de Lesseps, who knew the ground better, merely repeated his statement. In the offing appeared the indispensable Cherif Pasha, at that time Minister of Finance, a fat and lazy Turk, anxious for a quiet life and well aware that Gordon was not a man to assist to that desirable end. Smelling trouble, he entered the room and asked them hopefully if they were agreed. Gordon, already showing a pique that augured ill for his successful playing of the rôle of chairman, did not reply. Lesseps urbanely said, "Yes," at which Gordon stared and then contradicted him. Conversation, always in French, ensued between Cherif and de Lesseps, which ended in Cherif thinking the point was settled when the Frenchman consented to serve without the Commissioners so long as he received permission from Paris. Gordon mistrusted de Lesseps, made sure he was "ratting," and asked Standen to take him into a corner and speak to him. Gordon did the same with the unwilling Cherif, who was bored and huffed with Gordon's intractable attitude. A further parley between the Frenchman and the Turk ended in Cherif coming over to Gordon and telling him that de Lesseps had agreed to the exclusion of the Commissioners. Gordon further disgusted the easy-going Egyptian Foreign Minister by saying, as he accompanied him downstairs on his departure, that de Lesseps would "never stick to it."

Nothing could have been more unpropitious for the success of the *enquête* than this preliminary discussion. The omens seemed no better when Gordon met Baring in one of the many anterooms of his palace. Both bristled, though Gordon disliked Baring more heartily than Baring did Gordon. Gordon was an R.E., Baring an R.A., and the sapper disliked the gunner's "pretentious, grand, patronizing manner," which came the worse from a man who was in the nursery when Gordon was in the Crimea. And now this young man, who knew next to nothing of the country and its people, set himself up as the champion of the bondholders whose 7 per cent extortions were a scandal that cried to heaven. It is not surprising that at this first meeting they crossed swords, Baring objecting to the exclusion of himself and the other Commissioners. Gordon in a huff declared that he would obey the Khedive's orders, and Baring replied that this would be unfair to the creditors. "When oil mixes with water we will mix together," was Gordon's comment on this encounter with the man whom he considered as his enemy. Yet not Gordon but Baring was destined to rehabilitate the finances of Egypt, and to give the country a better government than it had ever known.

But Gordon had no intuition of the fruits that Lord Cromer's rule was to bear in the next generation, and he ran upstairs in no good humor to find de Lesseps closeted with Walker and Pasquali, the Khedive's financial agents. Gordon still found nothing to please him. He did not like Mr. Walker because he parted his hair in the middle and spoke too glibly of millions; Pasquali, he thought, had a ridiculous name — "Pasquali is the sort of person who is ready to sing some operatic piece." Besides, he was an Italian. But these feelings wore off as they talked, and he began to find Walker a pleasant fellow, though it worried him that de Lesseps paid not the least attention to their discussion and rattled on gaily all the time about his friend MacMahon. Discussion, however, clarified the situation sufficiently for Gordon to take up a pen and draft five proposals, the first being that Tewfik Pasha, Ismail's heir, should be president of the Commission. His indifferent French gave out after he had written out four of them, and the last and vital one — that the decrees concerning the payment of the interest on the debt should be temporarily suspended — was in English. So ended an unsatisfactory morning's work.

He and de Lesseps got on better in the afternoon. A private discussion between them showed that they both had goodwill for Ismail, and Gordon began to put down in writing the heads of their agreement when Lesseps, losing patience with his French, took the pen from his hand and drafted a memorandum which recommended cutting down immediately the interest on the debt to 4 per cent, an economy that would probably suffice to balance the Budget while the Commission was holding its inquiry. But the atmosphere grew rapidly worse on the following morning. Gordon called early on de Lesseps, who complacently showed him a warm letter of thanks from Ismail for having consented to serve on the *enquête*. Gordon knew that this had been written under a misapprehension, and de Lesseps showed how little in earnest he was by telling Gordon, as he looked at his young wife, that he was going out for the day in the desert. How could one respect a man who enjoyed a *fête champêtre*? De Lesseps gave him at the same time the copy of a telegram he had sent to Paris. When Gordon read it he saw that de Lesseps counted on the Commissioners of the Debt becoming members of the inquiry. "Oh, my dear old fellow," he protested, "this will never do!" "Well, at any rate, it 's gone," the Frenchman answered, "and now I 'm going too, and I shan't be back till night."

Gordon left the frivolous Frenchman, and went to the Abdin Palace with the telegram in his pocket. There he found Cherif, happily smoking in an anteroom. "Well, what news?" Cherif asked drowsily, using that familiar formula more from politeness than anything else, for when Gordon told him about the telegram it made no impression, and he continued to chat in Turkish with a fellow pasha as if he had no care in the world. Nothing in that calm atmosphere indicated a crisis. But it soon changed when Ismail heard of de Lesseps's telegram to Paris. Out came Pharaoh — as Gordon called the man whom Baring, with his classical tastes, saw rather as a Verres — and threw himself on the sofa, saying he was completely *bouleversé* by de Lesseps's telegram. Since de Lesseps could not be found, the upshot of the Khedive's deliberations was to put the whole matter in Gordon's hands, and Ismail's secretary received orders to send a telegram to this effect to Goschen, as the representative of the bondholders, telling him to arrange matters with Gordon.

Never afraid of responsibility, Gordon at once acted on the Khedive's instructions, and cabled to Goschen that he had recommended His Highness to suspend payment of the next coupon in order to pay the employees and to meet pressing claims. "I will arrange with you," he added, "for the Commission of Inquiry into the Finances." Such confidence was sublime. But repudiation had a much uglier look to Europeans of the nineteenth century than it has to their posterity to-day, and Goschen had a far clearer view of the realities of the situation than Gordon. So he simply answered, "I will not look at you. The matter is in the hands of Her Majesty's Government." Gordon, annoyed but not alarmed by such confidence on the part of the bondholders' representative, suggested to Ismail that his proposals should be carried out by decree. If trouble arose, said Gordon, he would telegraph to Lord Derby that he had recommended this course to the Khedive, and that he was responsible for what was being done. This naïve project to shield the autocratic Khedive behind the authority of an English Colonel of Engineers may have been magnificent, but it was not diplomacy; and Ismail, though ready to use Gordon, hesitated to set himself up against the united front of the Powers. So he retired for a couple of days to his harem, where, if he could not escape care, he would at least be invisible to his Governor-General of the Sudan.

Gordon was left struggling helpless in the diplomatic meshes. Threatening letters began to reach him from Paris. He knew that in Cairo the Europeans thought him a dangerous revolutionary. He scarcely saw anyone, but remained in the sulks, "wishing and wishing that my end had come." His only consolation was going to bed at eight o'clock and so avoiding dinner parties and the drinking of wine. He had, in fact, to admit defeat, a thing personally galling and full of suffering, as he rightly believed, for the Egyptian people. Not that he was without supporters in the House of Commons, but a Tory Government was in power, and from them he believed that he could not hope for any sympathy towards his plans. Before the firmness of Vivian and his French colleague, Ismail wavered, and Gordon, seeing that he had fought in vain, decided to make his own retreat and told the Khedive he would not serve on the Commission if Baring and the other representatives of the bondholders were members. In the end, when he learned that Ismail had "thrown him over," he laughed savagely "at all this farce." He saw that it had been so from the beginning. Yet it was trying to find that Ismail was bored with him, and that all the previous honors were now turned to coldness and neglect. He consoled himself with the reflection that it was for the best, since he would have been bound to quarrel with Ismail over the composition of the inquiry, which Ismail had always meant to pack. When Gordon left after an eventful fortnight, no honors were paid him at the station, and he even had to buy his ticket. "The sun which rose with such splendor," he wrote, "set in the deepest obscurity." Yet his self-confidence was not impaired. He might have been imprudent in speech, but he felt sure he could have unraveled the financial tangle if only the Khedive had been firm. He was less sure about his future in the Sudan, for he knew he had been too outspoken to have strengthened his position. Anyhow, he felt differently now both towards his province and towards his master, Ismail. All his old enthusiasm, he said, had gone. But this did not prevent him from being very severe upon the Raouf he had formerly dispossessed of his Governorship of Gondokoro. Raouf was now a pasha and the Governor of Zeila, on the Red Sea, to which place Gordon traveled from Cairo. And Gordon, a second time, threw him out. Raouf Pasha, however, had his revenge when he succeeded Gordon as Governor-General of the Sudan.

3. Failure

Gordon returned to Khartoum in more than his usual dejection of spirits. He was disheartened at Ismail's duplicity. They were now on the worst of terms, though Gordon believed that all the troubles which fell upon the Khedive during the course of that year and the next would have been avoided had the Khedive taken his advice. Yet he was determined not to remain if the Khedive were dethroned. Apart from knowing that he was working for a master who no longer appreciated his services, Gordon had all the worries of a creaking administration on his shoulders. The Sudan Budget showed an alarming deficit, there was trouble with Abyssinia, and the slave-traders gave constant anxiety. It was an impossible business, he decided, trying to govern unaided a country the size of Western Europe. Englishmen were of no use, for they either got swelled heads or drank; besides, there was not one in ten thousand who could stand the climate. He advanced all these reasons for having no lieutenants of his own calibre and social standing to help him; the first was his own explanation of the habitual difficulty he found in working with responsible subordinates. Lupton was the only Englishman he engaged, and he had previously been an officer on a merchant steamer in the Red Sea. One or two Europeans were serving under Gordon. The German doctor, Emin Bey, whom he made Governor of Equatoria, was destined to hold that province for years after Khartoum had fallen to the Mahdi. And in January 1879 Rudolf Slatin, a nominee of Emin's, started his romantic career as an inspector of taxes in the Sudan Government. There were also one or two Italians and the stalwart Gessi, whom Gordon loved, although his name did end in *i*. Clouds at one time unhappily darkened their friendship, for Gessi peculated, like the rest, and when Gordon refused to reëngage him he threatened to publish the 250 letters which Gordon had written him. In the end Gordon relented, and Gessi became his right-hand man again. But at headquarters Gordon stood alone, with none to share his counsels or his work; if in a moment of weakness he asked one of his Egyptian officers for an opinion, the poor fellow would give a sickly smile and answer, "Your Excellency knows best." All the Arabs were sheep.

That summer and autumn of 1878, Gordon lived a sedentary life in his capital, an office slave. He worked till half-past four — rarely going out, as he disliked the salutings and the inescapable semi-royal state, and after that had to struggle to keep ennui at arm's length till he went to bed. At one time he drew a great map of the Sudan; at another he occupied himself with pulling a clock to pieces and putting it together again, which made him wish, as he had often wished before, that his education had included some smattering of trades. What was the good, he asked, of teaching boys Latin and Greek and algebra? They ought to learn about things that were useful — the old heresy seemed plausible to him. Sometimes there were missionaries passing through Khartoum, and then he could talk with them on spiritual subjects, especially on his belief that the Bible pointed to Egypt's becoming a blessing in the midst of Palestine and Syria — which he still held in spite of Cairo's rottenness. Or, failing this, he could always tell his journal what he thought of the Christian Pharisees, "a hard, cruel set from high to low." Christ knew them for what they were worth; He was hard on them, but never hard on the slum people. Christ found fault with the invitations the respectable people gave Him to dinner, but He did not think it beneath Him to call on "Divorced," or worse than "Divorced." How sinful was mankind! "There is no such foul thing on the face of this earth than the purest man or woman" — Gordon underlined this emphatic, if ungrammatical, sentence in a letter to Augusta. So the Governor-General's speculations, not untinged with a bitterness he condemned in the Pharisees, ended in his declaring that the general doctrine of the Church regarding the existence of Hell was erroneous. Gordon was as ready to confront theologians as the pundits of finance or diplomacy.

In this condition of undesired leisure it was natural that his mind should turn to the past. He remembered China and the Chinese with a cordiality he could not feel for the Arabs, and in the autumn he wrote to Li Hung-chang, whom he had not seen for fourteen years. That mandarin, now the Viceroy of the metropolitan province of Petchili and the foremost statesman in China, assured him in reply that the benefits he had conferred on China continued to be felt, and said with what interest he had followed Gordon's achievements in Egypt, which, indeed, were known throughout the civilized world. They might not meet again, "but the responsibilities of life," the Chinese sage observed, "are so distributed in different individuals in different parts of the world that it is a wise economy of Providence that we are not all on the same spot."

Khartoum during that summer and autumn of 1878 was particularly unhealthy, and Gordon's health began to fail him. He suffered from fever in an epidemic that also laid his servants low, and was alone in his "huge house" for two days, being presented in his delirium with an endless succession of imaginary petitioners who would not take no for an answer, and often having " very blasphemous thoughts." At another time sleeplessness drove him to wander up and down his palace and "think, think for hours." And in December, when the climate of Khartoum is usually at its best, he was attacked by the worst influenza he ever experienced. He persisted in his old belief, gained from reading medical books, — medicine is as dangerous a science as theology for the layman, — that he was suffering from angina pectoris. In fact, the symptoms — "a rush of blood to the head and you think it is all over," and a pain in the chest — were afterwards diagnosed as coming from the liver, not the heart. It was evident that he must prepare to leave or die. In many ways he was disillusioned. He had the gravest doubts whether the Sudan could ever be properly governed and the slave trade killed unless Europeans were everywhere, and to this he believed the climate must always be an insuperable obstacle. With all his vision, Gordon could not foresee what preventive tropical medicine was to accomplish in the next generation, and even had it been granted to Gordon to realize what the Sudan was fated to become half a century later, it is doubtful whether he would have approved of the change. He saw that the natives would never like the rule of Europeans, however just it might be; Arab officials, more akin in race, and Moslems like themselves, undoubtedly suited the people better, in spite of their being corrupt and oppressive. It was a hopeless dilemma.

But Gordon did not want to leave until the slave-robbers of Shakka, who had again been giving trouble, were fairly smashed. On his last visit to Darfur, however, the machinery in that iron frame gave signs of stopping. At one time he thought the end had come. Then he recovered enough to write, "To die quickly would be to me nothing, but the long crucifixion that a residence in these horrid countries entails appals me." When Gessi's brilliant campaign against the Shakka slavers destroyed once for all that particular centre of the traffic, Gordon decided to leave.

His feelings for Ismail had softened as he had watched him carrying on for more than a year an unequal fight against the European Powers, and he admired the "splendid leopard" for his gesture in dismissing the two unpopular European Ministers whom England and France had forced him to take into his Cabinet. This *coup,* which occurred in the spring of 1879, was after Gordon's own Radical heart; his sympathies were still with the Egyptians and the Khedive against the encroachments of Europe. But he was more cautious than before, and though Ismail in his difficulties had three times asked Gordon to come to Cairo, he had steadily refused to venture again into that atmosphere of intrigue. He pretended to be aloof, and when, on July 1, 1879, he heard that Ismail had ceased to reign and received orders to proclaim Tewfik, the news, he declared, did not affect him in the least. But, all the same, he felt "very cross" when he reached Cairo at the end of August as he thought of the dismissal of his old master, and he was strongly inclined to refuse to take up his quarters in the palace which Tewfik, following his father's example, had placed at his disposal. Gordon, however, decided this would have been too rude, and the deference which Tewfik showed him soon induced a change of mind. That same evening he told the new Khedive he intended to resign, at which he saw that Tewfik was pleased "to get his land back from a too powerful satrap" — he knew that the people in the Sudan called Gordon "the little Khedive." But there was no doubt that Tewfik appreciated his energetic, if unconventional, servant, and once more Gordon basked in the capricious favor of an Oriental Court.

When he began his Egyptian chapter of high adventure it had all seemed to him a joke. Now in a freakish humor the pillar of cloud, which had ever guided him, returned to the same mood, and led him on one of the most extraordinary missions of his life. Johannis, the Christian King of Kings, was a madman to whom none of the wisdom of his ancestor Solomon had descended. Ismail's forward policy in Eritrea and in the Red Sea had not made him better disposed towards an upstart potentate belonging to the despised religion of Islam, and Tewfik, anxious to establish better relations, asked Gordon to go and arrange with Johannis a settlement of the questions outstanding between Egypt and Abyssinia. Gordon did not want to undertake the business; at the same time a chivalrous feeling for the young Khedive prevented his refusing it. Much against his will, therefore, he prepared to return southwards once more. As he steamed down the Red Sea he felt in a very angry state. He knew that Johannis was, like himself, a religious fanatic — a man who believed he had a mission to Christianize all Moslems, who actually forbade smoking in his country under pain of mutilation. With such a person it would be impossible to negotiate, and he realized that again he was engaged on a hopeless errand, that he was "in a hole out of which I see no exit." Gordon decided, in a vein worthy of Swift, that a more detestable creature than man could not be conceived. Then, turning to the Bible and

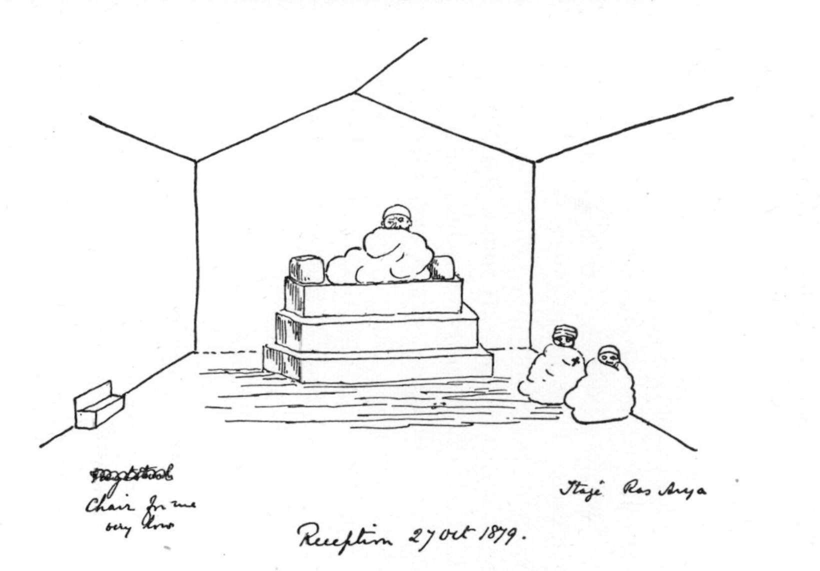

The King was perched up on the top of three angareps or stretchers, covered with silk, in a most commanding position. he kept his nose nearly covered, and only shewed part of his face. he had a white handkerchief tied tightly over his head. Ras Arya & the Itagé were huddled up side by side. Cows, mules &c are allowed entry into his Majesty's presence.

A SKETCH BY GORDON OF HIS RECEPTION BY KING JOHANNIS

(From a letter to Augusta Gordon)

seeing in himself another Job, he prayed to God to visit all the sins of Egypt and the Sudan on his head, to make him the scapegoat for the wickednesses of its peoples. This morbid state of mind was lightened at Massawa, where he broke a theological lance with the Swedish Protestant missionaries, telling them that, as man had no part in original sin, so he had nothing to do with his redemption. Could they explain the Atonement, Gordon asked them. If not, "let them hold their peace."

His anticipations of his mission proved correct. It was both tiring and tiresome, and Gordon's health suffered more than ever under the strain of marches in the mountains. He had palpitation of the heart, "which reduces one to zero," and heat rash that turned into boils and made him resemble Job more closely than ever. True, the primitive Christianity of the Abyssinians excited some sympathy, and he liked hearing the monks chant matins at 3 A.M. He found Johannis as mad as he had expected and much more melancholy — he was "of the strictest sect of the Pharisees, drunk over night and up at dawn reading the Psalms."

But Gordon sympathized with his grievances, and drew some amusement from the interviews he had with this saturnine King of Kings. Politically his mission was a failure, and he did not even succeed in his attempt to secure freedom for his fellow smokers among the subjects of the Negus. By December, after many hardships and dangers, he was back again in Massawa en route for Egypt and England.

Vivian had left Cairo, and his successor, Edward Malet, realizing Gordon was quick to take offense, sent the kavass and carriage of the British Consul-General to meet him at the station. The next morning the accomplished diplomat received a visit from the Governor-General of the Sudan, and was astonished when Gordon produced a silver filigree box, saying, "I have brought you a little present." Malet, who had never met Gordon before, politely refused the gift. Gordon continued to press it upon him with great earnestness, and Malet, seeing that even the ordinary questions of life appeared to Gordon in a light of their own, said at length he would buy the box, and asked Gordon what it was worth. "Three pounds," Gordon answered, and Malet thereupon produced three sovereigns from his pocket and took the box. Obviously Gordon was a peculiar man. And when Malet asked him to dinner Gordon's refusal heightened an impression of oddity that was still further strengthened when, as the British Consul-General's guests were about to sit down to the dinner in question, "His Excellency Gordon Pasha" was announced, and he quietly explained he had changed his mind. Edward Malet, a suave and punctilious diplomat, could not help feeling somewhat annoyed that Gordon's unexpected arrival caused them to be thirteen at table.

Gordon liked Malet personally, as he disliked Baring and Nubar, and the British diplomatic representative appreciated Gordon's character, in spite of its oddities. These had their inconveniences, as Malet found a day or two later when Gordon went to see him and told him that he meant to call out Nubar Pasha. The reason, he explained, was because at a reception the night before he had overheard Nubar let fall some disparaging remarks about Vivian. Malet attempted to make light of the matter, pointing out that Nubar had no particular reason to love Vivian, and that in conversation things were often said which were not meant to be taken too literally. Besides, diplomatists were used to having hard judgments passed on them, and Vivian would probably be the last person to mind what Nubar said of him.

Gordon brushed all these arguments aside. "But Vivian is a C.B.," he said, "and I am a C.B. too. I will not permit anyone to speak in such a way of a man who belongs to the same order of knighthood as I do." Thus, Malet observes, was Gordon a paladin, impelled by a vicarious chivalry to do battle for his whole order, and the British representative had considerable bother before he extracted a letter from Nubar to say that his observations on Vivian were to be taken in a Pickwickian sense. It is not surprising that others, less intuitive than Malet, thought Gordon mad, and that his storms with Nubar and the other pashas holding authority were attributed to a mind unbalanced. Gordon, however, as he left Alexandria, an unhappier man than ever before, was satisfied he had done two things: he had cut off the slave-dealers in their strongholds, and had made all his people love him. It was in this latter belief that he started four years later on his last visit to the Sudan, only to find that popularity is a plant that easily withers.

VI

THE KNIGHT-ERRANT

(1880–1883)

I must tell thee that there is no such thing as fortune in the world, nor do the things that happen in it, be they good or ill, come by chance, but by the particular providence of heaven.

CERVANTES, *Don Quixote*

The Knight-errant

"My God has been so faithful and kind all through my troubles," Gordon wrote to Augusta on January 8, 1880, "that I can recommend Him to you," a mood of resignation that was accompanied by a savage indignation at the folly and cunning of mankind, and it was in one of his blackest fits of depression that Gordon left Alexandria for Europe two days later. A certain M. Joseph Reinach observed him on their first day out, endlessly pacing the deck, the subject clearly of great nervous strain. Try as he would, remind himself that nothing really mattered, that the grave, six foot by two, yawned for all alike, he remained a man of action. Neither the influences of Christian optimism nor those of Stoic pessimism that found an uneasy equilibrium in his mind could subdue his passion for rule, and now that this was being thwarted he thought bitterly of the Egypt he was leaving behind him, of the ingratitude and weakness of the Khedive Tewfik, of the corruption of the *pashawat,* of the English in Cairo who were avaricious and blind, of the Foreign Office at home which never could see his point of view. Among all these hostile forces his own work in the Sudan would infallibly be wrecked. The misery of the unpaid officials, the poverty of the people at large, deepened the picture of moral squalor he painted for himself, and he decided that Ezekiel's savage chauvinism, which made the Lord God call Egypt "the basest of the kingdoms," would be justified so long as a constituent assembly of the notables of the country was not called "to stop the palatial intrigues and paralyze European ditto." Such were some of the ideas that ran through Gordon's head as he walked up and down the deck of the steamer on that winter's day.

Tired with his own thoughts, he began at last to talk to the Frenchman who had been watching the strange Englishman with such interest, and soon brought M. Reinach under the spell of his conversation. Gordon, he found, was the most amusing companion one could ever hope to meet with on a journey, an extraordinary person, *un diable d'homme,* who in some queer way talked both English and French at once. The ideas tumbled out pell-mell, sometimes seeming the fruits of a profound experience of men and things and sometimes the fantastic reflections of an overwrought brain. One moment he was praising God with exaltation, and the next expressing with equal vigor his contempt for the "mountebanks" of Tory Ministers, from Disraeli downwards, at whose hands he considered he had been so badly treated. Every hour he partitioned the world afresh — with special regard to the Ottoman Empire, still playing the part of the sick man of nineteenth-century Europe.

Gordon, for his part, found M. Reinach a good listener, and when they reached Naples carried him off to lunch with the exiled Ismail. The Frenchman was not less struck by Gordon's sympathy for the ex-Khedive than by his complete lack of interest in the sights and sounds of Naples and its environs. While they strolled round Pompeii together he talked the whole time of the Sudan and Egyptian politics. The gaiety of the Neapolitan street life, the beauties of Vesuvius and the Bay of Naples, alike left him unmoved. No saint of the seventh century could have been more oblivious of the superficial beauty of the world, or pursued his single idea in more ferocious isolation. It may have been owing to the Frenchman's persuasion, or possibly to the attraction the title of the opera would have for the student of the Old Testament, that Gordon went to see Halévy's *La Juive* at the San Carlo.

But the only recorded visit our hero paid to an opera house was brief; after an hour and a half he could "stand no more of it," and he left.

Gordon parted company with M. Reinach at Naples, and reached Rome alone and miserable. The Eternal City held nothing for him to justify the epithet. A severe attack of "the doles" laid him low for three hours, his recovery being helped by the thought that at the outside he should have only another seventeen years before his lease ran out — it does not appear on what calculations he based this figure — and there was always a chance of getting off sooner. Still, totally as he despised the world and all that was in it, he forced himself to go to St. Peter's, and felt an inward satisfaction when he found that masterpiece of the Italian Renaissance a poor thing. The Vatican Museum he did not even visit, and then with a sigh of relief he turned his back on Rome. Deciding that, come what might, he "would not be hunted," he took train for his lair at Southampton. There he looked forward to unburdening his mind of an evening to Augusta in the kitchen, the only place in which she allowed him to smoke.

A certain amount of lionizing he could not escape. It was the price he paid for the pleasure of showing his unconventionality, and when visitors were announced as he played with two of his nieces in his elder brother's Kensington drawing-room, it pleased this paladin to crawl under the Victorian drawing-room table, with a warning to the children not to disclose his whereabouts. "But mind, don't tell a lie," he added in his gay and boyish voice. The Prince of Wales, however, did not allow any distinguished man to fall through the meshes of his social net, and the interview that stands at the head of this strange history was followed by an invitation to dinner. Gordon refused it on the ground that he always went to bed at nine o'clock. The Prince laughed at this social fib, and merely changed the invitation into one for luncheon, so that Gordon's pride and the Prince's curiosity were alike satisfied.

In the few months of recuperation that followed his return home, Gordon was not less restless than he had been on the Mediterranean packet. He had finished with Egypt, had only to sign the official document of his resignation, his death warrant, as he called it — yet the glamour of Africa, with its immense fields for ambition, lay upon him as strongly as ever. Ismail had gone, but he saw in King Leopold a possible new master to serve, and he began negotiations in Brussels with that crafty Crœsus for his appointment as ruler of the Congo, negotiations that were never completely shelved for the rest of his life. He liked King Leopold, to whom he had been introduced by Lord Wolseley, a friend and counselor of the King of the Belgians. And he found that he liked Vivian, who had become Minister in Brussels, now that he and Vivian had no official relations. He even went so far as to promise Mrs. Vivian that he would think over her recommendation to marry. Not that he had any intention of putting his head into that particular noose. "Wives, wives, what a trial you are to your husbands! From my experience married men have more or less a cowed look," stands as a generalization of this time provoked by a particular instance of unwifely conduct.

From the heights of Lausanne, where he regained his health, this Colonel of Engineers, looking upon Lake Leman and the mountains of Savoy, decided that the world was too small. He longed with a great desire for death, because the future life, as adumbrated in the Bible, indicated it would be no idle place where one had to take holidays, but would consist of a city and Government — with the immortal part of C. G. Gordon surely occupying a post of importance. It would be, in short, something "grand and useful," and free from the hypocrisy of this earth.

Meanwhile he had to make the best of this insignificant

planet, so he busied himself, when not going about with a young nephew whom he had taken to keep him company, in drawing up a memorandum on the Near Eastern question, which then kept Europe in a simmer. It was a congenial task. Once before he had submitted a memorandum on this all-absorbing subject to Dizzy, who declared it was the work of a madman. Now he returned to the field he had known well for a quarter of a century, and set down a fairly accurate forecast of the Near East as it was to take shape after the Great War. No one paid any attention to it; but then, a man the retina of whose vision is sensitive to infra-red rays can hardly be astonished if others less farsighted consider his sanity doubtful. This done, he drew up another memorandum on the Sudan, which he gave to Lord Lyons at the British Embassy in Paris on his way home, an earnest document embodying the views Gordon had formed after seven years' first-hand knowledge of the country. It was a mistake, however, to end it as he did: "Anyhow it matters little; a few years hence a piece of ground six feet by two will contain all that remains of Ambassadors, Ministers, and your obedient, humble servant, C. G. Gordon." Such sentiments made Ambassadors frown and secretaries titter. Besides, did not Napoleon say that the man of action must always plan as if he were to live forever? In any case, Gordon considered his "orb" set — he believed he had made too many enemies in the official world ever to find employment again, except through King Leopold.

But, at the very time when he saw no further prospect of active work, Gordon's pillar was preparing to lead him a regular witches' Sabbath dance over half the earth. One thing during these months of leisure had cheered his spirits; Dizzy's defeat at the polls, he declared, was glorious news, little dreaming that his own destiny was to be interwoven with Gladstone's Ministry, which now came into power. At Lausanne, Gordon had drawn up such a Liberal Ministry as he could have wished for, Lord Hartington, his supporter, being Prime Minister. Though this was not to be, Gordon soon received impressive evidence of the esteem in which he was held by the Liberals. Without the least warning, Lord Ripon, the newly appointed Viceroy, offered him the post of official private secretary, one of the most important cogs in the vast administrative machine of the Government of India. No one could have been more unfitted for a position that required tact, self-effacement, and the acceptance of the diplomat's axiom that words are meant to hide, and not to express, truth. But Gordon, in his Radical enthusiasm, believed that a new régime was about to begin in India; and, not without misgiving, for he saw an endless succession of dinner parties, he yielded once again to the advice of Augusta and his brother Henry, and agreed to go. He was never apt to be rhapsodical over any new venture. In this case, however, he was more depressed than usual. "I am leaving," he wrote to his sister, "on May 13th (ominous date) with Lord Ripon. As a man thinks who has twenty-four hours to live, so do I with respect to this appointment. I am a good deal independent of place whilst I have His presence."

These misgivings did not only attack Gordon. While still in London, Lord Ripon began to feel uneasy over his choice. He had not in the least intended to give himself a master, but others did not disguise that they knew and welcomed it. Only the day before they left England, Lord Ripon discovered this when he introduced Gordon to Lord Houghton. That cultured aristocrat and man of letters expressed himself as delighted to hear that Gordon was to be his friend's private secretary, and could not congratulate Lord Ripon too highly on his luck. He was glad, he said, that Lord Ripon was going as Governor-General, but even more glad that Gordon was going as his secretary. It was not the sort of praise to commend itself to any man, and the Liberal Marquis winced at his friend's enthusiasm.

On the voyage out Gordon decided he would leave as soon as he could do so "in a respectable manner." He enjoyed the journey through Egypt, where he met Malet, who traveled with the Viceroy on the train to Suez, taking Malet into an empty carriage and reminding him of his refusal to accept the silver filigree box he had wished to present to him a few months ago. "You did ill to refuse," he said, "for I had also a suit of Damascene armor which I had meant to give you." He asked Malet if he would not now change his mind and accept a present. When the other said he would be delighted, Gordon took out a little ivory pocketknife with the initials C. C. (for Colin Campbell) scratched upon it, telling him that it had once been Lord Clyde's and had accompanied that General through the Indian Mutiny. And Malet, thinking over it afterwards, decided that Gordon's motive in this strange behavior was to establish a spiritual link between them through the magical properties inherent in inanimate objects — which, the diplomat reflected, he had perhaps succeeded in doing.

But Malet and Baring, Egypt and the Sudan, were soon left behind, and Gordon realized that he would never be able to feel for India as he had for those countries of the Bible. He did not know how long he could bear the "fiddle-faddle" of his present life — four months seemed the maximum. Besides, he had never been born to obey. "Holding the views I do, I could never curb myself sufficiently to remain in Her Majesty's service. Not one in ten million can agree with my motives, and it is no use expecting to change their views," he wrote, with something less than Christian humility as he looked forward in unrelieved gloom to the purgatory of social festivities at Bombay.

A week proved the limit of his patience. He found India was impossible, and the whole place full of lies, in which he was expected to participate. When Lord Ripon received an address, Lord William Beresford took it to Gordon and asked him to answer that the Viceroy had read it with much interest and would write about it. "You know perfectly well that Lord Ripon has never read it," Gordon replied, "and will not write, and I can't say those sort of things, so I shall resign and you take in my resignation." He hit Lord William on the shoulder, and said, "Yes, that is flesh. That is what I hate, and what makes me wish to die." It was clear to Gordon that India was to remain the preserve of the Anglo-Indian officials, whose avarice and luxury appalled him: they seemed not to have an idea beyond the rupee. "I declare I think we are not far off losing it [India]. I should say it was the worst school for young people. Everyone is always grumbling, which amuses me. The united salaries of four judges were £22,000 a year. A. B. had been five years in India, and had received in that time £37,000. It cannot last." So, in his wisdom, wrote Gordon a little over half a century ago. As for himself, he was no more than a "head spy" and his life "a living crucifixion."

Never had a Viceroy such an extraordinary private secretary with so disconcerting a knack of going to the heart of a problem! There was Yakub Khan, for instance, the ex-Amir of Afghanistan, in whose capital Cavagnari, the British Minister, and his staff had been murdered. Yakub was now a political prisoner in British India. Lord Ripon gave Gordon his *dossier* to study, and the conclusion he reached was that Yakub was innocent and should therefore be reinstalled on the throne of Afghanistan. Besides, Gordon realized that he was the only man likely to be able to keep order in that turbulent country. "Take him back yourself, my lord," he said. "You can easily do it with 3000 cavalry. If you succeed you will be looked on as the greatest Governor-General India ever had, and if you fail and are killed you will have a splendid marble monument put up to you." But Lord Ripon "did not seem to see the monument," and he would not accept Gordon's offer to do it himself with Yakub and some lakhs of rupees. What was the good of his staying in such a country? And, directly the Viceregal Court reached Simla, Gordon resigned. "Everyone will say I am mad," were his last words to Lord William Beresford, "but you will say I am not." And he pressed Lord Ripon, to whom he communicated his decision to leave while his lordship was cracking an egg at breakfast, to appoint Wolseley in his place.

Gordon, a free man once more, bethought himself again of Zanzibar — he could not get that Kenya project out of his head. But two days had not passed when Providence a second time intervened. China wanted him. Fifteen years had passed since he received the highest honors the Son of Heaven could bestow, and never the slightest hint that he could help any further that unwieldy empire to order its existence in a modern world. Now a telegram reached him from Sir Robert Hart via London. "I am directed to invite you here [Peking]. Please come and see for yourself. This opportunity for doing really useful work on a large scale ought not to be lost. Work, position, conditions, can all be arranged with yourself here to your satisfaction. Do take six months' leave and come."

It really was extraordinary — God, as he said, was helping him wonderfully, and before he had even replied to the invitation he had planned how the Chinese were to meet the threatened Russian advance into Manchuria, how the enemy's communications were to be cut, and how his own viceregal uniform, that he had never worn, would make an excellent present for Li Hung-chang. As the War Office was troublesome and refused to give him leave to go to China, Gordon wired that they should "arrange retirement, commutation, or resignation" for him, since to China he was determined to go. Then, not awaiting a reply, he embarked on a cargo P. and O.

boat for Shanghai. But before leaving Bombay he handed a *communiqué* to the press that must have caused disciplinarians in the service to wonder what the Army was coming to. "My fixed determination is to persuade the Chinese not to go to war with Russia, both in their own interests and for the sake of those of the world, especially those of England. In the event of war breaking out I cannot answer how I should act for the present, but I should ardently desire a speedy peace." He protested, too, against being regarded as one who wished for war in any country, particularly in China. "Inclined as I am, with only a small degree of admiration for military exploits, I esteem it a far greater honor to promote peace than to gain any paltry honors in a wretched war." Gordon's critics might well ask by what right a Colonel on the active list should use language like this. The War Office, however, was long-suffering, and when he reached Ceylon he found a telegram saying that his leave was granted so long as he engaged to take no military service in China, to which he answered grandly, "I will take no military service in China: I would never embarrass the British Government." Yet, as his mind went over and over the problem, he could not decide what to do about his commission; he determined, however, on one thing — he would repair the monument to the Ever-Victorious on the Esplanade at Shanghai.

No sooner had he arrived than all his castles in the air melted away. Far from China offering any opportunities for a reformer, it was exactly as it had been fifteen years before — corrupt, prejudiced, satisfied with its old ways. The years, too, had set a veil between him and those he used to know. His Chinese boys were grown to be great, moon-faced men, and the good-looking Lar Wang's son, whom he had sheltered after his father's murder and made his A.D.C., was now a red-button mandarin with a face like an ox. Only Li himself did Gordon find little changed, and his old feelings for the Chinese statesman swayed him not less strongly than before as he sat with him in his *yamun* at Tientsin and discussed the state of China. This was highly unsatisfactory, with the Dowager Empress, who had seized power when Gordon was first at Tientsin, still controlling a puppet Emperor. Li Hung-chang, soaked as he was in the traditional Chinese culture, seemed yet a dangerous Liberal to the reactionaries round the masterful woman who loved power more than she did her son, and Gordon, anxious to help him and his ally, Prince Kung, head of the Imperial Council in the days of the Ever-Victorious, decided to stay and do what he could to support him against the reactionaries. Gordon had hardly been a week at Tientsin before he cabled to the War Office that he could not "desert China in her present crisis," and wished to be free to act as he thought fit. Since this might include commanding troops in the field, he again resigned his commission in the British Army.

We are ignorant of his precise intentions. Some of the foreign diplomats seem to have been anxious that Li should march against Peking, and one of them is said to have suggested to Gordon that he should lead an expedition and depose the Emperor, a proposal that he turned down on the ground that, though he was equal to a good deal of filibustering, this particular plan was quite beyond him. But he was apparently frightened that Li might be persuaded to undertake some rash adventure, for a week later Gordon, no longer looking on himself as a Don Quixote come to save China, but simply remembering his friendship with Li, declared that the only thing which kept him in China was his fear for Li's personal safety.

How far the subtle and infinitely astute Li Hung-chang welcomed Gordon's protective feelings is doubtful, but it must have been on his advice that Gordon went to Peking and was there received by the Imperial Council. Its members were for war with Russia. Let them burn the suburbs of Peking (so as to protect the city against assault), remove the Emperor to a place of safety, show that they meant to resist *à l'outrance* — then, said Gordon, he would stay and help them. Otherwise China must give way. The grave mandarins urged the strength of the Taku Forts, the immense resources of the Empire; the eager Englishman grew more and more emphatic that China should yield. His language so frightened the interpreter that the trembling fellow upset a cup of tea, and positively refused to translate such intemperate words, so that Gordon, taking a dictionary, put his finger on the word "idiocy" and showed it to the Imperial counselors. Then, anxious as he had been two years before with de Lesseps to get things down on paper, he wrote out the terms of peace — five articles, including the payment of an indemnity which the mandarins could not stomach at all. It would be too much to say that Gordon's intervention was decisive. But he was satisfied that he had done his duty, and he pooh-poohed the advice of a member of the diplomatic corps that he should lie low while in Peking, for otherwise he might not escape with his life. "What does it matter?" he asked. "Neither you nor I will in all probability live more than ten or twelve years more, and what does it signify if we shorten that?"

Gordon returned to Tientsin and Li, and there began to find he was *de trop*. He hated himself, his fellow men, and the world more than ever; so depressed was he that the rumor went the rounds of his having suicidal tendencies. It was clear, in any case, that China had no work for him to do, and in the middle of August, 1880, after he had been five weeks in the country, he turned his face once more towards Zanzibar. But, before he left, his indefatigable pen had traced for Li's benefit the measures China should adopt in case of attack — quick movement of troops unencumbered by artillery, continual thrusts against the enemy's communications, night attacks not pushed home. "It is known that men armed with sword and spear can overcome the best regular troops, equipped with breech-loading rifles, if the country is at all difficult, and if the men with spears and swords outnumber their foe by ten to one." Thus did the greatest living master of guerrilla warfare foretell the massacre of Hicks Pasha and his 10,000 men at Obeid, which was to bring Gordon back to the Sudan and give him the death for which he longed.

Was he dead already? He said so when, on reaching Hongkong, he found a letter from the Military Secretary at the Horse Guards informing him that his resignation had not been accepted and ordering him to return to London. This "did not produce a twitter" in him — his only wish was that the Lord would come. Yet, struggle as he might to disentangle himself from the world, he could not succeed. If his reputation was sinking in official circles, the greater public esteemed him more than ever, and he was regarded with delight by an age in which there were no airmen or film stars to satisfy the people's lust for the romantic hero. His letters from the Sudan, which appeared that autumn in book form, filled out the picture sketched in the papers, and made him unique among those who were spreading the light of European civilization in the dark places of the earth. Gordon would not consent to its publication unless every word of praise were omitted — the only service, he said, that the editor of the volume could do him was to consider him as dead. This academic point agreed upon, Gordon supervised its publication and provided it with maps and notes.

It was wrong to allow Agag to get the better of him thus. But it was not easy to hew that masterful tyrant in pieces, to remain in obscurity, when the world wanted reforming so badly. At England's very doors lay Ireland in an extremity of wretchedness. Having nothing to do, Gordon decided to visit the west and southwest of that unhappy island. He walked about in the depressing November drizzle, deplored the heartlessness of the landlords, the poverty of the peasantry, decided that the Bulgarians, Anatolians, Chinese, and Indians were better off, and, with the speed of a special correspondent and the assurance of a politician, drafted a measure for the expropriation of the landowners. It would cost £80,000,000. But what was that to a country which had spent £30,000,000 on the expropriation of the West Indian slaves?

While his project was being published in the papers and commented on in leading articles, Gordon had fled into retreat at the vicarage of Twywell, in Northamptonshire, where lived his friend, the Reverend Horace Waller. If he did not there escape his uneasy mind, he first began to realize the importance of the sacrament of Communion, a tardy discovery on his part of the central feature of traditional Christian worship. He found much comfort in "the eating," as his innate Protestantism made him call it, and he decided that it should be taken at least once a month.

Though Gordon soon found Mr. Waller and his family to be worldly, Twywell began the process of "turning upside down" which culminated in what Scawen Blunt described as his "religious debauch" in Palestine two years later. Before this, Gordon confesses, he used to wander through his heart, finding nice walks and splendid palaces in which he reposed; then came the downfall of his Egyptian Palace, which was mouldy, faded, despicable, full of wholly earthly motives, so that he turned from the ruins in disgust. Next he sauntered into his last-visit-to-China Palace, until its splendor suddenly seemed tattered and mildewed. Lastly came drinking and smoking — and he resolved to cut down his allowance of cigarettes. He trusted for strength to keep his resolution and so "smite that immense serpent." Smoking was an abuse of one's body, God's temple, which Saint Paul told us must not be defiled. Smoking and drinking — it was a great snake, he told Augusta,[1] a yellow brindled one. Smoking he enjoyed, spirits he found difficult to do without. It was odd, he said, that "spirits and the French *eau-de-vie* (water of life)" were used for stimulants and taken to cheer the heart and raise the feelings when these were low from the absence of Holy Spirit.

So he took a vow, recorded it in his diary, and prayed for strength to observe it — the vow that he would abstain from spirits for six months and only smoke fifteen cigarettes a day. Later on he included sherry in his vow of abstinence, and even considered giving up claret. The six months' vow ended on November 18, 1881, and then he "had about ten days" during which, in spite of his prayers, he "was always open to attack on that flank." So he passed on himself another sentence of six months — and meditated abstention from wine as well. Such resolutions show that, if Gordon was strong enough to overcome his taste for spirits, the craving was always there, and that he indulged it to an extent reprobated by his own overscrupulous conscience.

Too much fuss has been made about this question, on which the Victorians, in any case, were far more sensible and less squeamish than their posterity. It is perfectly obvious that Gordon was not a drunkard or a dipsomaniac — his career, his incredible physical fitness, his almost uninterrupted health, in themselves answer such a charge. On the other hand, Gordon, in spite of his occasional vows, was far from being a fanatic for what is miscalled temperance. *Dulce est desipere in loco,* and though Gordon hated dinner parties, partly because they meant talking to women, he sometimes escaped from his loneliness and melancholy by observing this Horatian maxim. Had the accusation of drunkenness been made against him in his lifetime, he might well have cited Acts ii, 14–15, to his own satisfaction. For Saint Peter, on

[1] His letters on this subject referred to here are dated May 18, May 29, August 8, December 25, 1881.

the celebrated occasion when he and his fellow Apostles were accused of being full of new wine, did not protest that, boy and man, he had been a total abstainer for thirty years. He did not even allege that it was unthinkable he should ever be a victim of alcohol. He merely said it was preposterous to suppose that any reasonable person would be drunk at nine o'clock in the morning.

There was a more subtle temptation — the desire to write to the papers. His excuse was that he saw things more clearly than others — the necessity, for instance, of giving back Kandahar to the Afghans, or the redoubtable warlike qualities of the Abyssinians, or the way to stop slavery in the Sudan. And, if his pen was not busy on such subjects as these, there always remained more strictly professional questions; his memorandum to Li Hung-chang drew from himself an answering paper in the *Army and Navy Gazette* on the campaigning methods a regular army should use against an uncivilized enemy. At the moment his mind was running on the Basuto question, which he wanted to take in hand. But his telegraphic offer to the Cape Government remained unanswered, and he was left again wrestling with Agag, which he explained as "catering for notice and praise, hailing the tram of the world." He ran through the counts of this indictment against himself to Augusta. "Look what I have done!" he wrote: —

Stephano Treaty
Ripon
China
Hart
Egypt } January to January 1880–81
Ireland
Abyssinia
India

tabulating his sins not without complacence.

There were times when he did not think Agag such a bad fellow. For instance, he kept Dr. Birkbeck Hill, who was making the book out of letters Gordon had written to Augusta from the Sudan, as much as possible at arm's length, but he could not altogether maintain the fiction that he was dead, for he read the proof sheets. This was being much kinder to Agag than befitted a Christian. On one occasion a letter from the Prince of Wales's equerry brought that potentate "out for an airing," and he did not go in again until Gordon wrote a tract on the measure of the Spirit given to man. In the early months of 1881, he lived at 12 Victoria Grove, that pleasant little row of Regency houses off Gloucester Road, and mixed a good deal with the great world, yielding to the three-times repeated invitation of the Duke and Duchess of Sutherland to dine at Stafford House. One day as he was calling there he heard the Duke's butler coolly pointing him out to another visitor as Chinese Gordon — and "was not hurt." But while he mixed with people his ideal grew dim. He gave way to backbiting, said nasty things — for instance about that "objectionable after flesh Miss Venables," whom he met at his Aunt Amy's. The affection of a nephew did not prevent him from telling that lady herself one or two truths which, Gordon wrote to Augusta, she would not be able to stifle, in spite of her previous training. And Mrs. Freese too knew his displeasure, when in half an hour's conversation at Charing Cross Station he rebuked the carping spirit in her, "told her she was always ready, like many others, to use her tusk, and after getting others to show their pearls to rend them." An arm with a spear ready to throw should be the Gordon crest, he said to Augusta, and *Noli me tangere* their motto.

Yet all this worldliness stood in the way of the Christian life he was striving to lead, taking the Sacrament now three times a week and beginning to think that the High Church Party was "more in the right direction than the Low." He wrote a tract, *Take Eat*, on the all-important subject — the Communion, he said, was a love philtre for one's enemies. He went so far as discussing with a correspondent the doctrine of Transubstantiation, though he complained he could not spell it. If only he could have found work in Dockland he would have been content, but when he approached one East End vicar he realized, after interviewing the reverend gentleman's wife, that he could do nothing in that parish.

Then, feeling he was being hunted, he moved back to the comparative remoteness of 114 Beaufort Street, Chelsea, made vows he would write no more to the papers, and prepared a more rigorous retreat for himself in Palestine. Suddenly there came the chance of "exile to Mauritius," and in the middle of 1881 he was on his way to that remote station in the Indian Ocean, full of hope about his progress in the spiritual life. He saw now that it was wrong to "hang about Jordan" — or, in other words, to long for death — when he ought to have advanced into Judæa, into the uplands of the Spirit, where the oneness with Christ would be realized. He felt himself growing, and was glad he had no more hankering after Egypt (the mystical, not the real, Egypt, he was careful to explain). And as he pondered over the virtues of the Holy Communion — which he did now every time he ate — he decided that the whole operation of eating was full of wonder, "the death of the animal, etc., etc., all showing its mystic import."

Mauritius appeared to him as his Patmos, his place of revelation. It was, in fact, his first R.E. billet since Gravesend. But its professional duties gave him opportunity to make his subordinates work — the tone of the British Army, he opined, had much deteriorated; he was able also to traverse the whole field of Christian truth, to work out the analogies between the Old and the New Testaments, to affirm his faith in the Incarnation — a glorious mode, he said, of showing us what God is. And, to perfect himself in the Christian life, he took the tremendous resolution (underlined to show what it is costing him) of telling his sister to stop all the papers. In this way he hoped to starve his passion for politics, to make his "scabs drop off"; God had shown him what they were — "evil-speaking, lying, slandering, backbiting, scoffing, self-conceit, boasting, silly talking, and some few others."

The smiling and cheerful figure, full of energy and vitality, as he appeared to his fellow officers on the station, gave little enough indication of the scabs without and the fires within. He often told himself that he was wasting his time, and wondered what he should do when his now imminent promotion to General's rank became a fact. Go to Natal, to Syria, to remote Sinai? "Be rid of Colonel (or General) Gordon." Live in the East End of London? And always in these doubts his mind reverted to Zanzibar, the gateway to the Kenya uplands. Of all places in Asia and Africa this drew him the most, and, more than anything else in his wasted career, one regrets that he was never fated to follow his intuition.

In any case, he did not observe his vow of silence very strictly. When an idea seized him he had to express it; the good resolutions vanished as his eager mind played about a subject which touched his enthusiasms or his prejudices. Since he now disliked the Government of India, he decided, as he passed through Aden, that that stronghold ought to be no longer dependent on Bombay, but a Crown Colony with a special regiment of its own for defensive purposes. Then the fact of being in the Indian Ocean drew his attention to the strategic importance of its islands, and he came to the conclusion that it was a mistake to regard the Suez Canal as the main route to India; far better to return to the old practice and utilize the Cape route. Gordon, pondering in Mauritius over the question of Imperial defense, decided that our commitments in the Mediterranean were not worth the trouble they cost. Malta was no asset, nor Cyprus. Better to leave the Mediterranean to the Powers upon its shores, and make the oceans our Imperial highways. If Gordon had been stationed in Malta, instead of Mauritius, he would probably in his egocentricity have thought otherwise, but his doubts as to the utility of the Suez Canal in war were strikingly illustrated when, in 1917, owing to the dangers of the Mediterranean route, most of the traffic to India had to be sent via the Cape.

Putting all these points before his friends in England — one of them to be the first Lord Esher — helped to keep depression at bay. He refused to live in the hills, went on his arrival to a "piggery of a hotel" in Port Louis, and afterwards took a furnished house in that unhealthy and steamy little town. Naturally he avoided all social functions; the very idea of archery and lawn tennis made him unhappy. But it delighted him to take a party of subalterns or young naval officers on some expedition or other. An excursion of this kind he organized like a military operation, drawing up elaborate marching orders of times and places, not forgetting to ensure that proper precautions were taken to avoid chills and fevers, marking the places where overcoats and clean socks were to be left in the morning and picked up on the return in the evening. Gordon's own dress on such occasions, a pot hat and an old black morning coat, was in keeping with the originality of his character.

The months soon passed. He preached to the Chinese coolies on Sunday evenings on God's indwelling, but thought it better not to mention Jesus; he went to service in the Cathedral, and the text of the sermon made him realize that the Christian lived in a land of magic — so long as the Christian is subdued by the things of this world he does not enter the higher land, and, if he refuses them, then he enters it. What, then, was the meaning of "Seek ye first the Kingdom of God, and His righteousness; and all these things shall be added unto you," since in the Kingdom they would be unwanted? A visit to the Seychelles, where he found the forbidden fruit, the *coco de mer*, gave him the idea that the site of Eden lay near by in the depths of the Indian Ocean. He developed the theory with maps and plans to show how the four rivers that watered the Garden once flowed down the Red Sea and the Persian Gulf, afterwards pursuing their joint course through a thousand miles of what was in the age of man's innocence the dry bed of the Indian Ocean. All his life Gordon had speculated about the Deluge and the water levels ruling before that world crisis. The subject appealed to his professional mind.

In the meantime the normal progress of promotion brought its reward to Gordon, who became a Major-General at the comparatively early age of forty-nine. At first he half-believed that as G.O.C. he might stay on in Mauritius. He did actually command the station for some weeks. But he had no illusions about the jealousies of the officers drawn from the Line regiments toward those who belonged to the specialists' corps of artillery or engineers. He believed also that the Duke of Cambridge was personally hostile to him — expatiating on this at length to Augusta. He felt sure he would never be employed again. Besides, if employment did come his way, it would probably mean looking after Volunteers, which he could never bring himself to do. In this uncertainty he was preparing to leave when the mail brought him a telegram from Aden, the nearest cable station. It was a belated answer to one he had sent over a year before to the Cape Government. It asked him if he would renew the offer he had then made to settle the Basuto question. The War Office had already been approached and agreed to his going. Nothing could have been more unexpected or providential, and in two days Gordon started on a sailing ship for the Cape. From a rough and desperately uncomfortable voyage he learned that seasickness and incipient jaundice helped him to lose his self-conceit, to be more like Christ, but he reached the Cape sick and miserable. Though everyone was kind and complimentary, — well as he knew compliments to be but sounds of the wind, — he could not help wishing he were a "nail in Christ's footstool; how willingly I would have everyone to be higher than me in Heaven," he added, with the humility of a Saint Teresa, whom he also resembled in his passion for authority on earth. To make his selflessness more complete, he asked Christ, at his first Communion in Cape Town, to undertake Himself the post of Commandant-General (Gordon's new local rank) and allow him to remain "passive in the matter."

Gordon did not realize that, whether he acted as agent or principal, the one thing he could never do was to remain passive. In any case, a change of Ministry in the Cape Government supervened immediately after his arrival in Cape Town and charged the atmosphere with storm. The sympathetic Merriman, who had sent for him, was succeeded by one Scanlan, a man without sympathy either for the Basutos or for the mission, with which Gordon had also been entrusted, of reorganizing the Cape Forces. Disagreement was inevitable. But this did not prevent Gordon from getting speedily to work, and he had not left Cape Town a week when he addressed a memorandum to the Government outlining what should be done to solve the Basuto question. It was quick work — a little too quick, Gordon feared as he wrote it. He proposed to call a gathering of the chiefs, a Basuto Parliament; to allow this body to meet free from interference by any white officials; and to hear from it what exactly were the fears and grievances of the people. Their objections to being handed over without their consent to the Cape Government, as the Home Government had recently done in defiance of its treaty obligations with them, were too reasonable to make discussion on this point possible.

Such tenderness for native rights was little likely to commend itself to the existing Cape Government, which only desired to divide the Basuto chiefs in order to crush them more easily afterwards, while Gordon's wish was to see this fine native race, which he admired for its soldierly qualities, made secure against the avarice of the Boers and the other white settlers. So the local Premier sent on the memorandum to the Secretary of State for the Colonies, Lord Kimberley, who replied that the Basuto question was the business of the Colonial Government. It is unnecessary to enter in detail into the ensuing game of battledore and shuttlecock. Gordon continued to draft memoranda, the Government to ignore them. When he went to interview the leading Basuto chief, the Minister of Native Affairs seized the moment to persuade his native rival to attack him, with the result that Gordon's life was in danger from the outraged Basuto leader with whom he was negotiating. His efforts to reorganize the local forces were not more successful, and he had to submit to impertinence from one of his principal subordinates, whom he did not feel strong enough to place under arrest. Here was a change from the autocracy of the Sudan! Clearly he could not stand it for long, and yet as he read of the bombardment of Alexandria he congratulated himself on not being in Egypt. Through September he was wounded by the archers, and wondering what to do if war broke out with the Basutos; finally he decided he would take no part in any such campaign, and sent in his resignation. "What a queer life mine has been," he wrote to his sister, "with these fearful rows continually occurring." So, strengthened in grace but poor in pocket, — he had unwisely cut down his salary of £1200 to £800 before discovering that while at the Cape he received no British Army pay, — he prepared to leave for home. As he was about to go on board he asked the A.D.C. to the Governor, who had been one of his officers in China, whether he thought it suitable to the dignity of a Major-General that he should travel with only a sovereign in his pocket, for after paying his ticket that was all he had — and the A.D.C. promptly lent him money. His mission had ended in hopeless failure — the third he had suffered in two years. He did not worry over it. When at Khartoum he summed up his feelings about the matter in a letter to a friend: "I have quite forgotten the row at the Cape, what a fearful fuss about nothing it was, how badly I behaved — that is all my reflection."

Gordon for the first time returned to England without having added to his reputation. He consoled himself — according to his lights, he ought to have been thankful for it — by the reflection that neither praise nor blame made one better or worse. His future looked black. Unless he went to the Congo — and difficulties about the international status of the new state prevented anything's being done at the moment — his career seemed at an end. He would have to stay for three years on the active list in idleness to qualify for his pension. Though he professed to have no more ambition, he still in his heart of hearts hankered after Egypt, and it pleased him to think that, if everything there was going to rack and ruin, he had foretold it all. He wrote a paper entitled "Israel in Egypt" which showed the selfishness of Dilke's and Malet's policy. He meant to follow it with another called "The Exodus," but he did not think he would print either, since one should not rejoice over one's enemies — so he kept this frustrated ambition to himself, and decided to go to Palestine. "For me life is ended," he wrote. Now he was free to concentrate on that union with God which he had always professed as his goal, and he might hope for success, since no worldly cares now complicated his existence. He told himself that the reason he had hitherto been such an unhappy man was because he had thought it possible to make a bargain with Jesus — to give up half the world and gain a corresponding

National Portrait Gallery

GENERAL GORDON

E. Clifford

(A sketch, made in an hour, just before Gordon left for the East, December 21, 1882)

measure of Christ. This was of no use. Complete renunciation was the only way.

He reached Jerusalem in January 1883, and took a house which he liked because it was solitary and surrounded by barren, rocky hills. Yet from the first the note of disappointment persists. He is still unhappy. He does not care for sites, he says, and declares it is quite unnecessary for anyone to come to Palestine. "Put yourself in the actors' skin, and you feel as Peter and the others did." He has not seen where Agag was hewn to pieces before the Lord, but expects to find it, though the giant "is still alive in all of us." In spite of his determination to study, to make Old Testament geography clearer, to show where the Ark grounded, ennui soon attacks him, and after only two days in Palestine he decides that a year of the country will be quite enough. Then he will "retire to Bow (East End)."

Never before has Gordon shown us so plainly the true tragedy of his life as now, when he turns wholly to spiritual things only to find them insufficient. He wishes to be a contemplative, to spend the days alone reading and praying, and he is constitutionally unable to submit to the discipline that is as necessary for the saint as for the soldier. He persists in doing what seems best in his own eyes, in following his own fancies. "I hear," he writes, "that at my village the Greek-Russian Church gives the Lord's Supper to all who present themselves without query. . . . So I shall go there." He does not appear to realize that confession is as essential a preliminary to Communion in the Greek as in the Catholic Church, and that the priest in dispensing with it is merely an unfaithful servant. And a self-satisfied Gordon, who instinctively dislikes confession, adds the comment, "It is odd that no queries were asked when we poisoned ourselves in Eden; but that, when we wish to take the antidote, queries are asked."

Later on he moved down to Jaffa, where he was on friendly

terms with a Mr. Hall, a missionary. But they differed on the attributes of the priest's functions, and the cleavage grew too wide for Gordon to receive the Communion from the missionary's hands. His mind, with only religious speculation to exercise it, became an unhappy jumble. He is as far as ever from gaining the serenity of spirit which is the mystic's reward; it is hopeless, he says, to seek quiet in places — quiet is only to be found in one's self. Thus the life he has long planned turns to dust and ashes now that he begins to live it. He looks over the collection of books he has brought with him and his heart sinks. What good are they? It is better to trust simply to the Bible and concordance. Meanwhile he wonders how it is that, in spite of giving up all hindrances to a holy life, he is yet empty of any increase in spiritual joy.

Yet had he given them all up? Was he dead to the world? Suddenly his thoughts take an earthly direction, and he writes, "Wonderful are the works of God in the Sudan. He has upset the Egyptian people thoroughly and they will get their liberty from the oppressing Pashas," and he is tempted to put his view before Lord Dufferin, who has succeeded Malet as British Representative in Cairo. Then he remembers that he has put by earthly ambitions, and decides to occupy himself with making "a sort of concordance of catchwords" to establish the analogies between the Old and the New Testament. The oddest ideas strike him as he wanders about in an unhappy idleness: the beauty of the human form suggests a picture of all the angels examining a raised boy's body with "the greatest curiosity and amazement"; thoughts of the fighting which history has seen round Jerusalem make him think of the millions of bodies lying in its ravines, and how crowded they will be at the Day of Judgment.

Drifting was what Gordon accused the British Government of doing in Egypt — did he ever wonder whether the charge could not have been sustained against his own spiritual life?

He watched the excavations proceeding round Jerusalem, yet he never seriously examined the foundations on which he had tried unsuccessfully to make his own Holy City, his own Church with its single member — himself. If this were built on the canonical books of the Scriptures, who had given them their sanction? If the common traditions of Christianity were able to declare what was, and what was not, the voice of God, why should they be invalid in the case, for example, of the creeds which Gordon was far from accepting? Such doubts apparently never occurred to him; he was sufficient unto himself, so long as he had his Clarendon Press Bible in which to dig about for symbolism and prophecy.

No one had greater contempt for the amateur than Gordon, yet he was supremely unconscious that his religious speculations showed the amateur in his most exaggerated form. Protestantism is full of examples of earnest men for whom the responsibility of private judgment has proved too heavy a burden, of men who have in consequence stepped over the border line that divides sanity from madness. Clearly Gordon's queerness was becoming pathological, his religious mania was driving him off his mental balance, when he proposed, as an alternative to the British annexation of Egypt (which he said he did not recommend), that a canal should be made from Haifa to Akaba, on the Red Sea. Owing to the deep cleft of the Jordan, he protested, the thing would be easy. A cut from Haifa to that river, costing three millions, would let the Mediterranean into the Jordan Valley, so that the prophecy of Ezekiel (xlvii, 10) would be fulfilled, and the fish of the Dead Sea would be "according to their kinds, as the fish of the great sea [the Mediterranean]." "Such a canal," Gordon urged,

would close all attacks from Russia upon Palestine, except upon the line between Haifa and Zerin, and strangely enough would force her to attack on Megiddo (Armageddon). It would prepare the way for a united Europe to put this thus isolated Palestine under a common ruler, and would bring about the true prophecy of the Scriptures. All nations would come here and colonize. As for the Jews, they do not exist, to my mind, in those who call themselves so. I am a Jew a thousand times more than they are.

This was Gordon's solution for the Egyptian question in the autumn of 1883, when the victories of the Mahdi had made it critical. He sent it to Lawrence Oliphant, a man who also cherished his oddities. Oliphant, formerly of the Diplomatic Service and now living in Palestine, gave no opinion, so far as we know, on his Palestine Canal project. But he told Gordon that his duty lay in Egypt, and not in the Congo, where King Leopold had at last definitely decided he wanted Gordon to go. It was to make the final arrangements for the work to which he meant to devote the rest of his life that Gordon left Palestine in December 1883, and reached Brussels on New Year's Day, 1884, carrying with him, as a present for wicked King Leopold, a model of the Rock upon which the city of Zion was built.

He was nearer home than he imagined.

VII

KHARTOUM

(1884–1885)

I would that all would look on death as a cheerful friend who takes us from a world of trial to our true home. All our sorrows come from a forgetfulness of this great truth — I desire to look on this departure of my friends as a promotion to another and higher sphere, as I do believe that to be the case with all.

GORDON

Captain who loved the enemies you slew,
Soldier ordained "to kill and to be killed,"
Your duty here on earth at last fulfilled
Beneath the Arab spears that ran you through:
Pilgrim thinking only how to follow
In self-forgetfulness your Master's way,
Longing for death to end time's brief to-day,
And hungry for eternity's to-morrow:

Soldier and saint and sinner, when we see
— Now you have reached the quiet of your goal —
Your sternest fights were for the mastery
Of your own passions by the flesh enticed,
More brightly shines the splendor of your soul,
Servant of man and subaltern of Christ.

1. Sudan or Congo

During those early days of January 1884, Gordon on the whole felt cheerful. He was glad to have escaped spending Christmas and New Year's Day in England. Malet annoyed him because, when he called at the British Legation early in the morning, the servant told him His Excellency was just going to breakfast; and a subsequent invitation to dinner from the Minister also excited Gordon's criticism because Malet had written it on Foreign Office paper, which he had no right to use for private correspondence. Small things still excited him to censoriousness. His more justifiable annoyance with the War Office for refusing to allow him to enter King Leopold's service was tempered by gratitude to and admiration for that monarch. Leopold II was not only ready to compensate him for the loss of pension which his resignation would entail, calculated at something over £7000; he went so far as to offer to pay Gordon's hotel bill (he would not stay at the Palace, he declared, because he did not want the King's servants to see his old comb), and to defray the cost of his outfit. Gordon, always susceptible to the personal charm which royalties exercise by the right of their *métier,* thought Leopold a worthy and magnanimous prince. He was delighted with his Liberal views about Central Africa, with his interest in the model of the Rock, based upon the theory Gordon had formed that the topographical contours of the Holy City designedly suggested the female form with Golgotha as the head. And Gordon prepared to go to the Congo with the intention of never returning, sure in the conviction that "Our Lord has so ruled it."

His only extravagance in Brussels, where he had small baths for fifty centimes instead of large ones for a franc, was to order several copies of the photograph he had had taken in 1880. The Brussels photographer had caught with wonderful skill the restlessness lurking behind those eyes set far apart, the strength of the hard mouth, the broad, idealistic forehead, and the general untidiness which was in some way a reflection of his spiritual qualities. Gordon thought it rather a good likeness and sent three copies of the "Sheath" (his habitual word for his body) to Augusta. To her he went straight from Brussels, and on January 8 he posted from Southampton his official letter of resignation to the Military Secretary. He made his will, disinheriting, with Augusta's approval, five of his nephews and nieces, and prepared to catch a steamer from Lisbon on Feburary 5. He would deal the slave trade its deathblow — would end his life and find death in the Congo. "How divinely governed is all this movement by Our Lord!" he wrote to the secretary of the Anti-Slavery Society.

But things were happening of which he was hardly aware. It was true that he had many, many enemies in Egypt, and was looked at askance by the War Office and the Foreign Office. At the same time he had influential friends, who were continually working for him behind the scenes. So far back as November 1882, when Gordon was trying to stifle the hankering for Egypt after his South African fiasco, Lord Dufferin, then on a special diplomatic mission to Cairo, suggested that "some person like Colonel Gordon" should be found to set the Sudan upon its feet again. Nothing came of the proposal at the moment, but it was a straw in the wind. Gordon's name was again mentioned a year later, in November 1883, when the news came through that Hicks Pasha's army of 10,000 had been annihilated by the Mahdi, and the breeze of popular disapproval at the Gladstone Ministry's handling of the Egyptian question began to rise dangerously.

Permission of the Institution of Royal Engineers

THE LAST PORTRAIT OF GORDON
(*Taken in Brussels in 1880. In the Royal Engineers Museum, Chatham*)

That autumn Chinese Gordon, for the first time in his life and all unknown to himself, assumed size and significance in the deliberations of English statesmen. On November 27, 1883, Lord Granville, the Foreign Secretary, wrote to Gladstone, "Do you see any objection to using Gordon in some way? He has an immense name in Egypt, he is popular at home, he is a strong but very sensible opponent of slavery, he has a small bee in his bonnet. If you do not object I could consult Baring by telegraph."

In this demure fashion did Lord Granville begin to uncork the bottle which contained so formidable a genie.

2. Gordon Talks to W. T. Stead

There are three rival theories to explain why the Gladstone Ministry decided to send Gordon to the Sudan. The simplest is that it was one of those panic decisions taken in a hurry and repented at leisure. Edward Dicey, a hostile critic, quotes Lord Palmerston's saying that when he was told that something had got to be done he knew at once that what his informant wanted was permission to do something foolish, and Dicey adds that Gordon's appointment was, in the circumstances, the worst that could have been made. The fact, however, that Ministers were talking of Gordon in November 1883, two months before he was actually sent to the Sudan, rather militates against the panic theory.

Lord Cromer (then Sir Evelyn Baring), one of the actors in the drama, explains it in a different way. He admits it was a sin of commission to send Gordon to Khartoum — as it had been a sin of omission to allow Hicks to march upon El Obeid. But the responsibility, he asserts, lay chiefly upon the English press, and particularly on the *Pall Mall Gazette,* then edited by W. T. Stead. "The people of England, as represented by the press, insisted on sending General Gordon to the Sudan, and accordingly to the Sudan he was sent." Cromer adds that he twice refused to utilize Gordon's services, and it was only when he found that Nubar Pasha, Sir Evelyn Wood, and Watson Pasha, Gordon's old subordinate in Equatoria and now on the staff of the Egyptian Army, all favored Gordon's employment that he gave way. "In yielding I made a mistake which I shall never cease to regret. It may well be that, had I not yielded, the result would have been the same. The public feeling in favor of Gordon was so strong as to be almost irresistible." Such is Lord Cromer's explanation.

The third theory, propounded in his *Gordon at Khartoum* by Wilfrid Scawen Blunt, who also played a minor rôle in the events that were unrolling themselves in Egypt, is more subtle. He does not believe that Cabinet Ministers like Lord Hartington, Lord Granville, Lord Northbrook, and Sir Charles Dilke — the four members of Gladstone's Ministry in favor of a vigorous policy in Egypt — "went suddenly mad on Stead's persuading them that Gordon was a miracle man. Cabinet Ministers do not go mad in this way; their madnesses have much more method than that. Nor are they carried off their legs by a newspaper interview. It is they that inspire the newspapers, not the newspapers them." And Blunt follows hot on the trail of the intrigue for Gladstone's opponents within his Ministry to torpedo the policy of evacuation in Egypt for which the Prime Minister stood. In that intrigue he included Cromer himself, who, insisting in a dispatch of December 22, 1883, on the need of imposing a policy of withdrawal upon the Khedivial Government, said it "would be necessary to send an English officer of high authority to Khartoum with full power to withdraw the garrisons and to make the best arrangements possible for the future government of that country." What is this, Blunt asks, except the germ of the claim for the appropriation of the great Nile provinces to England herself? And he insists that by the end of 1883 the

Gordon mission was in principle decided, though Gordon was not named in it — indeed, Baring did not want him; an English officer was to go to Khartoum, not only to bring away the garrisons, as was afterwards pretended, but to reëstablish order and set up a new political régime.

Blunt sees the War Office in the centre of the intrigue against Gladstone. Gordon's friend Reginald Brett (afterwards Lord Esher), an adroit wire-puller, was private secretary to Lord Hartington, the Secretary of State for War, and Lord Wolseley, another friend of Gordon's, was Adjutant-General and had easy access to the Secretary of State. Gordon, a first-class fighting man, which was what they wanted, made an ideal tool, and accordingly when the four Cabinet Ministers, backed by the financiers whose interests were against withdrawal in Egypt, felt the time had arrived to start their campaign for a stronger policy in Egypt, Blunt asserts that they decided to add to its popularity by coupling with it the name of Chinese Gordon.

On January 1, 1884, the *Times* — according to Blunt, the obedient organ of the house of Rothschild, which was interested in the Egyptian debt to the tune of £9,000,000 — published a leading article upon a letter from Sir Samuel Baker advocating the retention of Khartoum and the Eastern Sudan, with the building of a railway from the Red Sea to Berber. In that letter Baker inquired why General Gordon Pasha should not be asked to assist the Government — the first mention in the papers of Gordon's name in connection with the crisis.

The next move came when Gordon gave his famous interview to W. T. Stead, that prophet of the new school of journalism. On January 3 the *Pall Mall Gazette*, following, as Blunt asserts, a hint from Esher, who had been connected with the paper, went over to the side of the Imperialist section of the Cabinet; and, on January 8, Stead, still prompted by

Esher, visited Southampton and saw Gordon at his sister's house in Rockstone Place. Gordon at first was unwilling to talk, but he soon yielded to Stead's persuasion, and the result was a review of the whole situation, with a plea for a fighting policy. "Whatever you decide about evacuation," he said, "you cannot evacuate, because your army cannot be moved. You must either surrender absolutely to the Mahdi, or defend Khartoum at all hazards." When Stead left, Gordon pressed a little volume into his hand. "This is my book," he declared, "and although I shall never be able to attain to the hundredth part of the perfection of that saint, I strive towards it — the ideal is here." It was one of the twelve copies of *The Imitation of Christ* which Gordon had told his sister to order for him.

The *Pall Mall Gazette*, making the most of its "scoop," headed the interview "Chinese Gordon for the Sudan," and in a leading article pleaded that he should be sent to Khartoum with full powers "to save what can be saved from the wreck of the Sudan." Its success was the greater because Gordon did not believe in the reality of the Mahdi's power, and made light of the insurrection. The Mahdi, he declared, would willingly accept conditions of peace. Such optimism suited the public taste, and from this movement began the Gordon cultus, which was to culminate twelve months later in a thrill of self-abasement on the part of that self-satisfied Victorian generation.

Before Gordon read the interview in the *Pall Mall Gazette* on January 10, his heart was troubled. After a life spent wrestling with Agag, that giant had thrown him once again. He decided he would see no more "reporters," and, profoundly dissatisfied, he betook himself to his friend, the Reverend R. H. Barnes, whom he had first met at Lausanne in the spring of 1880, for he no longer confided in Mrs. Freese. Coolness continued to overlay their old friendship. The last thing that lady had done was to criticize some of his Palestinian writings; she had "rent him," he complained, and Gordon was like all authors in preferring praise to criticism. Besides, not only was Mr. Barnes a pious and simple soul, possessing an uncritical admiration for Gordon; he was vicar of Heavitree, in Devonshire, the county in which Baker also lived. Gordon wanted to see him also. Thus both worldly and spiritual reasons drew him westward.

He spent a happy two days in Devon. On Friday, January 11, he received the Holy Communion in the parish church at Heavitree, the last occasion on which he partook of "the eating," and after breakfast went over to Exeter, where he called on the Bishop, Dr. Temple, with whom he discussed those missionary questions in which the future Primate was passionately interested. Gordon, realizing the serious obstacle offered by monogamy to the conversion of the Sudanese, asked Dr. Temple whether these Mohammedan converts might be allowed three wives, which would at least be one less than the four permitted by the Koran. The Bishop, however, considered the proposal uncanonical. Later in the day Gordon went on with Mr. Barnes to see Baker. He met them at Newton Abbott station, and as they were driving along the Devon lanes Baker pressed Gordon to go to the Sudan if the British Government required it. Gordon, the vicar records, "was silent, but his eyes flashed, and an eager expression passed over his face as he looked at his host." Late at night, "when he had retired," Mr. Barnes adds, "he came to my room, and said in a soft voice: 'You saw me to-day?' 'You mean in the carriage?' 'Yes; you saw *me* — that was *myself* — the self I want to get rid of.' "

If the British Government wanted him to go — there was no doubt in Lord Granville's mind, for he had, immediately after the Stead interview, again wired to Sir Evelyn Baring suggesting Gordon's name, and a second time had Baring replied saying he did not want him. Gordon, of course, was unaware of this when, on the evening he made his confession to his spiritual adviser, he wrote a letter to Baker outlining what steps he considered ought to be taken in the Sudan. Blunt thinks there must have been collusion between them, for Baker sent it on to the *Times.* This was powerful propaganda, and the readers of that paper could hardly fail to be convinced by the agreement between the views of the two greatest experts on the subject. Gordon's letter repeated what he had said to Stead: the alternatives were either to surrender absolutely to the Mahdi or to defend Khartoum at all hazards — "the latter," he said, "is the only course that ought to be entertained." As usual, Gordon, when he had chased the Biblical bees out of his bonnet, was right. But it was many years before his policy was carried out.

Events now moved rapidly, though always in the cloudy atmosphere of muddle and intrigue which to the end hung over Gordon's last mission. On January 15, in answer to a telegram from Lord Wolseley, Gordon went to the War Office, and there the two old friends discussed the question. When Wolseley asked him what he would do in the actual state of affairs, he answered, "I would send myself," and the upshot of the conversation was that Gordon agreed to go to Suakim, report on the military situation, and then return, always being under Baring for orders. After this mission was finished he was to be allowed leave to go to the Congo. Anyone knowing Gordon, as Lord Wolseley did, could hardly have imagined that he would docilely have carried out a perfectly useless visit to report and do nothing, which, in any case, was not consonant with Gordon's views as expressed in his letter to the *Times.* Blunt's suggestion is that the merely advisory capacity of Gordon's mission was camouflage designed to overcome Gladstone's reluctance. If that were so, it succeeded, as the Prime Minister gave way.

There only remained Baring. Lord Granville had told Gladstone the day before that it might be advisable to exert "a little pressure" on the British Representative in Cairo, if Gordon believed that he could by his personal influence excite the tribes to escort the Khartoum garrison and inhabitants to Suakim (a course of action which Gladstone should surely have foreseen would entail war with the Mahdi). And finally, on January 16, Baring yielded. Twice he had refused the offer to send Gordon; the third time he said: —

Gordon would be the best man, if he will pledge himself to carry out the policy of withdrawal from the Sudan as quickly as is consistent with saving life. . . . I would rather have him than anyone else, provided there is a clear understanding as to what his position is to be and what line of policy he is to carry out. . . . Whoever goes should be distinctly warned that he will undertake a service of great difficulty and danger.

The way was now clear. Gordon, after seeing Wolseley, had gone over to Brussels. On January 17 he was recalled by telegram, traveled over that night, and reached London at 6 A.M. on the eighteenth. Wolseley saw him two hours later, and told him what had been decided upon. At 11.30 he went to the War Office, and was taken by his friend to the Secretary of State. While Wolseley went into Lord Hartington's room for a moment, Gordon, as he stood with his back to the fire, suddenly asked the private secretary who was sitting at his desk, "Do you ever tell a lie?" He remembered his own experiences with Lord Ripon. But before the astonished young man had time to reply, Wolseley returned and introduced Gordon to Lord Hartington. There were present the three other Ministers, Blunt's conspirators — Lord Granville, Lord Northbrook, and Sir Charles Dilke. Gordon's own account of the interview runs: —

Wolseley came for me and took me to the Ministers. He went in and talked to the Ministers and came back and said

"Her Majesty's Government want you to undertake this. Government are determined to evacuate the Sudan, for they will not guarantee future government. Will you go and do it?" I said, "Yes." He said "Go in." I went in and saw them. They said "Did Wolseley tell you your orders?" I said "Yes; he said you will not guarantee future government of the Sudan and you wish me to go and evacuate it?" They said "Yes," and it was over and I left at 8 P.M. for Calais.

He received his instructions that afternoon — "a crafty document," in Blunt's eyes. For while the first paragraph ordered Gordon to proceed to Suakim [1] and report on the best method of evacuation (not forgetting to see what steps should be taken to counteract the slave trade), the second paragraph instructed him to place himself under the orders of Her Majesty's Minister in Cairo, to report through him, and to perform such other duties as might be entrusted to him by the Egyptian Government through Sir Evelyn Baring. "Such other duties as the Egyptian Government might entrust to you," says Blunt — one hears the Sussex squire's "View-halloo!" as he believes he sees his beaten quarry unable to escape him —

would have included Gordon's handing over the whole Sudan to the Mahdi, or his determination to smash the Mahdi, or again to "Sarawak the Sudan" on his own account or King Leopold's or the Queen's. Cromer was made responsible for all, and the Government at home retained the ordinary Parliamentary privilege of disavowing their own responsibility for things if things went wrong. Above all it enabled Granville to telegraph to Gladstone (who was ill in bed) with a free conscience that Gordon had been sent by the War Office simply "to report."

Did Gordon ever wonder on what foundations this last errand of his life rested? If he did, he gave no indication of

[1] In the Blue Book the word "Suakim" was altered to "Egypt."

it. He believed that his mission might "be for God's glory"; January 18, 1884, was perhaps the happiest day of his life. He felt "honored" in the morning at being received by Liberal Ministers, and when he left Charing Cross station on that winter's evening the Foreign Secretary, Lord Granville, bought him his ticket, the Duke of Cambridge held open the carriage door for him, and Lord Wolseley carried his suitcase. Wolseley's parting kindness for his friend of half a lifetime was to give him his watch and chain and his loose cash — for it suddenly transpired that Gordon had only a few shillings in his pocket.

So Gordon started on his last journey, and the newspaper readers of England learned next day with relief that Gordon had gone to disentangle or cut the knot which dervish fanaticism, Egyptian incompetence, and British dilatoriness had tied in the Sudan. From this time the legend round him grew apace. He was written up by journalists; the lessons of his life formed happy examples for preachers in a thousand pulpits. Books about his exploits and his selflessness began to appear. Tory politicians lauded his character and genius, using the prestige of his name as cover from which to launch attacks on the Government. The only people to grow doubtful were the Liberal Ministers who had chosen him as their instrument against the better judgment of their own Agent in Cairo. Gordon had not reached Marseilles before he was bombarding Lord Granville with suggestions in a way that was a little alarming to the staid Foreign Office. Gladstone afterwards voiced the opinion of at least a section of his Cabinet in saying it "was unfortunate Gordon should claim the hero's privilege by turning upside down and inside out every idea and intention with which he left England and for which he had obtained the Government's approval." But this anxiety to shift responsibility came later. At the outset the Gladstonians were as happy as everyone else. Gordon, they believed, would subdue the Sudan by the mere force of personality. While he was still crossing the Mediterranean, Queen Victoria recorded in her diary how she had seen Baring's cousin, Lord Northbrook, and he had read her some letters from Gordon, "whom he knows well. He says he is an extraordinary man with an enormous power over uncivilized people. His attempt is a very dangerous one."

3. Gordon Leaves for the Sudan

Gordon's intention, when he left London, was to go straight to Suakim, on the Red Sea, which Valentine Baker Pasha, Sir Samuel Baker's brother, held with an Egyptian force. How far Gordon counted on this to cover his evacuation from Khartoum is doubtful, for he had little enough belief in the fighting value of Egyptian troops. At the same time this was the only force protecting his line of communication, and obvious military considerations pointed to the necessity of Gordon's consulting with Baker in person. Through his personal friendship with certain sheikhs of the Red Sea Province, Gordon also hoped to be able to reach Khartoum. There he could do one of two things — treat direct with the Mahdi, if necessary bearding him at El Obeid, or put into operation his project for setting up independent sultanates in opposition to the Mahdi's power. There were various objections to both plans. A visit to the Mahdi was a highly dangerous proceeding, and was later categorically forbidden by Baring. On the other hand, petty sultans to take the place of the Khedive's Government were not easy to find. The only man who still might be able to wield power in the Sudan was Zobeir, the old slave chief, to whom the Egyptian Government had been considering giving a command on the Red Sea. But Gordon, two days after leaving London, telegraphed to Lord Granville suggesting that Zobeir should be sent to Cyprus, since he was his personal enemy and might be dangerous if left in Cairo.

Nothing, however, on that ill-starred mission went according to plan. Gordon's idea of going straight to Suakim, which Blunt considers was the only course that held out any hope of success, was prevented by Baring, who arranged for Sir Evelyn Wood to intercept him at Port Said and bring him back to Cairo. In a letter which Baring sent by Wood, he laid down the lines of Gordon's mission. He was to arrange for the evacuation of the Egyptian garrisons in the Sudan as rapidly as was consistent with (1) the saving of life and, so far as possible, property; and (2) the establishment of some rough form of government to prevent the anarchy and confusion arising from the withdrawal of the Egyptian troops. Baring was already acting upon the second paragraph of the written instructions Lord Granville had given Gordon. Hitherto there had been no mention of safeguarding property, and though the intention of setting up an alternative government to the Mahdi's was in the air, Baring's proposal was clearly an extension of anything hitherto officially put on paper.

But Gordon, still in high spirits, was in no mood to be critical or cautious. He accompanied Sir Evelyn Wood without demur to Cairo, where his old brother-in-arms, Sir Gerald Graham, met him at the station. They drove together to Wood's house, and Graham was delighted with Gordon's eager and boyish manner as he told his friend of the work before him. Except that the brown curly hair was now grizzled at the temples, the years did not seem to have touched him — he was the same Charlie Gordon that Graham had known in the Crimea. And before Graham, himself grown stout with middle age, was out of bed next morning he heard Gordon's voice cheerily calling him, and they were again discussing the Sudan and its problems. Gordon, as he had told Stead, still believed the Mahdi to be only a figurehead set up by the slavers; he thought the rebellion had little religious element in it, and he relied on his own prestige and reputation for just dealing towards the natives to win them over to his side.

Graham was far from sharing Gordon's confidence. It seemed to him a forlorn hope on which two Englishmen — for Colonel Stewart, a Hussar officer and a man with first-hand knowledge of the Sudan, had been chosen to accompany Gordon (his "wet-nurse" was Gordon's own designation of him) — set out to oppose the victorious advance of the Mahdi and his 300,000 fighting men. Gordon, indeed, appeared the only person who saw no danger in the work ahead. He was a changed man from the quarrelsome Governor-General of the Sudan who had left Cairo in such dudgeon four years previously. When he called on the Khedive Tewfik he apologized for his rudeness on that occasion, and the friendliest talk ensued. He was on the best of terms with Nubar, who embraced him. All their old griefs were forgotten, Gordon's contempt for Nubar's avarice, and Nubar's contempt for Gordon's methods of administration, which he had once crystallized in the dictum that Gordon would read the Bible all the morning and then get up and order a man to be hanged. No angry breezes ruffled Gordon's relations with Baring. For the moment everything went on oiled wheels. Gordon secured the firman from the Khedive Tewfik appointing him once again Governor-General of the Sudan — an essential preliminary to his mission, as Lord Granville had agreed, since he could do nothing whatsoever unless he was given powers by the Khedivial Government, which still held authority *de jure* over the Sudan. This firman was a generously drawn document, authorizing Gordon to carry out the Khedive's "good intentions for the establishment of justice and order," and "to secure the peace and prosperity of the Sudan by maintaining the security of the roads open to commerce"; of evacuation it said not a word. At the same time Gordon was also given two proclamations, one announcing his appointment in formal terms, the other declaring the Khedive's intention to evacuate the country after having set up an organized government. The publication of the second of these was left to his own discretion; he could withhold it or not as he thought fit.

Only one shadow lay across those two days in Cairo. Gordon met Zobeir by chance in Cherif Pasha's *selamlik* — and in the first moment of their encounter received a mystic feeling that here was the man to aid him in his task. With characteristic impetuosity Gordon went straight to Baring and asked him to arrange a meeting between them at which Zobeir should state his griefs. The following morning Baring received a memorandum from Gordon to the effect that, if anything more than evacuation was required, he considered Zobeir's presence in Khartoum a *sine qua non*. Gordon wrote, betraying in his style the tension under which he was laboring: —

> I would willingly take the responsibility of taking Zobeir up with me, if, after an interview with Sir E. Baring and Nubar Pasha, they felt the mystic feeling I could trust him, and which mystic feeling I felt I had for him to-night when I met him at Cherif Pasha's house. . . . I cannot exactly say why I feel towards him thus, and I feel sure that his going would settle the Sudan affair to the benefit of Her Majesty's and Egyptian Governments, and I would bear the responsibility of recommending it.

Baring repressed his astonishment that forty-eight hours before he had received a proposal through Lord Granville and emanating from Gordon that Zobeir should be deported to Cyprus, and arranged the meeting as Gordon desired. "The scene was dramatic and interesting. Both General Gordon and Zobeir Pasha were laboring under great excitement and spoke with vehemence," so runs the great proconsul's prose. Neither Baring nor Nubar, however, experienced any mystic feeling. Nubar, no doubt, recalled how Gordon's intuition played him false on a similar occasion eleven years before in the case of Abu Saud. And, though Baring considered the proposal to employ Zobeir plausible, the fact that Stewart, Wood, and Gordon's particular friend, Watson, were all opposed to it, seemed to him decisive, apart from the outcry that he knew Zobeir's employment would raise in England. Baring, in January 1884, little realized the storm that was to rage round the question of Khartoum a year later.

That night (January 26) Gordon took the train for Assiut on his way to the Sudan by the Nile route. Before he left he telegraphed to Khartoum, "Don't be panic-stricken. Ye are men, not women. I am coming. Gordon." Those who saw him in the evening at Sir Evelyn Wood's house said afterwards that he was silent and reserved. Later this was attributed to his failure to have his own way about Zobeir; more probably it was due to his personal dislike for Sir Evelyn Wood, whom he found "worldly." At the time he felt confident Zobeir would be allowed to follow him. Baring assured Gordon at the station that he would back up his request for Zobeir if, on his arrival in Khartoum, he was still of the same mind; and from the account left us by Sir Gerald Graham, who with his A.D.C. accompanied Gordon to Korosko, it is clear that the thing did not worry him. As they talked, or rather as the indefatigable Gordon talked and Graham listened, he laid down the alternatives as he saw them — either the assumption of authority in the Sudan by England (a course that Gordon in his heart of hearts clearly favored and which time has brought to pass) or its complete abandonment, which ran clean against every ideal he held for the future of Central Africa.

His nervous tension was shown by his indignation when Graham suggested that Gordon, in making himself the agent of the policy of abandonment, might be held responsible for all the evils that subsequently would befall the Sudan, and he asked Stewart and Graham's A.D.C. whether they did not think this suggestion monstrous. Gordon's physical endurance also impressed itself upon Graham that night, for while Graham and the others one by one began to doze, Gordon, who had brought no wrap with him, was prevented from sleeping by the excessive cold. Yet the following morning, when they boarded the steamer at Assiut, Gordon was the freshest of the party, and Graham has left us a vivid little thumb-nail sketch of him, standing on deck and talking with his A.D.C., Ibrahim Bey Fauzi. His eyes twinkled with fun, his features were relaxed in smiles, as in voluble but incorrect Arabic he rallied the young man, or with extended forefinger laughingly pushed some question home. Here was an irresistible natural charm of manner, utterly unlike the charm of the polished man of the world, yet for that reason perhaps all the more winning. No wonder Gordon's men would follow him anywhere.

Yet he had already shown another side of his character that morning. The other Gordon, the stern authoritarian, had been evoked by the conduct of the Darfuri chief who had come with them from Cairo. In pursuance of the plan for establishing independent sultanates, the Emir Abdul Shakour had been dragged from retirement in Cairo, given a splendid uniform with the largest decoration that could be found, and told that he was to return and sit in the seats of his Darfuri ancestors. Gordon felt some disgust when the wretched fellow appeared on the platform in Cairo with more than a score of women — such uxoriousness promised ill for the success of his political experiment. But at Assiut when the swarthy native, still wearing his gala uniform and his Medjidie order, which fell perpetually off his shoulder, pushed rudely past Gordon and took possession of the saloon on the steamer, he soon discovered his mistake. Gordon turned him out, commanded him to take off his uniform, and then had him back and made him understand that, whatever independence the Mahdi might subsequently allow him to enjoy in Darfur, he was at present under an Englishman's orders. But it was a poor augury for the success of the only scheme so far put forward to counter the Mahdi's power over the Sudan. Its failure was officially recognized when, on January 29, Baring received a telegram from Gordon, "The Emir Abdul Shakour has taken to drinking."

Graham, on that last journey, saw Gordon uneasy in mind, though untroubled for his own safety. He talked incessantly of the Sudan. At one moment he sketched a plan of operations for which he said that he intended to ask for five officers from home; at another he spoke of incorporating the Equatorial Province in the Congo, and as he developed his scheme for the establishment of a great state in Central Africa, under an international flag and with the King of the Belgians for its head, he seemed to Graham like a single-minded Napoleon, whose megalomania was counterbalanced by his immense pity for the natives. "You can see his kindness shining in his face when the natives crowd round him, kissing his hand," Graham wrote in his diary. He records also how Gordon, though intolerably chafed by the slowness of Nile travel, never showed impatience with the Arabs when they visited him, and sat for hours, as their fashion is, while they wrapped a grain of conversation in a mighty bundle of compliments. And when Gordon landed at Luxor and waited while the steamer coaled he spent the time, not in looking at the majestic ruins of Karnak, but in sitting at the hotel and once more discussing the Sudan with an archæologist working there.

Yet at the same time as Gordon, bemused by the vastness of the problem before him, thought of one hasty expedient after another, he was impressing upon his family and his friends that there was no danger. "I am as safe as at Southampton," he wrote to Augusta, "mind and keep that in view." One of the first pieces of news he received when he reached the frontiers of the Sudan was that the Mahdi was the nephew of one of his old servants, a camel guide. Nothing could have been more unfortunate, for it confirmed all his previous ideas about the personal insignificance of the new prophet, and outweighed the discovery he made at the same time that the whole population of the Sudan, and not simply the slave-dealers, were concerned in the rising — a fact that, in reality, undermined the foundations of his plans for checking the Mahdi. Gordon, however, professed no uneasiness as he entered the Sudan, and found it quieter than he had expected. It looked, he said, as if everything would be settled in six months. True, an untoward event occurred at Abu Hamed, where his camel ran away with him, but he was saved from a fall, which, he said, " would have been a bad omen with the superstitious natives." And, though naturally paying no heed to omens, Gordon deduced from the incident that God would bless his efforts; it indicated also that his mission would not be to his personal glory, which was as well since he "feared the insidious snake — pride."

4. Gordon Cheers the People of Khartoum

At Berber, Gordon halted. There he did two things, for both of which he has been blamed. He called together the local notables, and on February 13 secretly communicated to them the contents of the firman announcing the Khedivial Government's intention to evacuate the Sudan. " This document," says Colonel Stewart, who was present at the meeting, "caused the most profound sensation, but in so far as one could judge from what they said, nothing could exceed their delight. We have tried to fathom what those present really thought, and we are told that it was a mistake to have shown it." It was a leap in the dark, as Stewart told Baring — a fatal leap. Gordon's subsequent admission that he did "not know well its contents" — his own Arabic was scanty, and he was habitually careless about interpreters — shows that no one concerned in this ill-starred adventure, whether in London, Cairo, or Khartoum, escaped the atmosphere of muddle that enveloped it from the start. Subsequently Gordon came round to the same opinion, though he declared that he had never promulgated the firman. But the knowledge of its existence soon spread over the Sudan, and helped to persuade the still-wavering tribes to leave the setting sun of Egypt for the rising sun of the Mahdi.

His other mistake, which Blunt asserts made any amicable arrangement with the Mahdi impossible, was to write a friendly but condescending letter to the latest Prophet of God, offering him the title of Sultan of Kordofan, and sending him at the same time a robe of honor. To this the Mahdi made the obvious reply that there was no need for him to be Sultan of Kordofan, and in his turn sent Gordon a dervish dress, calling on him at the same time to surrender and turn Moslem — otherwise he and all his men would perish and suffer eternal perdition.

Something else that Gordon did at Berber called down criticism upon him — this time from his friends of the Anti-Slavery Society. The notables, taking advantage of the palpable weakness of authority, formally asked him whether the treaty of 1877, abolishing slavery in the Sudan after 1889, still held good. It was useless to answer yes, and, if Gordon said no, he at least helped to keep the local sheikhs quiet. One of his first acts in Khartoum was to issue a proclamation in confirmation of this decision and thus to annul the prospective effects of the Slave Convention. But the news that Gordon, once the champion of the anti-slavery cause, had now apparently thrown all his previous convictions to the winds caused much excitement in England. He was criticized in the papers, and, on the very day he reached Khartoum, Sir Stafford Northcote, the leader of the Opposition in the House of Commons, made party capital by asking, amid the cheers of his supporters, "whether General Gordon's powers extended to the issue of such a proclamation."

The outburst amused Gordon — complete rubbish, he called it. It seemed another example of the hypocrisy that flourished in Victorian England. His countrymen were preparing to abandon the Sudan to barbarism, thereby allowing slavery to flourish without restriction; yet when, to make his task more feasible, he recognized that five years hence slavery in the Sudan would still be legal, the Pharisees held up their hands in horror. Not a little did Gordon's former friends of the Anti-Slavery Society help to make his investment in Khartoum inevitable.

Gordon's arrival in that capital produced scenes of great enthusiasm. Crowds surrounded him as he walked from the quay to his palace; the people tried to kiss his hands and feet in approved Oriental style. "I come," he told them, "without soldiers but with God on my side, to redress the evils of the Sudan. I will not fight with any weapons but justice."

It was rhetoric, such as politicians use the world over. But he followed it up with more drastic evidences of his radical zeal.

The government books recording the taxpayers' arrears were burned, the whips and courbashes, those implements of the tax-gatherers, were given to the flames; and thus symbolically all the old bad ways of pashadom were forever abolished. Khartoum that night celebrated its freedom with the so-called illuminations, the strings of smoky hanging lanterns, which Gordon had often groaned over during his previous term as Governor-General.

5. The Disagreement about Zobeir

It was, however, one thing to wipe out the past, and another to provide for the future. In the first enthusiasm on Gordon's arrival, Frank Power, the young *Times* correspondent, falling an easy victim to Gordon's charm, asserted that the Mahdi had gone down before him. But a very few days in Khartoum convinced Gordon that his previous estimate of the Mahdi's power was mistaken. To the observer, looking at the question in cold blood half a century later, it is pretty clear that his mission was doomed to failure from the start. The words "too late," which Gordon had used to Baker in a Devonshire lane, were painfully true; by February 1884, the peaceable evacuation of the Egyptian troops and civilians from Khartoum, let alone from the stations farther south, was impracticable except by agreement with the Mahdi. Whether that agreement could have been secured at any time after Hicks Pasha's defeat is open to doubt; it was impossible after Gordon's offer of the Sultanate of Kordofan. But Gordon, whatever his failings as a statesman, was too good a soldier not to realize the dangers of the situation. He saw at once that Khartoum might at any moment be isolated; its long line of communications with the north depended on the uncertain fidelity of the tribes round Berber, through which lay the road either to Egypt or to the Red Sea. To make matters worse, Valentine Baker's defeat at El Teb, near Suakim, had now closed the route between that port and the Nile. True, when he sent Colonel de Coetlogon, who had organized the defense scheme of the town, back to Cairo, he told him he only did so because Khartoum was as safe as Kensington Gardens. The truth was that he felt a personal antipathy towards his brother officer — for one thing he had a young wife, and for another he was an alarmist. Coetlogon had said that Khartoum could not possibly withstand a siege by the Mahdi's forces.

The swiftness of events soon rendered any idea of evacuation impossible. Gordon had been only a week in Khartoum when he was forced to make armed demonstrations to overawe the tribes in the neighborhood. The situation, in fact, was already critical; how critical the proclamation he issued on February 26 shows: —

Since my arrival here about seven days ago, I have constantly advised you to the effect that good treatment and justice would be accorded to the natives, and that they should desist from rebellion, which only leads to war and bloodshed. Finding, however, that this advice has no effect on some people, I have been compelled to have recourse to severe measures, contrary to my own inclinations, so much so that the troops of the British Government are now on their way and in a few days will be in Khartoum. Whoever persists in wicked conduct will then receive the treatment he deserves.

Gordon's adversaries have not failed to adduce this as proof that his native pugnacity had already gained the upper hand. Sir Charles Dilke described it as an amazing lie; Lord Cromer long afterwards declared the statement to have been inexpedient, if not morally unjustifiable. Even his apologists admit it to have been inexplicable, or else due to a gloss by the Arabic translator. It is hardly necessary to assume as much. Gordon knew that General Graham was moving with a composite force against Osman Digna, the Mahdi's lieutenant operating round Suakim, and that by every precept of sound strategy it was essential to reopen the desert road between Suakim and Berber. If Graham reached Berber, Khartoum was within easy distance by river. Lord Wolseley had already drawn up military plans for a dash across to Berber, and submitted them to his chief, Lord Hartington, who had circulated them to the Cabinet.

In the meantime the telegraph between Cairo and Khartoum hummed with messages. Directly an idea entered Gordon's alert but impulsive mind, he could not rest until he had transmitted it to the British Representative in Egypt. There on Sir Evelyn Baring's table the pile of telegrams used to grow during the morning, and in the afternoon he would go through them, trying to extract from them what it was that Gordon really desired. Under their discrepancies one thing stood out clearly — Gordon still wanted Zobeir. He had been in Khartoum hardly an hour or two when he sent a long telegram pressing his view that Zobeir was the only man capable of ruling the Sudan. "He should be made a K.C.M.G. and given presents. . . . Zobeir's nomination under the moral countenance of Her Majesty's Government would bring all the merchants, European and others, back to the Sudan in a short time."

Baring, already inclined to support Gordon's request, came wholly round to that view when Stewart changed his previous opinion and agreed with Gordon that Zobeir was the only possible head of a Sudanese Government. But Lord Granville and his fellow Ministers were unconvinced by this agreement between the men on the spot. Public opinion, said the Foreign Secretary, would never tolerate the appointment of Zobeir Pasha; the idea made him and his fellow Ministers shiver at the anticipation of a press campaign led by their own Liberal supporters against the iniquity of reinstating a wicked slave-trader in his old haunts.

It is more than doubtful whether, even had Gladstone's Ministry acted with a determination equal to that shown by Gordon and Baring, Khartoum could have been saved in this way. Zobeir had lost prestige during his exile in Cairo, and he would almost certainly have been no match for Abu Fulaja, the "Father of the V-shaped Gap," whose smile melted even the hearts of Christian missionaries and whose victorious followers saw in him the Chosen of Allah. But such doubts did not assail Gordon, and Baring, for his part, though disinclined to trust Zobeir, seems to have felt equally confident that if the old slaver chief worked loyally with Gordon he would be able to head a local Sudanese Government.

But the courage of Ministers in London oozed right away as the progress of events in Khartoum reached their ears. Gordon's proclamation about the arrival of British troops "frightened the Cabinet out of its wits," and when he suggested at the same time to Baring that 200 British-Indian troops should be sent to Wady Halfa to assist in smashing the Mahdi, the phrase filled Ministers with horror. The British Agent in Cairo, with no electorate to think of, kept his head. It might be indiscreet of Gordon to talk about smashing the Mahdi, but Baring realized that sooner or later the thing would have to be done. England could not leave the Sudan permanently to the Mahdi and anarchy.

"Whatever may be said to the contrary," Baring told Lord Granville on February 28,

> Her Majesty's Government must in reality be responsible for any arrangements which are now devised for the Sudan, and I do not think it possible to shake off that responsibility. . . . I have no doubt as to the most advisable course of action. Zobeir Pasha should be permitted to succeed General Gordon. He should receive a certain sum of money to begin with, and an annual subsidy of £50,000 for the first five years, to depend upon his good behavior. This amount would enable him to maintain a moderate-sized army, and the whole arrangement would be an economical one for the Egyptian Government.

6. Abandoned?

Gordon's state of mind in all this fog of intrigue oscillated between the official and transcendental planes. When on the latter, he shows us the forebodings which warned him of disaster, though he tried to instill into the people over whom he ruled something of his own faith in the beneficence of the Almighty. On his first Friday in Khartoum he writes to Augusta telling her that it is the Moslem's Sunday. He has made, he says, to those who came to pay him their respects "a long sermonizing speech as to trust in God." He means to "order the troops to have regular morning and evening prayers, as the Turkish troops do"; "they worship the one God Jehovah," he adds, identifying on rather doubtful grounds Allah with the God of Israel. And he has the Arabic text, "God rules the hearts of all men," put up over his throne, so that when people come to him in fear, as they have begun to do, they may draw comfort from it.

There was much fear in Khartoum, and the responsibility for the safety of its people already weighed heavily upon him. At one moment he tries to console himself by saying he is glad the Sudan had got its independence through the Mahdi, at another the whole country seems to him a hopeless ruin. The peculiar pain which he had felt at other crises in his career, the pain arising from the excessive anxiety he "cannot help being in for these people," comes back to him at times. Yet he asks himself what was the good of faith if it could not ease such a burden. He writes to Augusta: —

> I think that our Lord, sitting over Jerusalem, is ruling all things to the glory of His kingdom, and cannot wish things were different than they are, for, if I did so, then I wish *my will,* not *His,* to be done. . . . Either I must believe He does all things in mercy and love, or else I disbelieve His existence; there is no half-way in the matter.

Yet his ideas will not run clear. Has God sent him to Khartoum? As he looks into his own heart he comes to the conclusion that ambition has put him where he is, and all he can do is to dismiss the matter by saying that "enough for the day is the evil."

Those last few short letters he wrote to his anxious sister in Southampton before the Mahdi's followers cut him off from the outside world show Gordon still probing into the foundations of the temple he had been trying to construct for twenty years. He is harder on himself than ever. Nothing now about drinking and smoking, but he resolves — as he had done once before in Mauritius — that never again will he read the newspapers. He hopes for his own good that he will be humbled, as early in March he still asserts his belief that he will find a pacific solution to his mission directly Zobeir joins him — Zobeir, as the Moslem and the hard man of war, he considers, will usefully supplement his own humane and tender Christian counsels. The comparison comes oddly from a man who was on the eve of directing a classic defense against enormous odds, but, like many another, Gordon knew himself indifferently well. For all the philanthropic and humanitarian sentiments which he had acquired during his career, he still remained at heart the same Gordon who had tasted the joy of battle in the trenches before Sebastopol and on the plains of the Yangtze. And when at last the middle of March came, and the dervishes swooped down on the Nile and cut off Khartoum from the outer world, his spirits rose. "We are all right," he begins a note to Augusta. "The enemy has established himself some 6000 strong nine miles from here, and we hear his drums from the Palace. We are well off for food, and the people are in good spirits. Oddly enough the supplies come in better than they did before, and we shall, D.V., go on for months." They could go on for months — until they were relieved. There was no more any question of evacuating the garrisons, except under cover of a military force capable first of defeating the Mahdi. On March 23, Frank Power, who lived with Gordon and now became his mouthpiece, wrote to the *Times*, "We are daily expecting the British troops. We cannot bring ourselves to believe that we are abandoned by the Government."

The superiority of the Mahdi's numbers made it impossible for Gordon to try to break their lines.

7. What the Queen, Gladstone, and Others Thought

At home, meanwhile, there was only talk. The situation in mid-March had already been described in messages from Berber as critical. On March 16, the prescient Baring told Lord Granville that the question would very probably arise of sending an expedition to Khartoum to bring away General Gordon and Colonel Stewart — the first mention of the Gordon Relief Expedition which kept England on tenterhooks the following autumn. A week later Baring sent a still stronger telegram, urging that an attempt should be made to help Gordon from Suakim, in the neighborhood of which Graham had already retrieved the defeat suffered by Baker Pasha, though the bravery of the dervishes who charged against the British squares showed that they were more formidable enemies than Gordon imagined. It was now clear that to reach Berber would be a difficult and risky operation. But it was possible, and, if British troops could not cross the two hundred miles of desert between the Red Sea and the Nile during the hottest time of year, it might be managed by an Indian cavalry brigade. Queen Victoria read the dispatch of her representative in Cairo, and at once telegraphed to Hartington, "Gordon is in danger. You are bound to try and save him. Surely Indian troops might go from Aden. They could bear the climate. You have incurred fearful responsibility."

Still the Liberal Ministers were not disposed to take action. Lord Granville told the Queen that the Cabinet considered it unjustifiable to send a British force as proposed, and that "objections, though not of the same character, existed to sending an Indian expedition." "It is believed to be impossible," he added, "for the tribes to take Khartoum by assault. The garrison has six months' provisions." Neither the Queen nor Baring remained silent at such pusillanimity. Baring pointed out that if Gordon and Stewart received the instructions which the British Government had transmitted through him "they cannot but understand them as meaning that they, and all with them, are to be abandoned and to receive no help from the British Government." He also emphasized the responsibility of the Cabinet. It had sent Gordon and Stewart on a dangerous mission; it had refused to agree to their request for Zobeir; and now it simply left Gordon "full discretion to remain at Khartoum if he thinks necessary, or to retire by the southern or any other route which may be available." He did not mince his words. "No one can regret more than I do the necessity of sending British or Indian troops to the Sudan, but, having sent Gordon to Khartoum, it appears to me that it is our bounden duty, both as a matter of humanity and policy, not to abandon him."

The Queen energetically backed him up. She told Gladstone that Sir Evelyn Baring only expressed her own feelings, and asserted that, "if not for humanity's sake, for the honor of the Government and nation Gordon must not be abandoned."

But Gladstone, with a Cabinet divided on the question, managed to avoid a decision. He had been pushed into Egypt against his will. He would not be pushed into the Sudan. Gordon had been sent there to report. Why did he not do so? The Cabinet was still ignorant of "General Gordon's circumstances, opinions, and desires." Let a telegram be sent to him to ascertain these — this, the Prime Minister told his sovereign, he was sure would "draw valuable information from General Gordon."

Abandoned — the ugly word, in Power's dispatch, crept into the *Times* on April 1, soon after the Government had clinched its decision not to send troops to Berber by withdrawing Graham's force from Suakim. But, when the Opposition brought the matter up in the House of Commons, Gladstone, with the knowledge that both Baring and the Queen had used the identical word, worked himself into a rhetorical fury over the exaggerations of newspaper correspondents. He complained that the time of the House should be wasted on Egypt in a way that was "out of all proportion to the pressure and urgency of the question," and vented his moral indignation on Sir Stafford Northcote for taking notice of unauthorized statements in the press. The idea that the Government had abandoned their agent was monstrous. Gordon, he said, was under no constraint of orders to remain in the Sudan, and was at liberty to exercise "a free judgment upon the matter." The eyes flashed, the voice of the old lion reverberated through the Chamber, and the Opposition, accused of taking its information from Fleet Street, wilted and collapsed. Gladstone had won what is known as a Parliamentary victory, and the question of Khartoum was thus left exactly where it stood before, except for the fact that Lord Hartington, speaking as Secretary of State for War, stated definitely that the Government accepted responsibility for Gordon's safety. It took, however, this entirely straightforward but slow-thinking Cavendish till the end of July to make up his mind that the time had come to implement his words.

In the meantime Gladstone could always continue his Fabian tactics. On April 23 he drafted a message for Gordon, now in the sixth week of siege, asking him to keep the Government informed, not only as to the immediate, but as to any prospective danger at Khartoum. The gist of the telegram was: —

. . . We do not propose to supply him with Turkish or other force for the purpose of undertaking military expeditions, such being beyond the scope of the commission he holds, and at variance with the pacific policy which was the purpose of his mission to the Sudan; if with this knowlerge he continues at Khartoum, he should state to us the cause and intention with which he so continues. . . .

As the message only reached Gordon more than three months later, it perfectly fulfilled Gladstone's intention of wasting time in the hope that thereby he need do nothing. Gordon was in no danger — that was Gladstone's answer to his critics. And until Gordon replied to his questions the Government could not be expected to act.

Unofficially, during the spring and summer, various suggestions were made to solve the problem. Colonel Burnaby, who had excited Gordon's strictures in Equatoria, and Mark Napier, a son of the victor of Magdala, had the idea of getting together a thousand sportsmen, "who would be ready to go a thousand miles to shoot a lion," and try to force a passage on camel-back from Suakim to Berber and so rescue Gordon. Blunt, to whom they propounded the idea, was unsympathetic; much as he liked Gordon personally, he thought the Mahdi was right and Gordon was wrong, and preferred "to see him perish rather than be the cause of sending a single dervish to death." The scheme, too, found little favor at the War Office, where Redvers Buller, temperamentally disliking Gordon, remarked that "the man was not worth the camels."

Blunt, indeed, had his own idea, which was to go on a mission of peace to the Mahdi, and on April 23, the very day that Gladstone sent the message asking for information, Blunt took to his friend Eddy Hamilton, Gladstone's private secretary, his own proposals for negotiating a treaty with the Mahdi Mohammed Ahmed. W. T. Stead attacked the problem from still another angle. Since little attention was paid to his suggestions that Gordon should be allowed to "Sarawak the Sudan," — in other words, to establish himself in Khartoum as an independent Sultan, in the same way as Rajah Brooke had in Sarawak, — he decided to enlist the aid of King Leopold. The little Fleet Street journalist with his self-appointed mission found no favor with the hard-headed monarch, who was unimpressed by Stead's offer of the Sudan as a gift from the British Government on condition that King Leopold should make himself responsible for Gordon's safety. A vehement discussion soon generated heat, and we have a picture of the tall and now angry King with the long nose and sinister eye towering over his pertinacious visitor "as a Cochin China rooster might tower over a little Bantam cock." Stead returned unsuccessful from his visit to Brussels. King Leopold said nothing about it at the time. But months later, when Gordon's fate was already decided, he one day referred to the interview which was to have saved the life of the man he had intended to be his satrap. "Oh, Stead!" he exclaimed. "It was terrible! How that man made me sweat!"

8. Gordon's Views

And what of Gordon? He did not think of Parliamentary tactics, of public opinion, or even of himself. He was perfectly willing to sacrifice his life, let alone his place. He had always held it was a soldier's duty to be killed, and he had not changed his mind, either about the ethics of his profession or about the utter worthlessness of the world since, as a youngster of twenty-two, he had gone to the Crimea. Death to him was nothing, less than nothing. It was the porch through which he would enter life; and if he saw the door already ajar and the radiance beyond it was not likely that he would allow any physical shrinkings from the death that he despised to prevent him entering that "bright, happy land."

Yet he could not, even when it came to the mere personal matter of dying, think only of himself. By his going to Khartoum he had prevented the garrison and the inhabitants from making their submission to the Mahdi. The example of Berber, which for two days after its fall was given over to fire and sword, showed what the Khartoumis must expect if they fell to the tender mercies of the Mahdi. It was all very well for Gladstone to say that Gordon was under no constraint to stay in Khartoum. Apart from the fact that technically this was untrue, since Baring had told him not to leave until further orders, there was no way of honor except to remain and share the fate of those who had accepted him as their leader. Had he been so minded he could have stolen away at any time to the very end. But Gordon was a soldier, and so long as he held the Khedive's firman as Governor-General of the Sudan he must consider the safety of every one of his subjects before his own. While Khartoum was still uninvested, Gordon wrote to Baring, "How could I look the world in the face if I abandoned them and fled? Could you as a gentleman advise this course?" Baring, who also was a gentleman, had not answered.

Directly the siege began, Gordon alone stood between Khartoum and its destruction. Everyone knew it. On the few occasions that he went outside the lines the people embraced his knees and kissed his feet, lest he should leave them to their fate. Yet he ruled in fear rather than in love. The thought pained him. When he saw men who came to him on business so frightened that their trembling hands were unable to hold the match to the cigarette he gave them, Gordon realized how sternly he behaved towards his officers and his officials. They were like dogs before him, and nothing, he averred, could obliterate from his memory the way he had treated them. His conscience smote him worst for his treatment of the two Pashas, Hassan and Said, who had gone in the middle of March to attack a rebel position below Khartoum. The operation was a complete fiasco, a mere handful of mounted Arabs putting the whole force of a thousand men to flight. Charges of treachery were brought against both the commanders, they were court-martialed, found guilty, and shot. Afterwards Gordon bitterly regretted signing their death warrants, and took to himself the whole blame for what he called their judicial murder. It was hard to rule and remain a Christian. "Happy, so far as we can see, are those men who swing in small arcs; unhappy are those who, seeking the field of adventure, swing between the extreme of evil and good." So he wrote in his journal when the siege was six months old. Thomas à Kempis was a more difficult master to follow than ever, now that war was the real Governor-General of the Sudan.

Not that Gordon had time to spend on his favorite reading. He was busy night and day, applying his professional engineering skill to the defenses of the town, laying mines, fitting up his little flotilla, — his "penny steamers," as he called them, likening them to those which at that time used to ply upon the Thames at London, — enrolling regiments of volunteers and of Negro troops, which were to prove the most dependable units of the garrison. So thorough were his arrangements that the single month which Colonel de Coetlogon had estimated as the limit of the town's capacity to withstand the Mahdi was stretched to more than ten. Upon Gordon's shoulders depended also the whole civil government. He had to arrange for the feeding of the people, to watch and control public opinion. He told the ulema what they should preach about in the mosques, issued paper money, made pashas and beys, gave decorations — and wondered how to answer the cries for bread of the women outside the Palace gates. Often he would go on the roof of his Palace and scan the enemy lines through his glass. He would have liked a hundred telescopes. Then at night there were the long lines of the ramparts to be visited, where he had to see that the sentries were awake and at their posts. Only in the afternoon was he able to snatch a

THE PALACE, KHARTOUM
(From the "Illustrated London News," 1885)

few hours' sleep. There hardly came a moment's relaxation of the strain. At meals he met the other two Englishmen, Stewart and Power. To Power he always seemed cheerful, but sometimes it happened that he could not eat from anxiety, and then he would "grow furious" to see that his example affected the others. "I am always frightened," he confessed, "and very much so. It is not the fear of death — that is past, thank God; but I fear defeat and its consequences. I do not believe a bit in the calm, unmoved man." But his messages to the outer world, which Gladstone found so infinitely consoling, betrayed nothing of these feelings; in them he was the confident soldier, ready to hold out for months and years.

At the same time, Khartoum, if it were not to fall, must be relieved before the autumn, and when Gordon learned that no British troops were being sent to Berber he naturally sought for another way out of the impasse. Early in April he suggested to Baring that an alternative to intervention by the British Government was for the Sultan, as Suzerain of Egypt, to assume responsibility for law and order in the Sudan. Did Gordon in following up this idea show, as Baring suggests, a flightiness quite out of accord with diplomatic realities? The truth is that the project of shifting the burden of the Sudan on to the Sultan's shoulders was an old one, and, at the beginning of January, Lord Granville had sent an official telegram to Baring which approved handing back to the Porte the administration of the shores of the Red Sea and the Eastern Sudan.

Under such circumstances there was nothing revolutionary in Gordon's falling back on this same idea. As he thought over it this solution attracted him more and more. Of course, the Sultan would want money, — say £150,000 a year, — and it was possible that Osmanli rule in the Sudan would not be remarkable either for humanity or for justice. Still, the Sudanese were an ungrateful and stiff-necked lot — "after the way these people have rejected my terms I would be inclined to let the Turkish harrow go over them," he told Baring on April 12.

Since there was no time to waste, Gordon three days later followed up this telegram with a direct appeal to the Sultan: —

Your Majesty, as Head of the Mussulman faith, must know far better than I do that the False Prophet threatens Your Majesty's spiritual authority. . . . The presence of 3000 of Your Majesty's troops, supported by the prestige of Your Majesty's name and at a cost of £300,000, would be sufficient to suppress the revolt and destroy the rebels. . . . We can hold out for five months and I believe, if Your Majesty sends these men, these men will not have to fire a shot; the rebels will dissolve as ice before fire.

Gordon did not leave the matter there. He dispatched a message to the Consuls-General of the Great Powers in Cairo asking them to press upon their governments the importance of giving financial support to the proposed Turkish expedition. He addressed a copy of the same appeal to the Pope. None of these calls for help reached the outside world, but in any case they must have come to nothing, for, on May 1, Lord Granville telegraphed to Cairo, "With respect to General Gordon's request for Turkish troops with a view to offensive operations, General Gordon cannot too clearly understand that these operations cannot receive the sanction of Her Majesty's Government and that they are beyond the scope of his mission."

The tone of asperity is undisguised. Indeed, the keynote of the whole of this disastrous story is the irritation felt by each party for the other. Ministers in England, Hartington being a notable exception, put the blame on Gordon, Gladstone in his self-sufficiency attributing some of it to Baring. That imperturbable diplomat deplored at once Gordon's flightiness and the procrastination of the Cabinet. And Gordon, as time went on, grew more and more bitter towards Baring, never appearing to realize that the true villain of the piece was not the British Representative in Cairo, but the Prime Minister in London. Then the fog of war descended upon the Sudan. Nothing more was heard of Gordon, and, as Gladstone had received no reply to his questionnaire of April 23, Liberal Ministers were able to forget Khartoum and the two Englishmen whom they had sent there. Gladstone was whipping up his party to attack the House of Lords — a much more exciting subject. And Gordon was left to his own devices.

9. Gordon's Last Victories

At one moment it seemed as if by his unaided genius he would succeed in saving Khartoum and defeating his encircling enemies. So strongly had he fortified the lines defending the town that the dervishes soon became chary of approaching them. After their first sanguinary repulses in the middle of April, when his system of mines proved highly effective, Khartoum was in no further danger of being taken by direct assault. And, by July, Gordon had infused such discipline into his troops and such energy into his subordinates that he felt strong enough to take the offensive once more. This time there was no recurrence of the rout for which the two Pashas in command had afterwards paid with their lives. Mohammed Aly Bey, the ablest of his native officers, carried out an extremely successful operation on the Blue Nile. The dervishes were defeated with heavy loss, and the fertile country southeast of Khartoum was to a great extent cleared of the Mahdi's followers, with the result that provisions again flowed into the town. At the same time the defeat of the dervishes at Halfaya, nine miles north of Khartoum, opened the way to the north.

Gordon prepared to follow up this offensive by operations on a larger scale aiming at the recovery of Berber. He planned to send Stewart and Power with 2000 men down the Nile. After they had taken Berber, which should not be difficult with the help of the armed steamers, they were to go on to Dongola. On August 26, Gordon sent a message to Baring asking that British troops should support this offensive from the north and be ready to garrison Berber when the Nile fell and it became more open to attack from the enemy. If no British troops came, Gordon explained that it would be necessary for Stewart to evacuate Berber and, after burning it, return to Khartoum. For the permanent government of the Sudan he insisted once more on Zobeir, adding that, if the Sultan sent troops, the Sudan could be handed over to them.

Such were the resourceful Gordon's military projects and political plans in August. Meanwhile, before letting Stewart, with his 2000 men, move upon Berber, he decided to clean up the Blue Nile country. A force of infantry on the left and Khartoum bank of the river, operating with the steamer flotilla, severely defeated the rebels in the neighborhood of Khartoum. Then it advanced a hundred miles up the river and captured the market town of Abu Harez. The spoils of this expedition included guns and ammunition, with large quantities of durra — a very welcome addition to the store of provisions in Khartoum. "We are going to hold out here forever," Gordon wrote apropos of these successes to the commander of *H.M.S. Euryalus* at Massawa.

This victory clears our vicinity on three parts of a circle. . . . There is one bond of union between us and our troops — they know if the town is taken they will be sold as slaves, and we must deny Our Lord if we would save our lives. I think we hate the latter more than they hate the former. . . . D.V. we will defeat them without any help from outside.

So, at the beginning of September, Gordon's prospects appeared bright — almost deceptively bright. He might have thought he was in China, fighting the Long-hairs; the same amphibious tactics were meeting with the same success. But there were vital differences: now it was Gordon who was cut off from the sea, and not the rebels; the dervishes, too, whom he defeated did not enroll themselves under his flag — dead or alive, they remained faithful to the Mahdi. Another reason for anxiety was that, when the Nile fell, Gordon's steamers, which played the rôle of cavalry for him, would lose much of their offensive power. Something more, therefore, was required than a mere local success, such as Mohammed Aly had won, if the main forces of the Mahdi, numbering their scores of thousands and at the moment awaiting the end of the inundation before advancing on Khartoum, were to be prevented from their purpose. A victory, for instance, over the Sheikh el Obeid, whose defection soon after Gordon's arrival had caused the tribes round Khartoum to rise, might well tip the scale permanently against the Mahdi. Besides, it was doubtful strategy to send the expedition under Stewart northwards and thus seriously weaken the garrison when this supporter of the Mahdi's lay within striking distance of the town.

On September 4, therefore, Mohammed Aly, now promoted a Pasha, set off up the Blue Nile with a steamboat flotilla and a thousand men, the flower of Gordon's troops, for an attack upon the sheikh's headquarters at El Eilafun, about twenty-five miles above Khartoum on the Blue Nile. Its success was only marred by the escape of the sheikh, and on the following day Mohammed Aly, hearing that this holy and dangerous man had taken refuge at another place twenty miles inland, decided to move against him. If he captured or killed the redoubtable sheikh, the Mahdi's cause in the Central Sudan would receive its deathblow. Mohammed Aly could not resist so tempting an opportunity, and though Gordon had warned him against going far from the river banks, and so losing the protection of the steamers, he decided to take the risk and advance against the sheikh in his lair. But he had to rely upon untrustworthy guides, who led his column into the scrub, where it was surrounded by dervishes in overpowering numbers and, after desperate fighting, cut to pieces. It was a repetition of the Hicks disaster on a smaller scale, and when Gordon heard of it he knew it was the end of his hopes. Nothing except outside intervention could now save the people of Khartoum.

10. Disasters Begin

Help seemed as far off as ever. The Gladstone Ministry, indeed, had been galvanized into taking a decision at the end of July, when Lord Hartington, goaded by Lord Wolseley and his own conscience, told the Prime Minister he would resign if a relief expedition were not immediately organized. Even then preparations were hung up while the military experts fought over the relative advantages of the Suakim-Berber and the Cairo-Assuan-Wady Halfa route for the advance on Khartoum. By September, the choice of the Nile route had been made, and Lord Wolseley had already reached Cairo and taken command of what was officially known as the Gordon Relief Expedition. The race against time had begun.

Of all these things Gordon had only scanty information when he decided to send one of his steamers under its Arab captain down to Dongola with dispatches. The French consul, Herbin, hearing of this, asked to be allowed to go too. Then Stewart suggested that he also should leave, a suggestion which Gordon jumped at, for it would enable him to make known his views — besides, he preferred having no other Englishman to cross his will. The *Times* correspondent, Power, was also added to the party. Weighing the chances,

Gordon decided that the *Abbas* was humanly sure to get through, while it was very probable Khartoum would fall, and with Stewart, therefore, he sent the official cipher key.

His last letter to Baring still attributed the blame to the wrong quarter: —

> How many times have we written asking for reënforcements, calling your serious attention to the Sudan! No answer at all has come to us as to what has been decided on the matter, and the hearts of men have become weary of this delay. While you are eating and drinking and resting on good beds we and those with us, both soldiers and servants, are watching by night and day, endeavoring to quell the movement of this false Mahdi. . . . The reason why I have now sent Colonel Stewart is because you have been silent all this while and neglected us, and lost time without doing any good. If troops were sent, as soon as they reach Berber this rebellion will cease and the inhabitants will return to their former occupations.

So, on the night of September 9, Stewart, Power, and Herbin steamed away from Khartoum on the S. S. *Abbas*, which Gordon had originally ordered in 1877 for his province of Equatoria. Two other armed steamers accompanied the *Abbas*, their business being to escort it past Berber, where the Mahdi also had two steamers which had been captured at the fall of that town. The *Abbas*, its hull specially strengthened to withstand rocks, towed a couple of Nile feluccas in which were some Greeks and Syrians whom Gordon had paid to act as a bodyguard to prevent any threat of mutiny from the crew of the steamer. Gordon gave careful instructions to Stewart. The two escorting steamers were not to return southwards until all danger from those belonging to the dervishes at Berber was past. If the *Abbas* was unable to get through the rapids between Berber and Dongola, they were to abandon it and take to the feluccas. They were only to land for wood in uninhabited places, and if they anchored it must be in midstream. As far as human foresight went, Gordon provided for the safety of those who were leaving him to face the Mahdi alone.

But his plans went awry, like everything else in this disastrous story. After passing Berber, Stewart, thinking all danger to be at an end, detached the two escorting steamers, though Gordon had told him to keep them for two days longer. The dervishes at Berber, seeing them repass southwards, at once sent out one of their own steamers in pursuit of the *Abbas*. Stewart, meanwhile, had cast off the two feluccas, and these, with the unfortunate passengers, now fell into the enemy's hands. Of this Stewart can have known nothing as the *Abbas* steamed rapidly downstream and successfully negotiated the Fifth Cataract. On September 18, they were within a couple of days of Dongola, and their troubles seemed nearly at an end when the *Abbas* struck a rock in mid-channel and could not be got off. For this contingency Gordon had provided the feluccas which Stewart had so rashly let go. The *Abbas*, however, had still a small boat in which some of those on the *Abbas* might have reached Dongola. But when natives appeared on the bank, waving a white flag, Stewart entered into parley with them. The local sheikh, professing to be friendly, said he would assist them, and invited the three Europeans ashore, though he made the sinister stipulation that they should bring neither arms nor escort. In spite of being warned by his native officers not to trust the sheikh, Stewart blindly accepted the invitation. He and the two others landed, went into the sheikh's house, and were immediately murdered.

It was one more of the unhappy mischances that helped to seal the fate of Khartoum, the more poignant in occurring when success was so near. Within a hundred miles of the scene of this tragedy a young officer in Gordon's own corps, Major H. H. Kitchener, R.E., at the time in charge of the advanced intelligence service, was preparing the way for the Relief Expedition. Had Stewart been fated to reach him, Lord Wolseley would have known how imperative was speed if Khartoum was to be relieved, and to what straits the town was by this time reduced.

11. Gordon and Gladstone

As Gordon sat writing in his Palace that morning of September 18, he little guessed the grim fate which had befallen his companions a few hours before. Such news of them as trickled through was good. He had learned from a spy that Stewart had captured an Arab convoy of 200 camels, and it pleased Gordon to picture the Mahdi's fury. Some qualms he felt about their safety, chiefly on account of Stewart's rashness, which might at any time land him and his companions in trouble; but it looked as if all had gone well, and by this time they must be near Dongola. Once Stewart reached Cairo, the Relief Expedition would surely be expedited. As he wrote in his journal, which he had begun to keep on the morrow of Stewart's and Power's departure, he was fairly easy in mind. He recorded how he had arranged for the removal of the Greek Consul and his nationals via Equatoria, and he wondered what was to happen after the garrison had been evacuated. Zobeir with a subsidy — or the Sultan? Otherwise the Mahdi in Khartoum would only be a step to the Mahdi in Cairo, in Mecca, in Damascus. . . . Who could put a term to the militant power of this religious fanatic? And yet, as Gordon thought of these world problems, pen in hand, he decided that his own presence in Equatoria with his faithful flotilla of steamers would make the Mahdi think twice of embarking on any great adventures. Still in Gordon's mind there remained the idea of retreating to the south and annexing the Equatorial Province to King Leopold's state of the

Congo. From this Gordon went on to discuss the previous and future existence of animals, and from that to ponder on the mystery of the Incarnation. Here was a pleasanter subject than the Sudan to meditate upon, yet he could not escape the latter for long, and he closed his daily entry with the remark that the Europeans captured by the Mahdi (Slatin was one of them, and Cuzzi [1] another) had "denied their Lord and deserved their fate in some measure."

We have a glimpse of another character in this drama on that same morning of September 18, 1884. The septuagenarian Gladstone, then stumping Scotland in his campaign against the House of Lords, was staying at Brechin Castle with Lord Dalhousie. The *Dundee Advertiser* that day printed a telegram from Cairo which gave in sensational form Gordon's messages of August 26 to the Khedive, Nubar, and Baring, which he had sent off when it seemed possible that he might retake Berber. The newspaper magnified the 2000 Turkish troops suggested by Gordon to 200,000, and described him as "careering up and down the Nile, crying for the blood of the Mahdi, and burning towns and slaying rebels to his heart's content." Gladstone's heart beat fast at this magnificent indignation. Here was confirmation for all his suspicions of Gordon's motives, for all his convenient convictions that Gordon was in no danger. "As he read," a fellow guest has recorded, "his face hardened and whitened, the eyes burned as I have seen them once or twice in the House of Commons when he was angered — burned with a deep fire as if they would have consumed the paper on which Gordon's message was printed. . . . Then he left the room and was seen no more that morning."

Gladstone had recently abused Sir Stafford Northcote, with all the scorn of a Hebrew prophet for the priests of Baal, when that respectable leader of the Conservative Opposition pre-

[1] Giuseppe Cuzzi had been British Vice-Consul at Berber.

sumed to take his information on the Sudan question from the newspapers. But Gladstone, although he was Prime Minister, did not wait for any official confirmation of the news he had read in the *Dundee Advertiser*. Without even a day's delay, he gave orders that Gordon was to be placed under Lord Wolseley, and that his powers as Governor-General were to be limited to the area round Khartoum. If Gladstone could not leave a troublesome servant to the fate he had brought upon himself, he could at any rate degrade him. And Lord Granville on September 19 telegraphed to Cairo the decision taken by Gladstone after reading a Scottish Liberal paper.

It is a quaint sequel to this reaction of Gladstone's conscience that when Lord Granville's order reached Gordon on November 25, two months before the end, he took it as meaning that the policy of evacuation had been abandoned and that the British Government meant to appoint its own officers to governorships of the various provinces of the Sudan. On the strength of it he tore up the firman given him by the Khedive the previous January announcing the evacuation of the Sudan. So the play of misunderstanding and cross-purpose went on to the end.

12. The Mahdi's Last Offers

All this while the real protagonist, Mohammed Ahmed, the man with the gap in his teeth and the charming smile, had been preparing for the *dénouement* of the plot he had hatched. Khartoum was his goal, and though his leisurely progress might deceive Kitchener, whose spies were only human in telling their paymaster what he wanted to hear, the growing might of the Mahdi was only too apparent in Khartoum. Gordon had long lost whatever moral respect he had ever had for his adversary, and he now looked on him as a charlatan, a robber, and a fanatic who put pepper under his nails to make the tears flow when he wished to impress his dervishes, and "cut off the lips of smokers and the noses of *snuffers*." With such a man negotiation was surely impossible. The Mahdi, on his side, continued to hope that Gordon might be induced to follow the example of Slatin and Cuzzi. At the end of June the Italian had been sent under a flag of truce with a demand for the surrender of the town. Gordon then refused to see a man he looked on as a renegade, and he sent his reply to the dervish commander by another hand: —

Giuseppe Cuzzi brought me yesterday letters, in which you call on me to surrender. As you well know, the Mohammedans who are with me do not wish to surrender, and do you expect that I, who am a Christian, should set the example?

If you have letters to send me again, do not send a European but one of your own people.

Further efforts followed in September. One day three dervishes came within the lines bearing a message from the Mahdi and for a second time offering the present of a dervish dress. Gordon received them in person, and listened while they told him that he had only to put on that robe, patched as a symbol of the poverty to which every dervish was sworn, to be received with honor in the Mahdi's camp. Even then a contemptuous refusal did not cause their master to give up hope of inducing Gordon to change his mind. Again he used Cuzzi as an intermediary, and a second time Gordon refused to see any Christian who had denied his faith. Then sheikhs and emirs of the Mahdi called on him in rising tones of peremptoriness to submit to the Prophet of God, and to them Gordon replied that the Moslem doctors of theology in Khartoum had proved from the Koran that the Mahdi was an impostor and an enemy of Islam. How then should he, a Christian, accept the Mahdi as Prophet?

As the false Prophet in person approached Khartoum, Gordon on the whole was relieved, for, if the Mahdi failed,

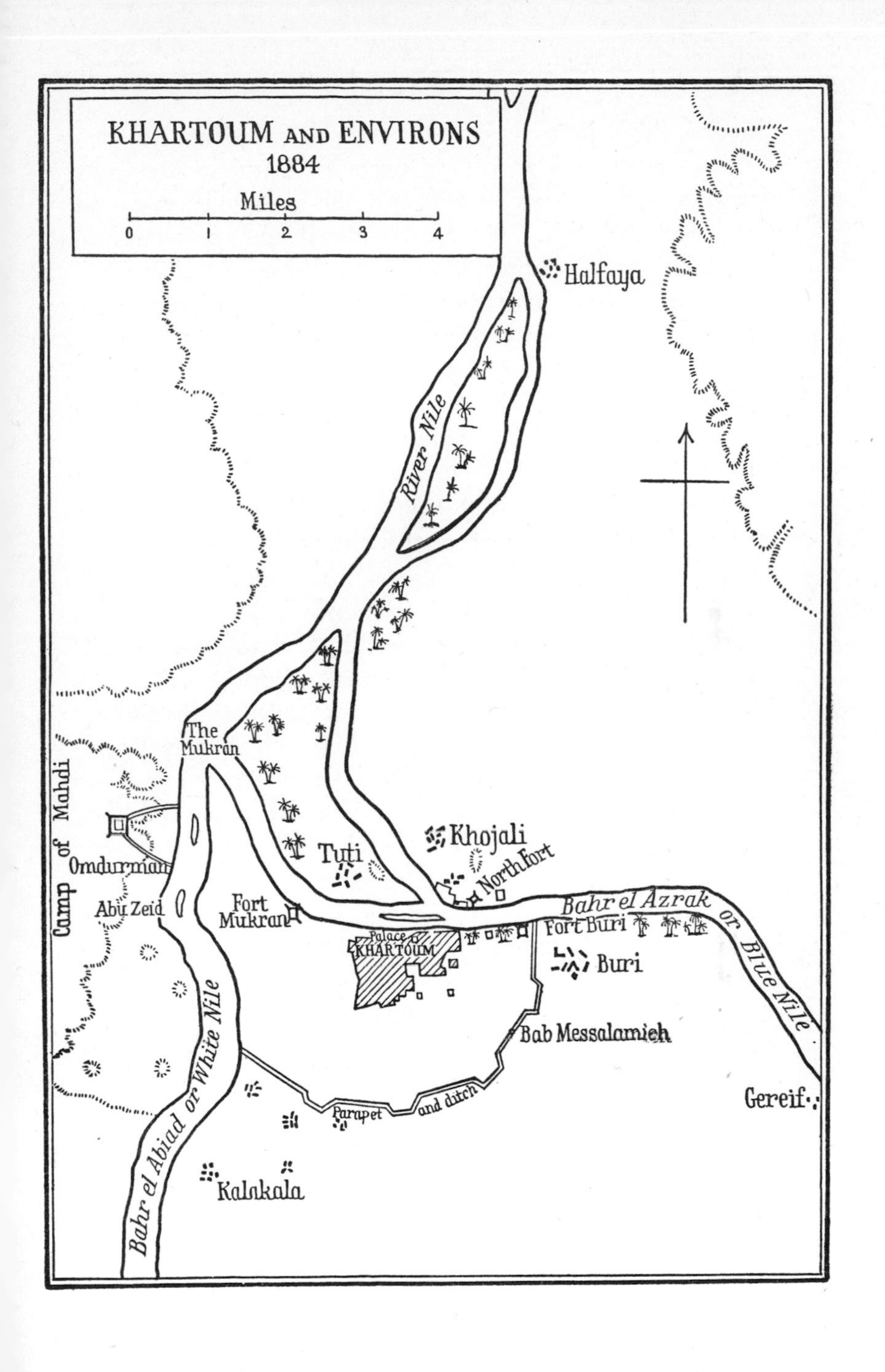
KHARTOUM AND ENVIRONS
1884
Miles
0
1
2
3
4
Halfaya
River Nile
The Mukran
Camp of Mahdi
Omdurman
Abu Zeid
Fort Mukran
Tuti
Khojali
North Fort
Bahr el Azrak or Blue Nile
Palace
KHARTOUM
Fort Buri
Buri
Bab Messalamieh
Parapet and ditch
Gereif
Kalakala
Bahr el Abiad or White Nile

there would be no necessity for a difficult expedition to Kordofan to crush him, and if he succeeded he might prevent a massacre such as Gordon knew only too well would ensue on the fall of the town. Gordon wondered what he would do himself in such an event. Blow up the Palace and all in it — or else be taken, bear witness with God's help to the Faith, and if necessary be martyred for it. He inclined to this alternative, for the other had more or less the taint of suicide — it seemed like taking the decision out of God's hand.

From the professional point of view, Gordon envied the Mahdi. Were he in the Mahdi's position, he said, he would laugh at all Europe, and he wondered whether he would be justified in coming to terms with the false Prophet on the understanding that he should allow all refugees to pass down the Nile, while Gordon should give over to him unhurt all the warlike material in Khartoum. But, as the place under his care had become a veritable arsenal, he decided that this would be a gift too dangerous in its consequences for Egypt, so he made up his mind that he would only surrender Khartoum with his life. In any case, Mohammed Ahmed, in spite of a certain streak of humanity that ran through his character, could never have agreed to such terms. Submission or death — these were the only alternatives the Mahdi, in virtue of his religious position, could offer to his enemies.

Finally, in mid-October, when Gordon had just discovered grave symptoms of disloyalty among the high officials of the town and been forced to imprison several "swells," the Mahdi decided to use his most cherished captive, Slatin Bey, the ex-Governor-General of Darfur, in one last effort to obtain Khartoum by peaceable means. Rudolf Slatin, like the other Europeans in the Mahdi's camp, had turned Mohammedan, though not before giving ample proof of his bravery and ability. Now, under pretense of demanding Gordon's surrender, he wrote offering his services to Gordon until death.

The two letters, one in French and the other in German, were duly delivered. But they remained unanswered. "The letters of Slatin have arrived," runs an entry in Gordon's journal of October 15; "I have no remarks to make on them, and cannot make out why he wrote them." Evidently not a Spartan, is Gordon's comment on the Austrian, for whom, despite his apostasy, he felt sorry. "If he gets away I shall take him to the Congo with me; he will want some *quarantine*," he said. But he would not hear of his joining the garrison without the Mahdi's positive leave, "his doing so would be the breaking of his parole, which should be as sacred when given to the Mahdi as to any other power, and it would jeopardize the safety of all those European prisoners with the Mahdi."

Gordon would not see Slatin — but he decided he would see Renan if he came to the lines. Gordon had this in common with the rationalist Frenchman, that both were bored with hero worship. They had tacitly agreed on this one afternoon at the Royal Geographical Society, in Kensington Gore, when Renan was being lionized and saw the look of commiseration on Gordon's face. Ever since then Gordon had had the feeling that they would meet again, and now it looked as if his intuition were to come true. For the story ran that a strange Frenchman had reached the Mahdi's camp — much to his astonishment, it was said, for he could not believe that any European should elect of his free will to join the dervish cause. It was less surprising to Gordon that Renan could have taken this step, since in his last book he had bid adieu to the world. What, therefore, more probable than that he should have gone to the Mahdi to escape from the civilization that both Renan and Gordon despised?

As Gordon recorded this fantastic surmise in his journal, one can see the pleasurable anticipation with which he looked forward to a conversation with the Arabic and Hebrew scholar. "Whatever one may think of his unbelief in Our

Lord, he certainly dared to say what he thought and he has not changed his creed to save his life." The meeting would have been a pleasant change from the detestable business of "killing people or devising means to do so." Anyhow, Gordon decided, if it were Renan "he would not approve of the Mahdi's pepper system."

13. "I Hate Our Diplomatists"

The pepper system — as Gordon thought over the events leading up to the crisis that now involved him and many thousands who had trusted him, he felt angry with the diplomatists who threw dust in people's eyes. "I must say I hate our diplomatists. I think with few exceptions they are arrant humbugs," is his verdict, which he illustrated with a pen-and-ink cartoon of Baring and his second-in-command, Egerton. But his anger reached farther than Khartoum. When, on November 1, he notes that there is only enough food in the town for another six weeks, he says: —

I could write volumes of pent-up wrath on this subject if I did not believe that all things are ordained and work for the best. I am not at all inclined to order half-rations with a view to any further prolongation of our blockade; if I did so it would probably end in a catastrophe before the time in which, if full rations are given, we should have exhausted our supplies. I should be an angel (which I am not, needless to say) if I was not rabid with Her Majesty's Government; but I hope I may be quiet on the subject of this Sudan and Cairo business with its indecision; but to lose all my beautiful black soldiers is enough to make one angry with those who have the direction of our future.

Three days later Gordon heard definite news of the disaster to the *Abbas*, and he knew that another point in the game had gone against him. The S. S. *Bordein*, which he had sent down some ten days before, returned on November 2 with letters from the outside world. One from Kitchener asked him who were on board the steamer that came down from Khartoum, and added that they had been killed. Gordon debated with himself the rights and the wrongs of the catastrophe.

If *Abbas* was captured by treachery, then I am not to blame; neither am I to blame if she struck a rock, for she drew under two feet of water, and fifty sailing boats used to go down yearly to Cairo with high Nile; if they were attacked and overpowered, then I am to blame, for I ought to have foreseen the chance, and prevented them going. But when they left we knew nothing of the Expedition, and I passed them under escort through Berber, which was the only apparent danger they had to meet.

As the conviction grows upon him that they were captured by treachery, he constructs in imagination the whole scene: —

The sheikh inviting them to land, saying, "Thank God the Mahdi is a liar" — bringing in wood — men going on shore and dispersed. The *Abbas* with her steam down, then a rush of wild Arabs and all is over.

It was sad, but, being ordained, he must not murmur. Holding the views he did about death, he could not pity Stewart or Power. As for himself, it might be Nemesis for the death of the two Pashas. Nothing lay heavier on his mind than this during those last months. "Being in authority and responsible, action is necessary, but mercy should temper justice." He followed this statement of the first principle of government with the confession, "I only killed two Pashas, and I declare that if it had not been for outside influences these two Pashas would have been alive now. They were judicially murdered." It was some consolation to give money compensation to their families.

It struck Gordon as paradoxical how in general they had managed to be successful while in detail they had suffered disaster on disaster. Writing to Mr. Barnes, the Vicar of Heavitree, on November 5, he says he had always felt that if they got through it would be "a scramble." Now every day their fate was more precariously poised. The question whether they could hold out until the Relief Expedition arrived was very doubtful. When the latest batch of letters came through on the *Bordein,* they had been wrapped in pieces of newspaper. These were found blowing about by a clerk, who saw that they were English papers of dates up to September 15. No question now of the sinfulness of such reading. Gordon had all along complained of the meagre reports from Baring and Kitchener, and now for the first time since February he was able to secure some general information about what was happening. It annoyed him to discover that the official name of the expedition was the Gordon Relief Expedition. It was not, he protested, being sent to relieve him, but the garrisons which he had failed to relieve. And when he read how Lord Wolseley had told an interviewer on August 31 that he hoped to relieve Khartoum before many months, Gordon wrote that Lord Wolseley "must have wonderful confidence in our powers of endurance, considering that when he is said to have made this utterance we had been blockaded six-and-a-half months, and we are now in our ninth month." Then, by one of those strange flights which Gordon constantly took from one subject to another, he reflected that the Sudan business had actually cost him £3000 beyond his pay at least, but he adds grandly that he "will not ask them or allow them to pay it." "I shall get it from others," he adds, "and I shall get another £1000 to buy Stewart's journal, if he has been killed or captured."

Gordon flared up whenever he thought about his mission, yet he knew bitterness was wrong. "God is not unfaithful, if we fall," he writes, "for it may be for His glory, and He does not promise everything we ask if it is not good for us to have it." At the same time he meant to act according to his own conscience, and not to obey orders if these clashed with it. The name of the Gordon Relief Expedition suggests it is to relieve him personally; when his safety has been secured, the work of the expedition will be over. He emphatically denies that he will be a party to any such meanness, and puts the case of the inhabitants as they would argue it: —

You (Gordon) came up here, and had you not come, we should have some of us got away to Cairo, but we trusted you to extricate us; we suffered, and are suffering, great privation, in order to hold the town. Had you not come we should have given in at once and obtained pardon; now we can, after our obstinate defense, expect no mercy from the Mahdi, who will avenge on us all the blood that has been spilt round Khartoum. You have taken our money and promised to repay us; all this goes for nought if you quit us; it is your bounden duty to stay by us and share our fate; if the British desert us that is no reason for you to do so, after our having stood by you.

He adds: —

I declare positively and once for all, that I will not leave the Sudan until everyone who wants to go down is given a chance to do so, unless a Government is established which relieves me of the charge; therefore if any emissary or letter comes up ordering me to come down I WILL NOT OBEY IT, BUT WILL STAY HERE, AND FALL WITH THE TOWN, AND RUN ALL RISKS.

14. Gordon as Autocrat

With all this incessant anxiety turning his hair grey, Gordon was still able to see another side to the daily life which went on in Khartoum under the shadow of catastrophe. There was humor to be extracted from the determination of its people still to pursue the Benthamite philosophy, to seek pleasure and avoid pain. The Post Office officials demand more pay. His own servant, already possessing one wife (which most men find is enough, says Gordon), asks for three days' leave to marry a second. Hansal — the Austrian Consul in Khartoum who flits occasionally through the story of Gordon's career in the Sudan — takes his daily morning ride, objecting at the same time to the bursting of the shells from the Arabs' Krupp guns, which he describes as *abrutissant.* A brave man, for all that, is Hansal, who dies at his post — though Gordon cannot like him and is relieved when false rumor asserts that he "means to go to the Mahdi *with his seven female attendants.*" Even in the gaunt existence Gordon now leads, small incidents give some color; it may be only a scorpion which stings the Governor-General in his morning bath and suffers death for its presumption — "we are now quits," is Gordon's comment; or a mouse that takes Stewart's place at table and eats out of his plate — it is far braver than any of his troops, except the Negroes; for cowardice he will back the bashi-bazouks and the Egyptian *fellahin* against any in the world. The enemy dervishes are not much better, for a hundred determined men, in Gordon's opinion, could carry the Khartoum lines at any time with ease. There are occasional exceptions, as in the case of the little dervish boy who, when threatened with instant death by his captors unless he denied the Mahdi, bravely shouted his faith in that Prophet. Sometimes dangerous things were done out of sheer incompetence to grasp a situation, as with the Khartoumi who, after going over to the Mahdi in accordance with Gordon's permission, calmly returned to visit his wife and family. He did not realize that a war was in progress, and that he might have been shot as a spy.

The thing was going to be a scramble. Of that there could be no doubt. At the end of November, Gordon calculated that their supplies would be exhausted by December 15 — the date which Wolseley had fixed for his final advance across the desert from Debba to Metemma, a five days' journey if no opposition was met with en route. From Metemma the river to Khartoum was open. So long as Gordon's theories about the essentially unmilitary qualities of the dervishes held, Khartoum might or might not be relieved in time.

Two events occurred in the second ten days of November to modify both these conclusions. One was the discovery that quantities of biscuit had been stolen from the government stores, the recovery of the spoil enabling Gordon to prolong his defense beyond the period he had estimated; the other, that the Mahdi's own dervishes were not the faint-hearts he had previously suspected. And this in the end proved decisive and sealed the fate of Khartoum.

He found out this unwelcome piece of news on November 12, the crucial date in the siege. Late the previous evening slaves brought in news to Omdurman that the Mahdi's own troops were about to attack. The information was passed on to the Palace, where it got no farther than the telegraph clerk. At 3 A.M. Gordon, having finished his rounds, was dropping off into a troubled sleep when he heard drumbeats in his dreams. He awoke to remember he was in Khartoum, and that the *tup-tup-tup* was rifle fire. Where was it? Would it die away? As Gordon lay speculating about it the fire became more intense. He wondered whether they would have enough ammunition — the lack of it was always the excuse of bad soldiers. It was no good worrying. He must get up and go on the roof of the Palace, his usual battle station. He discovered about the telegram, and gave the clerk a box on the ears. Then, as his conscience pricked him, he handed him a pound bakshish. The clerk, with all the humility of his twenty years, declared he did not mind if Gordon killed him — was he not his father? — and took the tip gratefully. Telegrams, orders, swearing, and cursing followed until 9 A.M. By that time the only two steamers he had left had got steam up and sailed out to assist the garrison at Omdurman, where the dervishes were attacking in force. One of them, the *Husseinia,* ran aground. All the morning the issue of the engagement hung in the balance. By noon Gordon declared he had lived years in hours, for if the Arabs captured the steamers, then Omdurman would fall, and after that the North Fort — then Khartoum itself. But, although the *Husseinia* remained on the sand bank, the battle did not end so disastrously as Gordon feared. At the same time the Mahdi's advent had clearly made a difference in the fighting qualities of his enemies. "I must say," he writes the same afternoon, "the Arabs to-day showed the greatest pluck." Then, to explain his previous misjudgment, he adds, "I believe that by the Arabs we may understand our own regulars captured in Kordofan and Darfur, etc."

15. The End

The situation took a definite turn for the worse in the battle of November 12, for the dervishes then managed to break through the lines connecting Omdurman with the river. That fort had been built 1200 yards from the Nile — an error which Gordon regretted. Now that its communications with the river bank were cut, Gordon could send it no more supplies of food or munitions. Its fall was therefore only a question of time. And, when Omdurman fell, Khartoum's days would be numbered.

"I could write volumes of pent-up wrath," he had declared on November 2, apropos of the failure of the Relief Expedition to relieve them; on this occasion his anger was pointed by observing through his telescope that the sentries on the North Fort were not on the roof. He sent over to have them flogged. But he knew that the whole lot — officers, men, civilians, and all — were at best lazy and at worst treacherous. He could bully, beat, and imprison. One of the reasons for everyone respecting him was that he freely used these time-honored methods of Oriental government. When a new armored steamer was launched at the Khartoum arsenal during this month, and the Khartoumis wished it to be called *Gordon,* he answered grimly, "I have put most of you in prison and otherwise bullied you, and I have no fear of your forgetting me."

The strain was great and incessant. Gordon had never had a light touch with his subordinates. He was always a difficult man to serve. Now he must have been a volcano to those around him. They were unable to realize that a general catastrophe might occur at any moment. They went on in the old humdrum ways; his staff actually remained at home on Fridays — their weekly day of rest — as if the profoundest peace reigned over Khartoum and the Sudan. "I may truly say I am weary of this life: day and night, night and day it is the same." Incompetence was everywhere. He saw it in Cairo as well as in Khartoum, and, from writing about his own incompetent staff, turns to abuse Baring. Then he crossed out what he had just scribbled — censoriousness was still his besetting sin. Happily the professional tastes now quickened, after their atrophy from long disuse, helped him to bear his enormous load of care, and he pictured to himself how he would like to be "in a real siege with no civil population or robbers of officers to bully" him. "To-night," he wrote at the end of November, "a sortie with fifty men would give the Arabs a dose which they would not forget." He adds sadly, "But it is no use, we are not up to it."

On November 25, steamer smoke was observed down the Nile. For the moment the people thought that it might be the Relief Expedition. Soon it was seen to come from the *Bordein* making another journey to the besieged town and fighting its way past the Arabs on both banks. After running the gauntlet it reached Khartoum in safety, but no redcoats were on board such as would have sufficed to show the Mahdi that he had waited too long, and that he must make the best of his way back to Kordofan. None of the promises Gordon had so often held out to the suffering inhabitants were fulfilled. The *Bordein* brought nothing from Dongola except a few private letters and two official messages. One from the British Government, after assuring Gordon that it was interested in his safety, asked his views and position, so that "if danger has arisen or is likely to arise" measures might be taken accordingly.

This message — it was a repetition of Gladstone's original questionnaire of April 23 — had been sent from Cairo on July 24. Luckily for Gordon's temper, it was in cipher, and Stewart had taken the key. The other came *en clair* from the Egyptian Government, having been sent off on September 21 as the result of Gladstone's orders after he had read the sensational account of a mythically rampageous Gordon in the *Dundee Advertiser*. Gordon missed the point this message made about limiting his powers as Governor-General to Khartoum and its neighborhood. "I am glad to see from your last telegram," said the Khedive, speaking with the voice of Mr. Gladstone, "that you have abandoned the idea of burning Berber, of which I cannot approve." And he added that Gordon would receive the instructions of the British Government through Sir Evelyn Baring and Lord Wolseley.

"There was a slight laugh when Kartoum [1] heard Baring was bumping his way up here," Gordon wrote on the day after the arrival of the last news he was ever to get from the outside world. "If Baring does bump his way up here as British Commissioner, I shall consider he has expiated his faults and shall forgive him." And then Gordon fills the backs of more telegraph forms — this was the only paper he had left — with his favorite theme of the transience of life.

In ten or twelve years' time Baring, Lord Wolseley, myself, Evelyn Wood, will have no teeth and will be deaf; some of us

[1] Gordon always spelled it so.

will be quite *passé;* no one will come and court us; new Barings, new Lord Wolseleys will have arisen, who will call us "bloaks" and "twaddlers." "Oh! for goodness' sake come away, then! Is that dreadful bore coming? If once he gets alongside you, you are in for half-an-hour" will be the remark of some young captain of the present time on seeing you enter the Club. This is very humiliating, for we, each one, think we are immortal.

When Gordon returns to the same subject a day or two later, he pictures the artilleryman-diplomat, who, like himself, had made a career outside his own corps, reaching Metemma on camel-back. Baring says to Egerton: —

"Metemma at last after the most fearful sufferings, every bone in my body dislocated with those beastly camels. Found here his journal, from which it appears that that duffer, the Mahdi, has at last roused himself, but I fear it is too late. As to the tone of the Journal, it is *simply deplorable,* and (do not mention it, please) he has actually made a sketch (brace yourself up to bear it) of our high priest. Excuse more, for what with the bumping of the camel and the depravity shown by this scoffer, I am more dead than alive."

The temperamental "oil and water" (so Gordon put it) antipathy he had always felt for Baring persisted to the end. But although he found fault with Kitchener, thought him mean towards his messenger-spies and casual towards himself, yet, thanks to Sir Samuel Baker, he appreciated the talents of the young Engineer officer. The proper Governor-General for the Sudan, Gordon says, would be Kitchener. If he were appointed and British sovereignty established over the land, all would be well — but you cannot do this, he adds bitterly, because of the ninety million sterling debt on Egypt, over which he sees Baring standing like a watchdog.

The future presented itself to Gordon as clearly as ever during those last weeks when the Mahdi's dervishes were closing in on Khartoum. But he did not see that his life was the sacrifice which would ensure the ultimate certainty of bringing the Sudan under the government he now desired. Alternatively to Kitchener, Zobeir, in Gordon's eyes, still remained the one man capable of withstanding the fanatical barbarism of the Mahdi's emirs. Zobeir or the Sultan — these were the only alternatives to a British Sudan.

Meanwhile Gordon continued to fight on. On November 26, he published a proclamation saying that the expeditionary force had reached Dongola and started in three divisions.

> They will soon be in Khartoum. . . . If God will, in the next few days the siege will be raised and your alarm will pass away. Know also that if Mohammed Ahmed should call me for three years to surrender Khartoum, I will not listen to him, but will protect your wives and families and possessions with all energy and steadfastness.

Unfortunately the British soldiers had been so long on their way that deferred hope had taken all the sting out of Gordon's promises. The people of Khartoum could not be expected to understand the delay when it passed Gordon's own comprehension. If the expeditionary force had reached Metemma, — as he calculated they should have done by the end of November at the latest, — a hundred men, he said, were all that was necessary. They had just to show themselves on the steamers, and the Mahdi would raise the siege. . . .

November passed and December began. With it came the last fortnight in which we still know from Gordon's own pen something of his hopes and fears, and of the daily events in his life. One day he is nearly blinded when the cartridge blows out as he is firing a Remington rifle. The fearless Gordon also admits to feeling uncomfortable when the Arabs shell his Palace, and he discusses the question whether it is mean to bob at gunfire, coming to the conclusion that "judicious bobbing" is not a fault. Every day shells fall near his wing of the Palace — the Mahdi has sent a company of his "pet dervishes" to keep Gordon under fire. A lucky shot may bring down the roof and bury the Governor-General in the débris.

But even this personal attention had its comic side. When, on December 4, the band came to give its usual Thursday-afternoon concert on the roof, there was an unrehearsed interlude. For the sounds of music drew the dervish fire, and the plucky little band (they were boys; all the bandsmen were in the lines) furiously threw down their instruments and rushed to arms. When the fusillade died down, the buglers gave the ironical call, "Come to us, come to us" — which renegade buglers in the enemy camp were able to repeat.

But if the Arabs were poor marksmen, and discouraged if angry soldiers, — for the spies' stories that the Mahdi was seriously thinking of striking his tents had some truth, — Gordon could not conceal from himself that the end was near. On December 5, he says that he is planning to relieve Omdurman Fort. "Things really look very black" — a successful sortie is his last resource. In any case, he has almost given up all idea of saving the town. Then on the following day he is reluctantly compelled to abandon the idea of landing at Omdurman — "we have not the force to do it." On December 12, as he watched what he called the Arabs' church parade, when the Mahdi led the weekly Friday prayer and held his weekly review in honor of the Yom-el-Gooma, Gordon devoutly hoped it would be the last he would have to witness. They had been 272 days besieged — long enough time. They were not, he admitted, over-great heroes ("if we analyze human glory, it is composed of nine-tenths twaddle, perhaps ninety-nine-hundredths twaddle"). Still the siege of Khartoum was just as good as that of Sebastopol. Now, unless help came soon, the town would inevitably fall. Within ten days their biscuit and durra would be exhausted. Starvation then would quickly do its work: "Now mark this, if the Expeditionary Force, and I ask for no more than 200 men, does not come in ten days, the town *may fall*; and I have done my best for the honor of our country. Good-bye. C. G. Gordon." That is the last entry in his journal — on December 14, 1884.

Early in November, Gordon had told Lord Wolseley they could hold out for another forty days. That period expired on Sunday, December 14, and then Gordon decided to communicate once more with the outside world by means of the *Bordein*. He wrote an official letter to the Chief of Staff, Sudan Expeditionary Force, which left no possible doubt of the situation in Khartoum. It ran: —

KARTOUM
14.12.84

SIR,

I send down the steamer *Bordein* to-morrow with Vol. VI of my private journal containing account of the events in Kartoum from 5 Novr. to 14 Decr. The state of affairs is such that one cannot foresee further than 5 to 7 days, after which the town may at any time fall. I have done all in my power to hold out, but I own I consider the position is extremely critical, almost desperate, and I say this, without any feeling of bitterness with respect to H.M. Govt. but merely as a matter of fact. Should the town fall; it will be questionable whether it will be worth the while of H.M.G. to continue its Expedition, for it is certain that the fall of Kartoum will insure that of Kasala and Sennur.

I have the honour to be, Sir,
Your most obedient servant,

THE CHIEF OF STAFF — C. G. GORDON
SOUDAN EXPEDY. FORCE

Gordon also sent a letter to Colonel Watson Pasha, his one-time subordinate in Equatoria. "I think the game is up," he said, and added that they might expect a catastrophe in the town in ten days' time or after. In his adieux he included Mrs. Watson and his lifelong friend, General Graham. To

Augusta, the inexorable sister with whom he had corresponded for over thirty years, he had so often spoken of death that now, when it seemed unexpectedly — perhaps joyously — near, he found nothing to say except that God ruled all for the best — and that his "affairs pecuniarily are not over-bright." A strange paradox that his only personal worry at such a moment concerned his bank balance, though not so strange when one remembers that he contributed largely to Augusta Gordon's support. Unfortunately the recipient, with little sense of responsibility for the legitimate curiosity of posterity, cut out the essential sentences, and this note on a single sheet of paper has come down to us in two sadly mangled pieces. His postscript, however, was in the grand manner. "P.S. I am quite happy, thank God, and like Lawrence, I 'have *tried* to do my duty.'" The phrase, with its concluding blank verse line, made a fitting end to what was destined to be an historic series of letters.

Thus the *Bordein,* carrying this mail and the last volume of the journal, — surely the most wonderful book ever written by the general of a desperately beleaguered city, — also addressed, like its predecessors, to his old friend Lord Wolseley, left Khartoum on December 15. It had done gallantly with its nondescript crew, most of them wearing Gordon's decoration for the siege, of which they were very proud, with its black slave ladies who cooked in the hold, its rats, its stench, and even its baby or two. But Gordon was destined to see no more the little steamer which had served him so well. How often in other years had he traveled on it up and down the Nile, sitting on the deck, his Bible next to him with the green and yellow bookmark embroidered by Augusta after the tartan of the Gordons!

One later message reached the expeditionary force at the same time as the letters of December 14. Written on a tiny piece of paper were the words, in Gordon's handwriting and over his signature and his Arabic seal, "Khartoum all right. Could hold out for years." Dated "29.12.84," it has always been looked on as one of many messages which Gordon hoped would fall into the Mahdi's hands, to the discouragement of that false prophet. Hence the Arabic seal. It was at the time welcomed by the English newspapers anxious to allay curiosity about Gordon's fate. But it did not deceive Sir Charles Wilson when it was delivered to him, together with the six volumes of Gordon's Khartoum journal, on January 21. On that day he effected his junction near Metemma with the steamer flotilla which Gordon had sent down to meet the expeditionary force. Khartoum was a hundred miles to the south, the river everywhere navigable — a three or, at the most, four days' journey. Had Sir Charles Wilson left at once, he should have reached Khartoum at the latest on Sunday, January 25. The town fell on January 26. Thus, even at this late hour, there was still time for the Relief Force to have justified its name.

But procrastination and mischance continued to dog the events connected with Gordon's mission. Throughout the autumn, time had been lost in the various stages of the advance. Gordon, like Napoleon and Marlborough, and, indeed, all great captains, believed in speed and surprise as the determining factors in war, and throughout he did his best to impress this fact on the British Staff. If Lord Wolseley had been in Khartoum and Gordon in command of the expedition to relieve him, there would surely have been a different story to tell, and one more flattering to the prestige of British arms.

One need not enter into the details of that advance up the Nile by 10,000 picked troops of the British Army — when Gordon believed that a tenth of that number, if properly handled, would have been sufficient. The enormous transport required for so large a body of men made progress exasperatingly slow, and it was not till January 8, 1885, that the flying column under Sir Herbert Stewart, which was to make the final dash on Khartoum, began to march across the 150 miles of desert in the bend of the Nile between Ambukol and Metemma.

But the deliberation of Wolseley's plans gave the dervishes time to concentrate, a danger of which Gordon, always emphasizing that speed was Wolseley's best ally, had warned him. At Abu Klea, one of the wells on the desert route, Stewart found some 10,000 dervishes drawn up against his picked force of 1800. That night of January 16 the two little armies faced one another. On the following morning Stewart cautiously advanced in square formation against the expectant enemy. The dervishes waited until the lines were about a mile apart, then charged. Stewart halted his men, and the British squares stood with fixed bayonets as they had done at Waterloo seventy years before. For the last time the old traditional tactics were used in war by the British Army, and it prevailed against a brave but poorly armed enemy, though not before the dervishes had broken one of the squares and inflicted serious casualties.

The battle of Abu Klea might have been decisive if it had been immediately followed up. Actually it had two very serious consequences. It delayed the advance of the relief column by at least a day. And one of its victims was Colonel Burnaby, Gordon's old acquaintance in Equatoria. Wolseley had given instructions that this experienced cavalry officer should take command of the flying column if anything happened to Stewart. When the latter, after successfully leading his men to the immediate neighborhood of Metemma, was mortally wounded by a stray bullet on the morning of the nineteenth, Wolseley's foresight proved of no avail. For the officer who should have succeeded him was already dead, and the very thing happened that Wolseley had wished to avoid.

The command, in the absence of any countermanding orders, automatically fell upon Colonel Sir Charles Wilson, a soldier belonging to the Intelligence Service who had never previously served in war. It was to him that the *Bordein,* now with the other steamers of Gordon's flotilla, handed Gordon's dispatches when, on the morning of Wednesday, the twenty-first, the British column actually reached the banks of the Nile above Metemma.

Had the dashing Burnaby been alive, there can be no doubt that the flotilla, with British troops on board, would have pushed on that very afternoon. Khartoum would have been reached on the twenty-fourth or twenty-fifth, the town revictualed, and the Mahdi, already discouraged by his reverse at Abu Klea, would quite possibly have started his retreat to Kordofan even before the steamers arrived and landed their British soldiers on the quay at Khartoum. But Burnaby was dead, and Wilson hesitated. Instead of following up the moral effect of the battle of Abu Klea and making an immediate dash on Khartoum, he hung about at Metemma. On the twenty-first and the twenty-second he used Gordon's steamers for reconnoitring north and south of his position. The twenty-third was spent in getting the steamers ready, and they did not leave for Khartoum till January 24.

There was controversy at the time over the reasons that prompted Wilson to delay at this critical juncture. The most plausible explanation is that put forward by Dr. Bernard M. Allen in his *Gordon and the Sudan.* He attributes the delay to the homely fact that Lord Charles Beresford was at the moment suffering from a Nile boil. Wolseley had chosen this daring young naval officer, who had been a popular hero since the bombardment of Alexandria, to take command of the steamers on their dash to Khartoum. Wilson, as senior intelligence officer, had received orders to accompany him. Now, on the morning of the twenty-first, when the impetuous and pugnacious Beresford should have been making everything ready for an instant advance, he was *hors de combat* through his local though painful affliction. But he passionately desired to lead an expedition on which his heart was set. In a day or two he hoped to be well, and he used his influence therefore with Wilson to persuade him to listen to unfounded reports of enemy activity north and south of Metemma. Such is the theory put forward by Dr. Allen, who has exhaustively studied every detail of this campaign. It is supported by General Stuart-Wortley, who was then serving as a lieutenant in the Relief Force, and was one of the three officers detailed by Wolseley to go through on the steamers to Khartoum. If it is the true explanation, it bears out Gordon's dictum that the most insignificant trifles often produce the greatest results.

In the meantime Gordon, only a hundred miles away, was in a desperate plight. When he sent the *Bordein* to Metemma on December 14, the amount of food in store was 83,525 okes of biscuit and 546 ardebs of durra. The daily needs of the garrison and people were about 50 ardebs of durra and 10,000 okes of biscuit. It was obvious, therefore, that in ten days the town would be faced with starvation. "Know, O thou enemy of God, there is no escape for thee from death at our hands, and from death by lack of food." This the Khalifa Abdullah, the Mahdi's chief-of-staff and the brain of the besiegers, had written to Gordon early in December. Daily his words looked more like coming true. By obtaining the unripe durra crop on Tuti Island, which Gordon still held, and laying it out to ripen in the sun, starvation was staved off for a few more days. Early in January, Gordon made various sorties against the enemy lines, but these were in the nature of forlorn hopes. At the same time he gave leave for any of the townspeople who so wished to join the Mahdi, and Gordon wrote a letter — his last — to Mohammed Ahmed, whom a year before he had rated so lightly, asking him to treat them kindly. This the Mahdi seems to have done.

Khartoum could not hold out much longer — everyone knew that except the Relief Force, in which optimism prevailed until Gordon's last messages, received on January 21, showed how precarious was its state. By the second week in January, donkeys, dogs, and rats began to be used for food. The soldiers were served out with a gum ration which had been found serviceable at the siege of El Obeid. A meal made from the pith of date trees proved less satisfactory, for it induced dysentery with all its attendant evils.

In this extremity Gordon still looms up through the stories of survivors as a superhuman figure, insensible to fatigue, going the rounds of the lines, encouraging the troops to hold out until relief came, visiting the hospitals, and cheering the civilian population by walking through the streets and visiting the notables in their houses. He spent much of the time on his roof, watching the enemy's camp and looking where the Nile stretched away northwards for the steamer smoke which would mean that their agony was at an end.

But the days passed and still there was no sign of the British, while the enemy's grip gradually tightened. On January 15, Omdurman, the key of Khartoum, capitulated after its commander had signaled that his provisions were exhausted and Gordon in reply had ordered him to surrender.

Still the Mahdi hesitated to make an attack on the now weakened lines, which Gordon weeks before had said would fall to a hundred determined men. On January 20, news of the battle of Abu Klea reached the Mahdi's camp, and though he celebrated it with a salute of a hundred and one guns, the weeping women whom Gordon saw through his telescope told a different tale. A woman spy subsequently confirmed the news of a British victory, and on that night of January 20, when Sir Charles Wilson was outside Metemma, joy reigned in Khartoum.

In this state of affairs, when the fate of the beleaguered town was precariously balanced, a serious and, as it proved, a decisive event occurred. The weakest part of the lines was where these abutted on the White Nile. Gordon knew this well, and had taken various precautions to strengthen it. As the flood receded, the trenches were carried into what at one time had been part of the river bed. For a thousand yards the works were pushed out as the water level dropped. Then the Nile ceased to recede regularly, and a sand ridge appeared 300 yards from the east bank, from which it was separated by a shallow channel; if the Mahdi's troops landed by night on the ridge and waded ashore, they would be within the lines. When one of Faragh Pasha's officers on this sector deserted to the enemy, Gordon knew that he would communicate to the enemy the secret of this vital weakness. Gordon in his anger demanded an explanation of Faragh, and a stormy interview with his Sudanese general, who was in favor of surrendering on the Mahdi's terms, ended in his striking Faragh. The Sudanese is reported to have left the Palace in a rage, which we may well believe. Of what really happened we know nothing, for Faragh too was one of the victims of the massacre. Gordon, however, could not have considered as proved his connivance with his traitorous subordinate, since Faragh remained in command to the end.

According to the account compiled by Kitchener, on Saturday, January 24, the very day on which Wilson started from Metemma, Gordon held a meeting of the notables of Khartoum, and discussed the situation with them. These men, though by now deeply committed against the Mahdi and uncertain whether, even if they recognized him as the Successor of the Prophet, he would not sell them into slavery, seem to have supported Faragh Pasha's view. It was better to throw up the sponge. But Gordon would not hear of it, and declared he would never surrender. He was *shadid* — his will was still unconquerable.

Sometimes Gordon, peering into the future, used to think with horror that he might live to an extreme old age. What would he be like in 1919? That date in the remote future made him shudder. How terrible if he were then still dragging out an unhappy life! But God was to be kinder to him than he knew. For not in his most roseate vision had Gordon expected to be allowed off parade when he was just fifty-two. Even during these last few months he had not really expected death; if Khartoum fell, he anticipated the same fate as had befallen Cuzzi and Slatin — with the difference that he would never deny his Master. This might entail martyrdom, but Gordon's only reference to the subject shows that he thought it unlikely. At the back of his mind there was the conviction that he and the Mahdi were fated to meet face to face — and in such an encounter anything might happen. The Mahdi was, like Gordon himself, a searcher after truth, and he too had forsworn the world. When Gordon felt mystic intuitions about any man, — and we know that he had them at one moment about the Mahdi, — they usually prompted him to believe that somehow from their meeting fruitful results would spring. Vague fears of this kind perhaps inspired the more violent men round the Mahdi, who knew better than their master that Gordon would always be preferred by the Negroes to any Arab masters. For the Mahdi had given orders that the Pasha of Khartoum was to be spared, and he is said to have been angry when he heard that his orders had been disobeyed.

At the same time Gordon, as he admired the hawks sweeping in splendid circles high above his Palace on their incessant watch for carrion, wondered whether they were destined to

"TOO LATE!"

Telegram, Thursday morning, February 5: "Khartoum taken by the Mahdi. General Gordon's fate uncertain."

(From "Punch," February 14, 1885, by permission of the Proprietors)

pick out his eyes he feared he was not the best of sons and the penalty laid down in Proverbs might be his. Yet these speculations amounted to little. In spite of himself, he was still a soldier. His business was to kill and be killed, and he meant "to go down with his flag flying."

Sunday, January 25, the last day of the siege of Khartoum, came, and with it signs of activity in the Mahdi's camp. The dervishes were crossing the White Nile and massing at the southwest end of the lines. Reports of Gordon's own movements on that day differ. One account says that he was ill, suffering probably from the dysentery produced by the food substitute which starvation imposed upon the garrison. He did not appear in public, but had interviews with many of the leading men. In the evening he crossed over on some business or other to Tuti Island in the *Ismailia* — which he now kept with steam up at the Palace, ready to leave with the European civilians when the dervishes carried the lines. The report of this visit led to the rumor in the town that he had abandoned Khartoum to its fate, and helped to deepen the general depression. On the other hand, we are told that he continued actively to visit the lines, encouraging the troops, and enrolling as many civilians as he could to help man the defenses. In any case, we may be sure that he went to his usual lookout on the Palace roof, where night and day he had spent so many hours, and pointed his telescope northwards. But he saw no smoke, for that evening the *Bordein* was still fifty miles away — forty-eight hours too late. On the night of the twenty-fifth, the final orders for assaulting the town were given by the Mahdi, and at 3.30 on the twenty-sixth, attacks were simultaneously delivered against the west and east gates. The east gate held. But at the west, when the defenders saw that the enemy had penetrated to their rear by landing on the sand bank, resistance ceased, and the town then lay at the mercy of the dervishes.

Through some failure in his telegraphic communications with the lines three or four miles away, Gordon in his Palace appears to have been ignorant of what was happening. He must have heard the firing, as he had so often heard it before. But in the dark, and cut off from his commanders, he could do nothing.

There is again divergent evidence as to the last scene of all. He had apparently arranged to retire to the church when the town fell, and to hold out in that semi-fortress as long as possible. Some say that he was walking towards Hansal's house, which was by the church, accompanied by some twenty kavasses, when a body of dervishes dashed up and discharged a volley, Gordon being the first to fall. Another account, the more reliable, runs that the dervishes swarmed into the garden of the Palace, overpowered the black troops on guard, and, screaming for the Christian Pasha's blood, rushed the outside staircase. Gordon came out to face them, and as he asked, "Where is the Mahdi?" a dervish ran him through with his spear. The time must have been about 5.30 A.M., a little after dawn, with only a feeble twilight as yet in the sky.

In accordance with the usual Arab treatment of arch enemies killed in battle, Gordon's head was cut off and taken as a trophy to be exposed in the Mahdi's camp. In the slaughter of that morning, however, disputes arose between the wild savages who had dispatched their dreaded enemy as to the identity of the head. It was probably to make sure on this very important point — for, if Gordon's head were not stuck up for all to see, the fact of his death would soon have been questioned — that a number of dervishes appeared before Slatin's tent carrying an object in a cloth.

They undid it, and one of them asked, "Is not this the head of your uncle the unbeliever?" Slatin tells us that he gazed silently at the ghastly sight. "His eyes were half opened;

the mouth was perfectly natural; the hair of his head and his short whiskers were almost quite white."

And Slatin, mastering his emotion, answered, "What of it? A brave soldier who fell at his post. Happy is he to have fallen. His sufferings are over."

THE AFTERMATH

The Aftermath

Extract from Queen Victoria's journal: —

Osborne
5th Feb. 1885

Dreadful news after breakfast. Khartoum fallen. Gordon's fate uncertain! All greatly distressed. Sent for Sir H. Ponsonby, who was horrified. It is too fearful. The Government is alone to blame, by refusing to send the expedition till it was too late. Telegraphed *en clair* to Mr Gladstone, Lord Granville, and Lord Hartington, expressing how dreadfully shocked I was at the news, all the more so when one felt it might be prevented.

Queen Victoria to the Marquis of Hartington (sent also to Gladstone and Granville): —

5th Feb. 1885

These news from Khartoum are frightful, and to think that all this might have been prevented and many precious lives saved by earlier action is too frightful.

Sir Henry Ponsonby to Sir Evelyn Baring, March 19, 1885: —

The Queen was in a terrible state about the fall of Khartoum, and indeed it had a good deal to do with making her ill. She was just going out when she got the telegram, and sent for me. She then went out to my cottage, a quarter of a mile off, walked into the room, pale and trembling, and said to my wife, who was terrified at her appearance, "Too late!"

Entry in Gladstone's diary, February 5, 1885: —

After 11 A.M. I learned the sad news of the fall or betrayal of Khartoum. H[artington] and I, with C. [Gladstone's wife], went off by the first train and reached Downing Street soon after 8.15. The circumstances are sad and trying. It is one of the least points about them that they may put an end to this Government.

Gladstone to Queen Victoria: —

10 DOWNING STREET
5th Feb. 1885

Mr Gladstone has had the honour this day to receive your Majesty's telegram *en clair,* relating to the deplorable intelligence received this day from Lord Wolseley, and stating that it is too fearful to consider that the fall of Khartoum might have been prevented, and many lives saved by earlier action. Mr Gladstone does not presume to estimate the means of judgment possessed by your Majesty, but so far as his information and his recollection at the moment go, he is not altogether able to follow this conclusion which your Majesty has been pleased thus to announce.

Mr Gladstone is under the impression that Lord Wolseley's force might have been sufficiently advanced to save Khartoum had not a large portion of it been detached by a circuitous route along the river, upon the express application of General Gordon, to occupy Berber on the way to the final destination. He speaks, however, with submission on a point of this kind.

In further paragraphs of what Lord Morley calls this vindication of his conduct, Gladstone blames (1) the military for not having chosen the Berber route, (2) the climate, and (3) treachery within the Khartoum garrison.

He concludes: —

There are many reproaches, from the most opposite quarters, to which it might be difficult to supply a conclusive answer. Among them, and perhaps among the most difficult, as far as Mr Gladstone can judge, would be the reproach of those who argue that our proper business was the protection of Egypt, that it never was in military danger from the Mahdi, and that the most prudent course would have been to provide

Gordon's Statue in Trafalgar Square
Hamo Thornycroft

it with adequate frontier defences and to assume no responsibility for the lands beyond the desert.

Lord Cromer, writing over twenty years later, says: —

Well do I remember the blank feeling of grief and disappointment with which I received the news of his death, and even now, at this distance of time, I cannot pen the record of those sad last days in Khartoum without emotion. . . .

Rarely has public opinion in England been so moved as when the news arrived of the fall of Khartoum. . . . When General Gordon's fate was known a wail of sorrow and disappointment was heard throughout the land. . . . On this, as on other occasions, the Queen's language truly represented the feelings of the nation.

Lord Cromer's verdict: —

Mr Gladstone's error of judgment, in delaying too long the despatch of the Nile Expedition, left a stain on the reputation of England which it will be beyond the power of either the impartial historian or the partial apologist to efface.

Queen Victoria to Miss Augusta Gordon: —

OSBORNE
17th Feb. 1885

DEAR MISS GORDON,

How shall I write to you, or how shall I attempt to express *what I feel!* To think of your dear, noble, heroic Brother, who served his country and his Queen so truly, so heroically, with a self-sacrifice so edifying to the World, not having been rescued. That the promises of support were not fulfilled — which I so frequently and constantly pressed on those who asked him to go — is to me *grief inexpressible!* Indeed, it has made me ill! My heart bleeds for you, his Sister, who have gone through so many anxieties on his account, and who loved the dear Brother as he deserved to be. . . . Would you express to your other sisters and your elder Brother my true sympathy and what I do so keenly feel, the *stain* left upon England, for your dear Brother's cruel, but heroic fate!

Ever, dear Miss Gordon,
Yours sincerely and sympathizingly,
V. R. I.

Mr. Gladstone to Sir Henry Gordon: —

10 DOWNING STREET
22nd Feb. 1885

DEAR SIR HENRY GORDON,

As long as a hope could in any way be entertained that your excellent and distinguished brother had survived the betrayal of Khartoum, I was unwilling to forgo the slender consolation it might afford; and I have also been delayed in writing this note for two or three days by an inquiry on a kindred subject. But I cannot longer forbear from addressing to you my humble tribute to his memory, insignificant as that tribute must be when rendered to one, whose fame has not only become a national possession, but gone forth throughout the world.

A longer paragraph follows extolling Gordon's character and emphasizing the "betrayal" of Khartoum by the painful reflection, "How ill his generous confidence was requited by some of those for whose welfare, though they were of foreign race, it was his desire to live or die!"

From W. S. Blunt's *My Diaries*: —

10th Feb. 1885

It is announced that Gordon is certainly dead, and there are sensational accounts of the sack of Khartoum. I am inclined to think it just as well, in the cause of peace, that the worst should have happened.

Lord Wolseley to Lady Wolseley: —

This affair seems to me like a nightmare. At one time I could almost feel Charlie Gordon's hand in mine.

Li Hung-chang to the British Minister in Peking: —

25th Feb. 1885

Being deeply afflicted by the news which I have just received of the untimely end of Gordon, my old and trusted friend, and noble, heroic and unselfish companion in arms, to whom China owes a debt of lasting gratitude, I hasten to express to you, as her Majesty's representative, my sympathy in the loss which the great British nation has sustained.

The Khedive to Sir Henry Gordon: —

Feb. 29, 1885

Egypt and myself honour the death of General Gordon as the hero of this age, the grandest character we have known, the friend and defender of our people.

From the *Times*, March 14, 1885: —

Yesterday [Friday, March 13] there were in our cathedrals services of a somewhat unusual, but in every way seemly, kind. At the request of the Archbishop of Canterbury, the day was generally observed as one of mourning for the loss of General Gordon, and special services were held in commemoration of him and of the soldiers who have fallen in the Sudan. . . . It cannot be doubted that as his figure recedes into the past, until it stands beside other illustrious soldiers, its proportions will continue to appear noble and beautiful, and that criticism will not much detract from its present fame. . . .

The vote to General Gordon's family has been settled. The grant by Parliament of £20,000 was unquestioned. . . .

INDEX